Policy in Love

*This book has been supported
by a grant from the National Endowment for the Humanities,
an independent federal agency.*

Policy in Love

Lyric and Public in Ovid, Petrarch and Shakespeare

by Christopher Martin

 DUQUESNE UNIVERSITY PRESS
Pittsburgh, Pennsylvania

Copyright © 1994 by Duquesne University Press
All Rights Reserved

No part of this book may be used or reproduced,
in any manner whatsoever, without written permission,
except in the case of short quotations
for use in critical articles and reviews.

Published in the United States of America by

DUQUESNE UNIVERSITY PRESS
600 Forbes Avenue
Pittsburgh, Pennsylvania 15282-0101

Library of Congress Cataloging-in-Publication Data

Martin, Christopher, 1957–
  Policy in love : lyric and public in Ovid, Petrarch, and
Shakespeare / by Christopher Martin.
      p.   cm. — (Duquesne studies. Language and literature series
; v. 17)
  Includes bibliographical references (p.) and index.
  ISBN 0-8207-0260-9
  1. Lyric poetry—History and criticism. 2. Love poetry—History
and criticism. 3. Ovid, 43 B.C.-17 or 18 A.D.—Criticism and
interpretation. 4. Petraca, Francesco, 1304–1374—Criticism and
interpretation. 5. Shakespeare, William, 1564–1616—Criticism
and interpretation. I. Title. II. Series.
PN1356.M37 1994
809.1'4—dc20   94-30961
                                                                CIP

for
Lydia,
Mae and Clinton Martin

Contents

	Acknowledgments	xi
INTRODUCTION	Sounding an Audience	1
ONE	Blind Hands, Blank Pages: The *Amores*	13
	Quod licet: Ovid's Elegiac Compromise	17
	Non iudicium, sed animus: Conditions of Restraint	34
	Survival and the Imperial Audience	56
TWO	*Un uom del vulgo:* The Community of Petrarch's *Canzoniere*	70
	Conspicuous Triviality	75
	Nel commune dolor: Death's Witness	97
	The Appeal of Mortal Things	116

THREE	And Men's Eyes: Shakespeare's Politic Lover	130
	Children of State: Convention and Contract in the Procreation Sequence	137
	Public Means and Rival Claims	154
	Public Manners and Dark Conceits	176
AFTERWORD	The Poetics of Intimacy, and Its Publics	192
	Notes	196
	Index	221
	About the Author	228

Acknowledgments

I thank my colleagues in the English Department at Boston University for leaving me space throughout this book's conception, research and composition, and for their encouragement and counsel once the penultimate product began to circulate. I desire no better associates, and look for no better companions. Practical assistance toward the book's final version came first from James Siemon, who rescued me from one especially hazardous oversight in the Ovid section; and last from John Paul Riquelme, who, as chair, somehow conjured time (from where I'll never know) to synthesize others' recommendations with his own consistently insightful pointers to give my arguments better shape—I am glad to be ever in his debt.

I have also benefitted from kind institutional support. The project got underway during a fellowship sponsored by Boston University's Humanities Foundation, and was enriched immeasurably by a residency at the University of Padua, where my thinking about the *Canzoniere* predictably found the right kind of inspiration: I thank Franco Giacobelli (and his family), the perfect host. The staff of Padua's Biblioteca di Palazzo Maldura were consistently receptive to the needs of a foreign scholar, and I owe them the same gratitude that I extend to the personnel of Harvard's Houghton collection and the Folger

Shakespeare Library. Back home, I found myself graciously accommodated by those who helped keep me local, especially Rhoda Bilansky, in charge of interlibrary loan at Boston University's Mugar library.

Outside the university, I am grateful to all those who have offered reassuring words, particularly James Nohrnberg and Arthur Kinney. Duquesne University Press's consultant reader, Raymond B. Waddington, balanced scrupulous criticism with friendly receptivity. The civility and understanding consistently displayed by Susan Wadsworth-Booth and Albert Labriola have set for me a standard of editorial professionalism.

This book about audiences took its essential sustenance, however, from those to whom it is dedicated, my wife Lydia and my parents Mae and Clinton—the only ones whose approval I ultimately covet, anyway.

INTRODUCTION

Sounding an Audience

I begin with a poem first published in 1619, nearly a century after its composition and three years after Shakespeare, the last author this book concerns, had ceased writing once and for all. It belongs to Jan Everard, a Dutch youth who under the name Janus Secundus would become the sixteenth century's supreme Latin poet. His masterful recovery of classical love lyric's rhythms and manners earned him an authority that rivaled Petrarch's hegemony over vernacular fashions, even though an item like "Ad grammaticos, quur scribat lasciuius" (To the grammarians, why he writes wantonly) exposes a temperament radically distinct from his Italian predecessor's.

> Carmina quur spargam cunctis lasciua libellis,
> Quaeritis? insulsos arceo Grammaticos.

2 Introduction

> Fortia magnanimi canerem si Caesaris arma,
>   Factaue diuorum relligiosa virûm,
> Quot miser exceperemque notas, patererue lituras.
>   Quot fierem teneris supplicium pueris.
> At nunc uda mihi dictent quum basia carmen,
>   Pruriat & uersu mentula multa meo,
> Me legat innuptae iuuenis placiturus amicae,
>   Et placitura nouo blanda puella uiro,
> Et quemcumque iuuat lepidorum de grege uatum
>   Otia festiuis ludere deliciis.
> Lusibus at laetis procul hinc absistite, saeui
>   Grammatici, injustas & cohibete manus:
> Ne puer, ob molleis caesus lachrymansque lepores,
>   Duram forte meis ossibus optet humum.

[Why should I scatter sexy poems in all my little books, you ask? I'm fending off insipid grammarians. If I sang of the mighty arms of magnanimous Caesar, or the devout deeds of saintly men, how many bad marks I'd be it for, poor wretch, how many corrections I'd have to endure! How often I'd be a torment to tender boys! But now since moist kisses dictate my poem to me, and the penis often itches in my verse, let the young man about to please his virgin friend read me, and the sweet girl about to please one just become a man, and whichever of the band of charming poets it pleases to play away the idle hours in merry delights. Get far away from the happy playing here, harsh grammarians, and stay your unjust hands, so that no boy, thrashed and weeping because of my gentle graces, will wish perhaps that the earth lie hard on my bones.][1]

The epigram brazenly postures as a product of the very institution it rejects. Whatever ideals humanist training had envisioned for itself, in practice the churning out of Latin verses by young boys under the guidance of uninspired pedagogues became one of its more depressingly verifiable hallmarks. Few would find in such numbing exercise the spark needed to kindle genuine poetic creativity; Janus, by contrast, actually sets out to do something with his education. And the first thing he does is shut down the classroom.

Modeled upon classical love elegy's *recusatio*—the poet's acknowledged eschewal of orthodox poetic topics in favor of eros's more personalized demands—Secundus's performance also transcends the convention. Far from apologetic about his inability or reluctance to honor public expectations, this *auctor* actively combats the appropriation of his work by a repressive and tasteless (*insulsus*, literally "saltless") authority incapable of preserving his lyrics' true flavor. The price of canonicity, he feels, is too steep: endorsement only brings its own form of censure and erasure (the feared *notas* and *lituras*), along with the curses of a captive readership. To rescue both text and audience from torment, he schemes to insure against any threat of approbation. A metonym for the grander purpose that all of his *carmina lasciua* intend, the *mentula* or "prick" is wedged provocatively near the elegy's exact center and serves a specific Priapic function, alluring those disciples of the phallic god while scaring off all the uninitiate who would presume to transgress upon real poetry's sacred turf.[2] In the place of a now ostracized professorate, Secundus convokes a freshly learned company, interested in the conjugation of more than just verbs, to rehearse his books' alternative, genuinely stimulating paradigms.

Secundus applies his learned expertise with a literal vengeance; yet the attack remains a deeply problematic one, since it cannot help but pay a kind of perverse homage to those same grammarians he expels. This author relies upon them, if not for circulation, at least for the skills and lexicon necessary to his work's composition and continued accessibility. Lovers' graduation into the verses he writes presupposes a grammatical discipline available only through such a hostile agency. Though thumbing one's nose at the teacher may prove an immediately satisfying act of rebellion, it becomes after a point an insubstantial gesture: the poetic sneer's bravado thinly masks Secundus's awareness of an inescapable dependency.[3] "Ad grammaticos" articulates an antagonism far more involved than the surface opposition between its dusty targets and the randier company Janus courts, and in so doing adumbrates a sense of contingency shared by the three lyric poets this book examines, before a despised and revered audience who arbitrate the cultural survival they all expressly seek.

Lyric poetry stands self-consciously apart as a residual genre especially resistant to an audience's claims or demands.[4] Classicists and modernists alike have paralleled the evolution of a lyric voice with the growth of literary individuation and subjectivity outside the pale of conventional ideologies: lyrists discover themselves in reaction to, rather than in conformity with, recognized mores.[5] Theodor Adorno felt obliged to open a 1957 discussion of lyric poetry and society with an apology for treating this "sphere of expression whose very essence lies in either not acknowledging the power of socialization or overcoming it through the pathos of detachment" in the context of public "bustle and commotion."[6] When lyric takes for its subject erotic relationships (as it so often does), the sense of privacy may well become complete, constricting the work's immediate circle to the poet and a specific object of affection: "She'is all States, and all Princes, I," in Donne's quintessential exclamation, "Nothing else is." To intrude is, in no uncertain terms, to recognize one's status as an outsider and (like the sun itself in his poem) a "Busie old foole."

T. S. Eliot's cautionary recollection that "a good love poem, though it may be addressed to one person, is always meant to be overheard by other people," adjusts this focus.[7] As a poet withdraws more emphatically toward the genre's asocial margins, sensitivity and responsiveness to an audience's presence is heightened rather than diminished. We do not belong there; still, our attendance is instrumental. Although love poets may invent imaginary recipients of their obsessive affections and extravagant passions—may even find such a situation creatively preferable to the existence of real-life paramours—they cannot so easily subsist upon the thin fare of an imagined readership. For their work to survive they must continue to entertain an all-too-independent jury that sits perennially in judgment on the fate of that work. The need to parley, of which the love poet remains intuitively aware, occasions the crafting of various "policies" that enable effective negotiation with an audience. The sense of giddy liberation gained from one's ability to sidestep convention also exacts a price, and the self-reflexive apprehensions and strategies designed to meet these fears inform several of European literature's most enduring statements.

The following studies reenter Ovid's *Amores*, Petrarch's *Canzoniere* and Shakespeare's *Sonnets* to examine the way these "politic" writers anguish over, bargain with and dramatize a relationship between authorial subjects and the demanding audience that they conceive. I am concerned, that is, with the poet's process of negotiating in the poetry the competing demands of intimacy and audience. My thesis is that lyric poets—like all of us—are politicians in a broad sense even in their private dealings, especially when they expose these to public view. Love poetry's political character is determined by the writer's awareness of the way that the audience responds to an artist's self-presentation. Each of the poets I discuss regularly presents poetic speakers in emphatic ways as distinctive figures to be judged, pitied, disparaged, or otherwise strongly responded to. These personae are, moreover, ironically sensitized to their vulnerability before the public who, sooner or later, must evaluate their performances. Ovid, Petrarch and Shakespeare are all authors who invite the approach through audience at the same time that their poems concern private affairs. It is this seemingly contradictory combination that first attracted my attention, and that unifies the following commentary.

The great extent to which classical Latin authors "were intensely conscious of their audiences" is pointedly reaffirmed in the scholarship freshly compiled by Tony Woodman and Jonathan Powell.[8] Writing specifically about the lyric, W. R. Johnson has moreover shown how Horace, whose practiced recusancy stamps so much of his work, returned by career's end to a basic professional awareness "that a poet who is separated from his intended audience is a lyric poet in a very paradoxical way, that lyricism requires real performance in a real community."[9] It is Ovid, however, who in his *Amores* presents the most sustained enactment of the complicated negotiation that this "community" requires. Brashly confident about his command of the medium and the enduring fame this mastery will secure, he displays throughout the attenuated work that has come down to us a subtle insecurity, founded in his acute awareness both that the public alone can validate his claims to success, and that his own expertise is seriously compromised by the self-destructive human tendencies he discovers over the course of his erotic reflections. The *Amores* brings into sharp focus an image of the speaker and his society as victims. Literary experience comes to parallel—in a manner more striking than is conventionally allowed—the sexual maneuvering that Ovid takes as his ostensible subject. No matter how skilled the poet claims to be as a seducer, the recipient of his advances alone decides just how successful his efforts will finally prove, and this knowledge renders all strategies desperate in ways that belie his presumed confidence. Rather than artistic talent and audience receptivity meeting one another mutually on the field of aesthetic surety, the artist's unwitting capacity to undo himself may just as well aggravate an already hostile or at least indifferent readership. Confronting a blindness that pervades the public landscape that Ovid depicts, his persona discovers the arbitrariness of victory, sexual or artistic.

Petrarch would never know the grim rewards of social

and political ostracism that Ovid's verse in the end ironically won for him, and on the surface the *Canzoniere* projects a more withdrawn and inflexible sensibility. Yet, behind the writer's bristly disdain for the *populo*, we again recognize a temperament sensitive to the urgency of public reception. To understand more fully the poet's procedures and their appeal, we must return to the ambivalence at the heart of this work: the decision to write in the popular tongue but to keep himself removed from the baseness of the crowd. Petrarch lines the "fables" that mediate between writer and audience with a subtle intimacy designed to win sympathy for the beleaguered lover's plight while maintaining the author's valued privacy. Again, contingency plays an important role, by simultaneously making evident the inevitably controlling nature of context, and by intensifying the private experience of the survivor. His sequence invites the audience to rechart the space opened by this effort at dissociation, more precisely, as a region of shared sensibilities, a field communally bounded by the comic and tragic discoveries that his love for Laura enables. Using William J. Kennedy's essential insight that the "inextricable union of character and audience, the one mirroring the other and contributing to its aesthetic advancement, is Petrarch's particular art and his legacy to the lyric tradition that sprang from the *Canzoniere*"[10] as a point of departure, I detail how, even at his most uncompromising, Petrarch's persona implicitly affirms a fundamental need to bargain with the audience to whom he at best openly condescends.

Petrarch is central to my study, structurally and argumentatively, for he presents the model of the poet's double necessity for acceptance and separation, public recognition and privacy. Shakespeare, in his *Sonnets*, brings this question of artistic dependency to a level of intensity which, though not exactly greater than that managed by Ovid and Petrarch, is certainly distinctive. Bruce R. Smith has noted that the dissemination of the *Sonnets* "offers a radical demonstration of how a text, once out of a writer's hands, 'belongs' to nobody," and locates these poems in "a highly equivocal position on the border between public and private."[11] Although Smith will (in company with most of the sequence's commentators) focus upon the "private" concerns, Shakespeare traces patterns of public interaction in a fashion at once more dramatically explicit and yet even more subtle than his predecessors. The speaker of these poems measures longevity by prolonged exposure within the public eye—which entails the young man's obligation to procreate and so pay "the world's due," the poet's own need to see that his lines endure "so long as men can read," and the mistress's duty to live up to the public image of her that he presumes to offer. As the speaker's opening claims on all of these registers are one by one exploded, he beholds his own temperamental unsuitedness to the dynamics of compromise. The insularity that comes to typify his situation must be revaluated ironically, through a skewed preoccupation with public responsibility that takes precedence over matters of subjectivity more recently celebrated in the criticism. "Policy" governs the tangled emotions of Shakespeare's infatuated persona, opening another window through which we can observe the poet's own parodic vigilance of his potentially recalcitrant witnesses.

Besides my own critical regard for these three writers as the most innovative and founding exponents of the genre of love poetry, more specific considerations ground my rationale for their inclusion over other contenders for a place in such a study as Propertius, Dante or Donne. Though they emerge from vastly different contexts and mark radically divergent attitudes toward the erotic circumstances they chronicle, each of the works I choose focuses its concern for an audience at a crucial moment in the tradition of western love lyric. The *Amores* caps the vogue of Augustan elegy that traces its line back to

Catullus and (by extension) to Callimachus, orchestrating and playing variations on what had become its characteristic tropes, while extending the manner to its metaconventional extremes. Ovid's exile concluded a phase of love poetry that would nonetheless continue to exert an influence over European lyric for centuries. And just as Ovid signals the terminus for one style, so Shakespeare caps the principal vogue inaugurated by Petrarch over two centuries before.[12] Petrarch had devised his work not only as an alternative to the Dantesque reformulation of courtly love lyric, but himself recast the classical erotic and poetic obsession Ovid had so profoundly examined. More importantly, I detect a peculiarly concentrated self-awareness in the poet-lover's engagement with his audience that draws me to these works. Though available in contemporaneous or intervening lyric poets, this strain is developed most efficiently and consistently in the unified contexts of the *Amores*, the *Canzoniere* and the *Sonnets*. By attending to authors who fix questions of public and private duality firmly at the center of their art, I wish to open considerations that reach beyond these three periods and cultures under study—encompassing both those who contributed to the lyric voices fashioned by Ovid, Petrarch and Shakespeare, and the artists whom these voices, in turn, have influenced.

This book's concern is not, however, with matters of influence, the poets' retrospective glance toward their predecessors (however inevitable this becomes to an appreciation of any author's poetic), a topic that has found ample treatment elsewhere.[13] Rather, this study takes up something more forward looking, the imagining of another, future party with whom the poet will have to contend no less fiercely—the *polis* who figures most prominently in the "policy" of my title. In a work that would be Englished in 1586 as *The French Academy*, Pierre de La Primaudaye reflects upon the "manie significations" of *policy* from classical times down through his own century. Charting its various references to "a Burgesie" and to "the maner of life used by some politicall person," he abstracts its overall aim as "to unite and frame us to the companie of men so long as we live amongst them."[14] Building upon the very awareness of this "companie" that these poets display, I investigate the complex exchange that they must entertain with an enduring polity, if their works are themselves to endure.

Audiences have always proven difficult entities to think about and discuss critically. Viewed from one perspective, writing is of course a peculiarly discrete exercise. This point has compelled Walter Ong to argue, with typical wit and insight, that the audience of a written text is "always a fiction," the projection of an authorial party "casting them in a made-up role and calling on them to play the role assigned."[15] However, a text often derives much of its animus from the writer's consciousness that a very real, potentially benign though frequently hostile readership needs to be countenanced and dealt with. For poets generally, and particularly for the three writers examined here, the "audience" becomes a Protean entity that variously embraces specific, immediate recipients (the Roman emperor, an elite company of humanist friends, an actual or fictional young man or mistress), a larger contemporary society, and the considerably vaster image of a posterity who must arbitrate their works' merit through time. In a crucial sense, the term's very elasticity comes to signify a conceived body that nonetheless stubbornly resists all attempts at poetic fictionalization, mocking rather than substantiating the artist's bid for control. My own shifting use of the term throughout the book intends to mirror the strategic turns that my subjects themselves make in their multiple, often ambiguous, always complex orientations toward audiences of various sorts, in a way that I hope never confuses the arguments. In so doing, I want to reinforce how, when regarded from another vantage, the audience envisioned by the artist is never a fiction.[16]

The focus on audience emerges from my primary interest in rhetorical criticism, though the approach also lends itself to a pragmatic or affective methodology (*reader-response criticism*, so-called). Neither of these dispositions adequately serves my orientation, however, and while traces of one or the other critical slant may come to the foreground at various moments in the argumentation, I do not employ either in any consciously systematic way. Rhetorical criticism's prevailing emphasis upon the devices that poets deploy to maintain control of their audiences failed to address my own concern with artists' apprehension over the dubious utility of these very devices.[17] Affective criticism, in contrast, concentrates upon the "dynamic interaction" between reader and text, yet remains too one-sided in its focus to illuminate the authorial concerns I pursue.[18] Only William J. Kennedy, in his landmark *Rhetorical Norms in Renaissance Literature*, has struck the kind of median pose with which I best identify. Kennedy calls to our attention the "dramatic interest" enabled by the way a poet shifts through a succession of roles, counterpointing the variety of roles crafted simultaneously for the audience.[19] Although I depart from what seems to me his study's ultimately conservative outlook toward poets' "constraint" of their readership, Kennedy's model stands squarely behind my own work, and his influence is pervasive.

Toward the book's close, in the context of a discussion of Shakespeare's sonnet 152, I observe that an "oath" signifies something more than a promise, and that "perjury" transcends the status of a lie. These terms, so vital to this particular poem and to the sequence leading up to it, touch down in the communal nexus that all of these chapters address. I anticipate the statement here, at the outset, to suggest the principles that connect and guide the readings that compose the commentary: that supposedly private relations need the corroboration of an audience, whether tiny or immense, in order to be established and maintained; that the negotiations involved substantially define the relations and are not just defined by them; but that those negotiations cannot be understood simply as the imposition of social and historical elements in some straightforward way on the lives and the language of poets and readers. With this in view, we are best poised to engage the lyric predicament that these three writers so fruitfully confront.

ONE

Blind Hands, Blank Pages

The Amores

> Poets are not, as officious mythology would have it, sons of Apollo, but of Marsyas.
>
> George Steiner[1]

His frankly obscene verses would, generations later, inspire lyric talents with a model for their own harsher cadences: "scis Romana simplicitate loqui"—you knew how to talk *Roman*—Martial recalled nostalgically. A reputation for sexual misconduct tainted no less his public demeanor. Even supporters were obliged to acknowledge the adulterous appetite he notoriously indulged, though they strove awkwardly to formulate excuses: that he liked (for example) to keep tabs on important men, and felt he could best do this by securing the erotic confidences of their women. Enemies of course capitalized upon such indiscretion, but as time passed opposing voices became fewer. At the very hour of his death, one biographer informs us, he thought life a joke. His office, he knew, sanctioned all these privileges. He was *princeps*, Augustus, who would one day be remembered as heir to the glory of Romulus and Alexander, and—he was not above anticipating to his intimates—as a god.

However intense his private lusts, Caesar Augustus prosecuted in deadly earnest an unprecedented agenda of moral reform. His radical legislation *Lex Iulia de maritandis ordinibus* and *Lex Iulia de adulteriis coercendis* of 18 B.C., devised to help restore the ethical superiority and domestic integrity of the state's mythic past, would for all their questionable efficacy eventually snare his own daughter and granddaughter, banished for the disgrace their infidelities cast upon the royal household.[2] The man who steadily incorporated imperial administration was prepared, moreover, to impress into his service whatever writerly talent surrounded him—an uncommonly deep pool, he discerned—by setting himself up gradually between 20 B.C. and A.D. 9 as "the literary patron of first resort."[3] Like his moral program, the *princeps*'s aesthetic vigilance also inflicted its casualties. In A.D. 8, by which time he had survived Virgil and Horace to become Rome's preeminent poet, Ovidius Naso was relegated to the remote Black Sea outpost of Tomis, capping the literary golden age over which Augustus presided with the Latin world's most infamous censorship case. Whether it was solely his ostensibly targeted *Ars amatoria*, a versified erotic handbook published almost a decade earlier, that occasioned the emperor's severity, Ovid's own laments from exile would mourn chiefly his verses' failure to please their imperial audience.[4]

Even against Augustan elegy's characteristically subversive backdrop, Ovid's "clear and emphatic rejection of the *topos* of *aureum saeculum*" set him up as an easy target for a political wrath disinclined to brook this manner of protest.[5] Ironically, long after the magnitude of Ovid's literary achievement had eclipsed the more parochial circumstances of his nonconformist's fate, critics by and large took the emperor's cue in their resentment: if not expressly immoral, this poet proves at best ruefully irresponsible—an irritation that continues to prejudice contemporary assessments.[6] In his influential study of Latin elegy, for instance, Georg Luck qualifies his praise with an indictment of Ovid's "wastefulness of talent," the abuse of an imagination so potent "that it can dare to squander itself even on nonsense, on luxuriant affectations, on all kinds of egomanias and capricious obsessions."[7] Similarly, Molly Myerowitz's sensitive exploration of the *Ars amatoria* cannot ultimately avoid the impression of Ovid as one "remarkably oblivious to the primary struggle of man with external nature," a somewhat cavalier indifference rudely disrupted by the shock of exile.[8] Those rarer advocates of the poet's seriousness have either bracketed altogether his elegiac collection, the *Amores*, or find themselves hard put to discover any real substance behind this work's speaker.[9] Even the brilliant treatments offered recently by Leslie Cahoon and Mary-Kay Gamel can champion Ovid's earnest sophistication only by denigrating the male lover's "heartless" lyric voice, fashioned deliberately by the author-ironist to invite a "feminine" critique of conventional attitudes.[10] Though their revisionary approach effectively shatters presumptions about the *Amores'* status as a comic trifle, it does so by deflecting abuse previously heaped upon the dubious poet himself onto his persona. In the process, they bury a complex psychology that, in my own reading, these poems provocatively elaborate.

The work's most recent editor expresses surprise "that it should have been the *Ars Amatoria* rather than the *Amores* which fell foul of the regime, for the *Amores* seem to be rather more out of line with Augustan ideals."[11] The *praxis* that its individual moments realize indeed contrasts the *Ars'* gnosis, imparting to the collection a more unyieldingly confrontational feel. Yet in the *Amores*, this archly uncompromising poet dwells assiduously on the idea of compromise. The landscape that Ovid's *amator* struggles through sensitizes him, despite the often predatory egotism he displays, to the contingency he never fully escapes. These lyrics collectively gauge the losses—calculated or otherwise—often sustained in pursuit of elusive goals. Only through an agile willingness to alter aspirations and expectations is his character able to cope; and if the flexibility by which he endures stokes the survivor's self-confidence, it also harbors a shamed self-contempt for the easily compromised integrity his actions must, in consequence, betray.

Attention to this rich duplicity, evolved throughout his amatory revelations, rescues Ovid's persona from caricature as a "hollow" figure or chauvinistic straw man. Alternately celebrated and derided by critics for the casual, somewhat jaded command he seems to enjoy—"he remains always in control of his emotions, always aware of the impact he is having on his addressee and his audience," in one representative formulation[12]—the *Amores'* speaker is in fact beleaguered by the futility of his efforts to secure a sense of control over experience. Inspired—in fact compelled, in the introductory poem's mythology—to write elegy, he regards an audience who is now suspicious of such lesser verse forms with an apprehension that keeps in check the boastfulness his poetic ego indulges. The poet-*amator* can no more presume upon his readers' acceptance or understanding of his work than he can upon his mistress's favor, and his sexual failures and displacements presage darker artistic fears.[13] Beyond the perils and limits posed by external agencies, however, the poet uncovers an even more insidious hazard in the violent means by which a will to dominate or control asserts itself, an appetite that ironically recoils to threaten self-destruction. From within and without, purchase upon a coveted self-mastery is, for the elegist, inexorably eroded.

To preview the peculiar complexity traced beneath the *Amores'* "lighter" (*leuior*) concerns, we may enlist briefly the paired elegies 1.11 and 12. In the first, the lover dispatches to his mistress a pair of wax tables inscribed with an invitation to meet covertly; and though he enjoins a full reply—"odi, cum late splendida cera uacat," he declares [11.20: I hate it whenever the surface of a fine page is left empty]—he will settle for her abbreviated expression of consent, "ueni." When they subsequently return bearing word of her cautious refusal, he discards the once honored tablets with a curse, "uos cariosa senectus / rodat, et inmundo cera sit alba situ" [12.29–30: may age's decay consume you, and fitting neglect fade your wax].[14] Loathing a blank page, the artist ends up petulantly obliterating his text. Desperate to survive, to leave their distinguishing mark, the *caecas manus* ("blind hands") that he describes in another elegy only work relentlessly to their own undoing. Conditioned by a fear of obliteration himself, Ovid crafts a persona held in suspension between preservation and annihilation. The poet understood, judiciously and passionately, his own potential, and had reason—long before his poems from exile would express this awareness less covertly—both to trust and fear selfish urges from the very start.

Quod licet: Ovid's Elegiac Compromise

The first thing readers of the *Amores* must keep in mind is that elegy—like love itself—was for Ovid a matter of compromise. The work as we have it originates in a spirit of calculated loss:

> Qui modo Nasonis fueramus quinque libelli,
>   tres sumus: hoc illi praetulit auctor opus.

> ut iam nulla tibi nos sit legisse uoluptas,
> at leuior demptis poena duobus erit.
>
> [We, who until lately were Naso's five little books, are now only three: so the author himself preferred it. You still may not get any pleasure out of reading us, but at least the pain of doing so has been lessened by two.]

The poet's inaugural statement is at once bold and deferential, precise and duplicitous. Branding the collection with these lines, Ovid points up the ambivalence of his editorial endeavor. On the one hand, his announcement implies a firm authorial mastery. The attitude expressed is not "What I have written, I have written," but rather "What I have written I may change as I please"—a sentiment well-suited to one who would become the great poet of *mutatio*. *Naso* alone determines what form his publication will take: nothing comes between *auctor* and *opus*, a point reinforced by the words' juxtaposition in his second line. On the other hand, the ensuing couplet radically qualifies this assertion of freedom. Its self-effacing apology, however ironic, dwells upon the actual reduction that frustrates his posture of command. What prompted the revision to begin with may have less to do with the personal aesthetic preferences he at first boasted than with a need to accommodate public tastes. Claim for the writer's sovereignty over his text modulates instantly into a negotiated settlement with an audience whose *poena* he has striven to alleviate. While we admire the poet's strength in making such an extreme concession—a stamina whose lack Ovid would bemoan in later work[15]—we are also startled by the sacrifice its bare *tres sumus* conveys: what used to be five has dwindled to three. Our author has bid dearly in his drive to maintain a readership, a gesture that (he grants wryly) may still not pay off. We enter, in short, a work whose original integrity has been violated by the poet's exemplary act of discipline.

Ovid's epigram recalls, as Gian Biagio Conte has

observed in his study of classical *imitatio*, the spurious lines prefixed to Virgil's *Aeneid*.[16] The allusion's richness extends beyond the offhand disrespect for Virgilian manner that Conte remarks. Ovid's parody is essentially self-directed, deepening by means of comparison the awareness of potential failure acknowledged in his own lines. Where the epic sets its author forth as one whose acclaimed career has mounted upon a ladder of sequential professional successes, the *Amores'* Naso presents himself as a thoroughly compromised figure, who instead of expanding confidently beyond past achievements struggles to defend an earlier collection's attenuated remains.

The *Amores'* ability to endure whatever amputation their author performed at the same time defines their strength. Adaptability is a virtue of little concern to the epic writer, secure upon the heights of his "favored" genre. The love poet, by contrast, requires an extraordinary agility to survive the threat of obliteration perpetually overshadowing his recusant mode, and must rest content with a different sense of self. By deftly figuring just such a temperament, the epigram previews key aspects of eroticism developed in the ensuing poems. The present text's announced character—altered, violated, reduced—now mirrors the emotional mutability, personal betrayal, and various social and artistic demotions (from battlefield to bedroom, from epic to elegy) that its poetry concerns. Our imaginations are best stimulated by matters partially concealed: this simple awareness shapes Ovid's sexual poetics, captured for example in *Amores* 1.5's dimly lit erotic revelations; the point stands behind our lingering critical desire to reconstruct the "original" five-book text. Had a longer first edition not existed (we infer), the author would have fabricated the idea of one to accommodate his epigrammatic overture.[17]

Near the end of the *Amores'* second book, Ovid's speaker comes as close as he ever will to formulating the overarching ethic by which he lives and writes, when he professes to his fellow poet Macer "quod licet," roughly

"I do whatever I'm able." The term *licet*—suggesting at once "what is possible" and "what is permitted"—enjoys an elasticity and ambiguity that the elegies persistently measure. Personal capacity and public ordinance seldom agree in Ovid's world, and the negotiation obliged by this tension fills out the collection. Nowhere do the poet-lover's confidence and insecurity meet to test and delineate his critical flexibility more than in the elegies bounding the individual books, pressure points to which I direct the remainder of this section.

Where Ovid's prefatory epigram speaks of retrospective curtailment, the *Amores*' initial performance retreats to another episode of "subtraction" to distinguish his text's mythic pre-history. What we unexpectedly find in the first poem is a poet's conservative self-image suddenly jeopardized by Amor's subversive drive to supplant epic purpose with elegiac craft:

> Arma graui numero uiolentaque bella parabam
>   edere, materia conueniente modis.
> par erat inferior uersus; risisse Cupido
>   dicitur atque unum surripuisse pedem.
>
> (*Am.* 1.1.1–4)
>
> [Arms and violent warfare I was preparing to declaim, in heavy meter, subject and style balanced. My lines were of equal length, until for laughs (it's said) Cupid made off with one of the feet.]

Resentment at this forced reduction to a lame meter—bastardized hexameters, really—smoulders throughout the next 16 lines.[18]

The *uates*, his prescribed ambitions hobbled by the loss of one metrical foot, now limps in a circle, an ironically literal image of *ambitio*. And were this stylistic embarrassment not bad enough, the redirection of *materia* that it entails further needles his dignity. His refusal to take up a topic so unfamiliar to him as amorous conquest—"nec mihi materia est numeris leuioribus apta, / aut puer aut longas compta puella comas" [19–20: nor is my subject matter—neither boy nor beautifully groomed girl—fit for these lightweight numbers]—asserts professional integrity while allowing Ovid a swipe at contemporary epic writers who, though possessing as little subject matter for sincere panegyric as his persona does for love elegy, are hardly deterred by their poverty.

Irritated that Cupid's plans should impede his own, the poet diminishes epic contention to a petty squabble over jurisdiction; but his noisy protests cannot challenge the interloper's laconic authority, and this early lesson in humility disciplines the attitude he henceforth adopts. His peevish query, "sunt tibi magna, puer, nimiumque potentia regna: / cur opus adfectas ambitiose nouum?" [13–14: why do you ambitiously look to exceed your already overextended domain?], only wins him Cupid's arrow and mocking reply, "'quod' que 'canas, uates, accipe' dixit 'opus'" [24: he said, "Here's something to sing about, poet"]. The confrontation with Eros's insuperable force issues in a facile acquiescence by the poet, who departs as docile as he had previously been feisty, his *opus* agreeably situated between elegy's alternating lines of six and five: "sex mihi surgat opus numeris, in quinque residat" [27: My work stands up impressively in six feet, then subsides into five].

Amores 1.1's encounter teaches the futility of opposition. The next poem studies how to negotiate terms. This elegy's opening movement, often criticized for the *amator*'s obtuse inability to recognize his own love-melancholy's obvious symptoms, actually discovers his need to verbalize passion's maddeningly inexplicable circumstance. The initial question, "Esse quid hoc dicam" [What can I call this?], betrays the awakened lover's sense that, could he articulate his feelings, he might yet avoid love's quandary. Failing this, the damage control he undertakes (in the aphoristic wisdom padding lines 9–18) encapsulates his ethic of self-preserving compromise:

22 Blind Hands, Blank Pages

> cedimus, an subitum luctando accendimus ignem?
>   cedamus: leue fit, quod bene fertur, onus.
> uidi ego iactatas mota face crescere flammas
>   et uidi nullo concutiente mori;
> uerbera plura ferunt quam quos iuuat usus aratri,
>   detractant prensi dum iuga prima, boues;
> asper equus duris contunditur ora lupatis:
>   frena minus sentit, quisquis ad arma facit.
> acrius inuitos multoque ferocius urget,
>   quam qui seruitium ferre fatentur, Amor.

[Should we give it up, or by fighting back fuel the stealthy flame? Give it up: the skillfully mounted burden sits light enough. I've watched an agitated torch blaze, only to subside when left alone. Fresh oxen who resist their first harness suffer more pain than those who accept their lot; the tractable horse's mouth doesn't feel the reins like that of the wild mount. Love deals much more harshly and bitterly with those who resist than with the compliant.]

His pliability becomes part of a crafty ploy to win concessions. Conquered, the poet nonetheless economizes his energy. If the *amator*'s resignation to what he sees as insurmountable odds casts him in a less-than-heroic light, it can also shield him from the force of Cupid's full power, thus enabling him to purchase greater liberty than he might otherwise enjoy.

With 1.3, the *amator*'s propensity for compromise channels finally into the mainstream of conventional seduction bargaining. He cannot even utter a plea to Venus without impulsively trimming his expectations: "Iusta precor: quae me nuper praedata puella est / aut amet aut faciat cur ego semper amem. / a, nimium uolui: tantum patiatur amari" [1–3: The request is fair: may that girl who has recently preoccupied me either love me back or at least substantiate my eternal devotion to her. All right, I've asked too much—just let me love her]. By the time he addresses his mistress, Ovid's speaker is well-prepared to qualify his self-presentation, informing her of his modest social and financial standing. Unlike the passages in Tibullus and Propertius on which the disclaimer is modeled, this speaker's words betray not a proud indifference to standard values, but a recognition of abashed contingency and a consequent eagerness to cut deals[19]: the poetry he can offer in her praise will compensate, he hopes, for the illustrious ancestry he lacks. From his perspective, the poem's later boasting is credibile because of this initial confession. Fears that *nimium uolui* seem to shape his discourse. He desires the woman both sexually and as a means to writing worthy verse, but feels compelled to specify his limitations along with his credentials, balancing a wry modesty against a puff of the artistic gift he exploits.

The *Amores'* opening progression dwells upon compromise. A rather different voice, it would seem, completes book 1's frame. *Amores* 1.15 defies any audience to scorn the poet's vocation. Now, by contrast, Ovid's speaker mocks the triviality of the military and legal professions so widely revered: "mortale est, quod quaeris, opus" [7: the work you look to is transient]. His hostile audience's resentment (*liuor edax*) feeds off their resentment toward the poet's self-validating office. They exercise no jurisdiction over work that hovers above their petty ingratitude, an assertion steeling his empassioned final statement:

> pascitur in uiuis Liuor; post fata quiescit,
>   cum suus ex merito quemque tuetur honos:
> ergo etiam cum me supremus adederit ignis,
>   uiuam, parsque mei multa superstes erit.
>   (*Amores* 1.15.39–42)

[Envy can only feast on the living; its mouth is closed when death abandons each to a just evaluation: therefore even when the pyre has consumed me, my best shall remain standing, quite alive.]

For all its self-reinforcing conviction, such a secure pronouncement remains suspect.[20] Two factors suggest this. First, the larger context: the poet's chiding resistance here sounds too much like his attempted repudiation of Cupid's influence in the first elegy to be wholly persuasive; and we question the insistence that art is not subject to loss (*iactura*) in a work already said to have lost two books. Second, and more subtly, Ovid concludes his roster of "enduring" poets with a reference to Gallus, the first major practitioner of Latin love elegy, who had recently been disgraced and hounded to suicide for allegedly treasonous political ambition.[21] Gallus's fall confirms the poet's point regarding worldly pursuits: following the military-political career prescribed by the mob has indeed proved "mortal" work for his dead colleague; it is only as a poet that Gallus will survive. Concurrently, however, Gallus has become a virtual emblem of the self-destructive potential of the hunger for fame, and of the conservative audience's authoritative power. Gallus's aspirations perhaps set him up for the tribunal that arbitrated his fate, but at this historical moment of canon reformation, the same body might also oversee and adjudicate the literary wealth that the age will pass on. Peter Green observes that "for Ovid to ignore the fact that official *damnatio memoriae* had made Gallus something of an 'unperson' ... was, to say the least, tactless"[22]; but Gallus's unsequential, terminal position in the recalled lineup of writers underlines precisely Ovid's daring, calculated move.

Amores 1.15's reference to this disgraced figure both valorizes the fellow artist and qualifies the assertions of immortality inherent in its very encomium. Ovid feigns to dismiss his accusers, aware all along that his contempt rings hollow in the face of their judicial prerogative. Ovid may resist the lure and trap into which Gallus fell, but the myrtle crown adorning his head still "fears the cold" ("sustineamque coma metuentem frigora myrtum" [37]), belying his pose of cavalier defiance. Though adversarial readers are his subject in the elegy, he is also ultimately subject to their tastes and outlooks. Even a poem like this can never fully suppress this consciousness.

At the opening of the *Amores'* second book, Ovid renews his ownership of the work as surely as he had set forth in the epigram. In 2.1, he relates how an attempted return to the epic (and publicly condoned) ambitions sketched in the first elegy is short-circuited by more pragmatic, less grandiose erotic concerns. Specifically, the poet returns to the *gigantomachia* he was preparing to compose only to have his epic of an attempted displacement of the gods itself overthrown by his mistress's sudden refusal to grant him access to her chamber. Turning from an abortive mythic siege of the heavens, he faces the literal prospect of besieging the woman's closed doors. Her mundane gesture ironically accomplishes what the *centimanus* ("hundred-handed") rebel Gyas could not:

> in manibus nimbos et cum Ioue fulmen habebam,
>   quod bene pro caelo mitteret ille suo.
> clausit amica fores: ego cum Ioue fulmen omisi;
>   excidit ingenio Iuppiter ipse meo.
> Iuppiter, ignoscas: nil me tua tela iuuabant;
>   clausa tuo maius ianua fulmen habet.
>   (2.1.15–20)

[I had in hand the thunder and lightning with which Jove would defend heaven. Suddenly, my lover decided to slam her doors on me, so I let Jove take care of himself, put him out of my mind. Please overlook this, god: nothing of yours served much use against that closed door's greater bolt.]

Love directs him back toward the *nequitae*—a pervasive term that correlates the lover's irresponsible moral imbalance and the literal "unevenness" (*ne-aequus*) characterizing his elegaic lines' matter and style. His insistence that he really was primed for the canceled epic project—"et satis oris erat"—is at once a boast and an embarrassed confession: compulsion, rather than a lack of talent, forces him to scramble unwillingly for the lightweight *tela* best suited to him.

When hyperbolic assertions of poetry's awesome power lapse into the assurance that verses can at least help charm open an angry lover's door, this speaker is not being reductive, only making clear what he settles for. His earlier caution of *nimium uolui* rings somewhere in the background. Likewise, the ensuing catalogue of epic heroes ennobles more than discounts his resignation: Achilles, Agamemnon, Hector, Odysseus are routed by a mistress who, we may gather from her lover's abrupt exile, rebuffs epic's encroachment upon the turf she means exclusively to occupy. Leslie Cahoon's indictment of the speaker's callous promotion of sexual expedience over heroic suffering is miscalculated[23]; it is the demands of an erotic relationship that summon him from mythical vistas. Recognizing this, the poet once more adjusts his aspirations. The rewards of such unpretentiousness, after all, are great, "magna datur merces."

An aggressive procedure of audience selection opens the *Amores'* second book. The "seuerae" are proscribed, as Ovid's infatuated persona looks to a more qualified and invested readership: "me legat in sponsi facie non frigida uirgo / et rudis ignoto tactus amore puer" [5-6: may the virgin who doesn't freeze up before a lover read me, along with the naive boy ready for love's new feeling]. The bravado of his peremptory dismissal also masks a somewhat nervous longing for validation. If the young lovers whose favor he solicits discern in him their own erotic furor, then the poet can take shelter in the commonality of his experience, despite being condemned by the harsher authorities who judge his verses. Not unless armed with some form of anticipated approval can he confidently turn his art away from celebrated epic goals to private ends. He replaces a literature justified by didactic or panegyric intent with one that invokes more proximate realities: a poetry of identification and differentiation, not indoctrination. No self-flattering whim, his gesture betrays a hunger for acceptance, for a reassurance that his work is viable. Censorious or supportive, his audience never moves very far from view. To actualize the security that he feigns, the singer of personal *nequitae* requires this chosen, alternative readership's attention as jealously as his own mistress evidently monopolizes his.

The last of the "programmatic" introductory poems is also Ovid's most elaborate. *Amores* 3.1 revises 1.1's dialogic scene into a *paragone* between Tragedy and Elegy, antagonistic personifications campaigning for the poet's allegiance. Although Elegy is never officially vindicated, her performance identifies splendidly the "lesser" form's strength and attraction. Against Tragedy's unyielding majesty, Elegy displays a uniquely supple ability to endure an inferior station's hardships. Readiness to cope with her acknowledged deficiencies empowers the genre in a way known only to those who must constantly settle for second-best, like the poet whom Ovid imagines.

Tragedy follows Elegy into the private, sacred *silua* to which the poet has withdrawn, but nonetheless aggressively presumes to speak first. She reprimands him for retreating into the infamy his love verse has occasioned ("nequitiam uinosa tuam conuiuia narrant, / narrant in multas compita secta uias" [17–18: they talk about your vices at drinking parties as well as on street corners]) instead of pursuing a theme worthy of his genuine brilliance ("materia premis ingenium; cane facta uirorum" [25: your material shortchanges your talents—sing about real men's accomplishments]). Described as *uiolenta* in demeanor, she becomes a virtual surrogate for the *seuerae* deflected in 2.1. Her stately appearance seems out of place amid the sylvan informality, and her aggressive bombast seems partly a function of her nervous discomfort with such relaxed surroundings.

By contrast, Elegy sports a casual disarray the writer finds both soothing and seductive:

> uenit odoratos Elegia nexa capillos,
>   et, puto, pes illi longior alter erat.
> forma decens, uestis tenuissima, uultus amantis,
>   et pedibus uitium causa decoris erat.
>
> (7–10)

> [Elegy arrived, her perfumed tresses braided, and (I think) one foot lengthier than the other. Admirably shaped, the filmiest of gowns, love's own face, and her lameness itself somehow harmonized with her charm.]

Just as the poet's description of Tragedy's gait conveyed an image of sure-footed, "heavy" formality, his references to Elegy are sidelong and qualified ("puto," "si memini"). Her accommodating nature best emerges, however, with the self-revelation she begins at line 35. First observing how Tragedy—unwittingly, it seems—has addressed her charge in elegiac meter, Elegy points out how "tamen emerui plus quam tu posse ferendo / multa supercilio non patienda tuo" [47–48: I've achieved my success by putting up with everything your pride couldn't handle]—such indignities as being nailed to doors, stashed inside of garments, and torn by angry recipients. Deferential by instinct, Elegy makes no claims on the artist's allegiance; she "fertilized" him, but suggests she's ready (unlike her rival) to let go when he sees fit.

Appropriately, the poet concludes with his own effort at arbitration. Affirming Tragedy's *grandius* status, and his hope to fulfil her wishes, he simultaneously bargains for a little more time with Elegy—"exiguum uati concede, Tragoedia, tempus: / tu labor aeternus; quod petit illa, breue est" (67–68). Where we might (again) have expected a sound defeat for Tragedy, we instead see the elegiac temperament at work, attuned to negotiation and compromise. In the face of all this deference, Tragedy, along with the *seuerae* for whom she speaks, is "moved" to grant his request. The poem manages no less than—though no more than—a truce between the more respected literary activity he has neglected and the provisional craft governing his current poetic.

A disarmingly unpretentious self-awareness wins in 3.1 the desired postponement; in honor of this deal, the farewell to elegy deferred herein becomes a reality in the collection's final poem, where the poet announces officially "Quaere nouum uatem, tenerorum mater Amorum: / raditur haec elegis ultima meta meis" [1-2: Look for a new poet, mother of tender loves, my elegies have now completed their course]. He voices a concern for freedom in the self-glorification of his Paelignian heritage that touches, as well, his aesthetic concerns. Allegiance to the "alternative" poetry he has perfected, and has until this moment embraced, involves in part a temperamental drive to challenge orthodoxy. His entirely volitional turn now toward the "area maior" substantiates his confidence in a career's future promise, self-assured in "post mea mansurum fata superstes opus" [20: a work sure to remain standing after I'm gone].

The powerful racecourse analogy opening this elegy nevertheless renders dubious whatever liberation he now proclaims: for the passage recalls and balances *Amores* 3.2, wherein Ovid's speaker steps from the previous poem's secluded *sanctum* into the circus's wild public intimacy. Discussed almost exclusively through the amator's elaborate seduction ploys as he courts a female spectator attending the races, this famous elegy also strikingly locates the individual's rather jostled position in a larger social realm. The audience he attempts to fend off still presses from all sides, and he must make his advances before their suspicious or indifferent gazes. More significant even than this point, however, is the gesture with which Ovid ends 3.2: after his mistress's horse has lost, the crowd asserts its right to demand a new start. The horses are called back, and in a second heat the lady's choice succeeds. For better or worse, the audience commands the performers, who are never securely finished with their race until the spectators say so.

Backed by this awareness, we penetrate the bravado of 3.15's speaker as he relinquishes his volume's *materia* and *modus*. Like the charioteers of 3.2, he awaits his auditors' verdict and indulgence, knowing that they may instruct him to start anew—not on another, fresher project, but on the work he has already completed to his own satisfaction. His turn to the "area maior" he enthusiastically anticipates may, at their command, need to be postponed. Behind the rather flimsy myth of the poet's hegemony lurks the more imposing and intimidating reality of his censorious audience's veto power.

It's not over, even when it's over. Such is the *Amores'* final attitude. *Amores* 3.15's *ultima meta* only brings us back around to the collection's initial epigram, which proclaims these poems a second run, an effort renewed by the poet's choice—or his audience's insistence. Publication signaled for Roman authors a "loss of control," Kenneth Quinn has argued, a work's "abandonment to its fate."[24] The *Amores'* informing sensibility intimates that the artist's public capacity always limits his "control," always obliges his anticipation of the readers' verdicts. The writer who would soon become mutability's greatest celebrant nurtured, early in his career, an appreciation of shifting texts and contexts, of both the promise and threat that change posed to his own artistic longevity.

What of the *Amores'* second book, which concludes in a manner quite unlike its flanking units? The remarks on poetry capping books 1 and 3 of the extant collection retreat here to the penultimate elegy 2.18, leaving 2.19 to an outraged mock-attack upon a husband who too casually accommodates his wife's affairs and thereby bores the womanizing *amator*. Moreover, 2.18 looks not, as do 1.15 and 3.15, to the poet's envisioned abandonment of elegy, but instead disrupts the pattern by devising yet another apology for his generic truancy. To grasp its full significance, we must understand 2.18 as the central moment in a three-poem sequence ending the central book, where specific poetic concerns are absorbed into the speaker's pained reflection upon his compromised stance, harboring all the rich implication of *quod licet*.

In 2.18, Ovid's speaker self-deprecatingly compares the lesser ventures he has undertaken to the epic project of his friend Macer: "ignaua Veneris cessamus in umbra, / et tener ausuros grandia frangit Amor" [3–4: I linger in Venus's idle shade, and tender Cupid enervates grand designs]. Boasting an ability to write in more elevated genres, he simultaneously confesses the fruitlessness of his attempts to do so under present circumstances, restrained securely in Cupid's camp by his mistress's blandishments:

> sceptra tamen sumpsi curaque tragoedia nostra
>   creuit, et huic operi quamlibet aptus eram:
> risit Amor pallamque meam pictosque cothurnos
>   sceptraque priuata tam cito sumpta manu;
> hinc quoque me dominae numen deduxit iniquae,
>   deque cothurnato uate triumphat Amor.
>
>   (13–18)

[Still, I took up the scepter as my subject, and our tragedy grew with care, and I was ready for whatever the task might be; Cupid laughed, however, at my cloak and painted boots, and the scepter was swiftly snatched from my hand, and my unfair mistress's decree steered me back in another direction, so that Love dresses down the tragic poet.]

With line 19's *quod licet*, however, the poet casually reverses his deferential tone. His *Ars amatoria* and *Heroides* have already secured a significant notoriety; by the poem's end, he boldly points up the erotic foundation of Macer's epic subject, the Trojan War, and confides that his friend will—"si bene te noui"—soon retire to the pleasures of elegy's lighter mode. *Amores* 2.18 pivots, finally, upon the idea of resignation to genres best suiting one's talents and temperament, rather than struggling against the odds. The speaker is, by the end, apparently content with the combined enjoyments of his lady's affections and his acclaimed (if admittedly *leuior*) poems. Such a bartered contentment should, he implies, attract even someone like Macer to consider the advantages of an alternative public *castrum*.

A regard for what can be managed—*licet*—informs also 2.17, on the poet's enthrallment to Corinna. He will concede everything, including his name ("sim licet infamis" he states three lines in, "infamy I can afford"), to secure her affections. The absolute authority that the author grants Corinna—"te deceat medio iura dedisse foro" [24: pass your verdicts on me as if in the forum itself]—extends to exclusive rights over his verse, an assurance that, to judge from the possessiveness displayed in the next poem, she takes very seriously. Poetry is, of course, all he has to offer in exchange for her love, but the public approval his works have encountered (he abstains from his abject posture long enough to reflect) gives hope that this little may prove just enough. Elegiac meter itself demonstrates the compatibility that unequal pairings can on occasion reach, he muses: "aptari magnis inferiora licet" [14: the trivial can be suited to the great].

The *Amores*' world is a grand network of recognized deals and capitulations, of bargain and acquiescence. Markedly, this very sense of easy compatibility comes under fire in book 2's closing poem. The elegy is less facetious than its outrageous argument—that unless the husband begins to guard his wife more carefully, the poet will cease his seductive maneuvers against her—has uniformly led commentators to believe. In context, the poet's flat statement "quod licet, ingratum est; quod non licet, acrius urit" [3: what's permissible isn't appreciated; what's prohibited burns more harshly], sounds like a direct indictment of the mentality he has himself expressed throughout. What excites his fury is the husband's passive acceptance of his ludicrous fate. The husband evidently subscribes to the idea pressed in 3.4, that any effort to confine a woman will only fire her appetites all the more; thus, he perhaps mirrors too unsettlingly the poet's own professed resignation to human faithlessness. The woman he pursues here, significantly, is not the Corinna to whom he had, only two poems earlier, sworn exclusive devotion. The adaptability implicitly or explicitly celebrated throughout signals from another perspective a pathetic lack of character—a lack he potentially shares with this absurd anti-rival.

The single movement formed by these final elegies both fortifies and qualifies the poet's confident self-image with an aura of doubt or even self-contempt. The pride he takes in his survivor's instinct, accommodating whatever limitations he encounters, masks his anxiety about antiheroism, about slipping from an expert diplomacy into the base pliancy of a time-server. The side Ovid chose in the *agon* between elegy's *leuior* concerns and epic's magnanimous reach was in its Augustan context a risky one, requiring a paradoxical fortitude that always needs to serve as its own reward. Along with this courage, the "counter-classical" sensibility packs a contrasting burden of insecurity that no manner of bluster can appreciably lighten. The *Amores'* speaker, if not his creator, does mourn his inability to see beyond the corruption, duplicity and cynicism of Rome that obstruct Virgilian heights. The shame of 2.19's *leno*-spouse refracts his abuser's own thwarted drive to command something more than *quod licet*, something beyond "idle" sensuality and its crippled meters disdained by colleagues like Macer. In his books' peripheral moments, Ovid focuses a self-scrutiny that will recurrently inform the elegies they contain, poems that will explore even more subtle instances of limitation and failure.

NON IUDICIUM, SED ANIMUS: CONDITIONS OF RESTRAINT

An instinct for negotiation serves to absorb the shocks that *amator* and author must sustain in Ovid's contentious world. The poems considered so far frame books preoccupied with the social, physical and psychological boundaries that persistently test the poet's abilities to cope. As the frame-poems also intimate, Ovid is most intrigued inside this general scenario by those points at which discriminatory powers break down, by failure to surmount boundaries that appear to be, in the end, not negotiable. Ovid's elegies inquire aggressively into the factors conditioning all deficient constructs, verbal or otherwise.[25] The defeat they at once enact and anatomize seriously challenges any doubts about their author's profound self-consciousness.

Ovid's own eccentricity fascinated and disturbed antiquity, who thought it worth caricaturing in a parable still broadly familiar to students of Latin literature. In his *Controuersiae* 2.2 the elder Seneca recounts how Ovid, accosted once by a group of concerned readers who sought permission to delete three lines from his works, agreed on condition that he be allowed separately to exempt three particular lines from their censure. When both parties simultaneously revealed the verses they had singled out, the selections (of course) matched. Distracted by its comedy, we have given too little thought to what the anecdote aims seriously to capture. Seneca himself, evidently embarrassed by the perversity of this *uir summi ingenii*, writes the episode off as an instance of self-indulgent antagonism, illustrating how Ovid lacked restraint rather than critical judgment ("non iudicium defuisse...sed animum"). His peremptory estimate—echoed by Quintilian's pronouncement that the poet, stuck on his own ingenuity ("nimium amator ingenii sui"), achieves only in his (since lost) *Medea* the heights he was capable of "si ingenio suo imperare quam indulgere maluisset" [if only he'd managed rather than indulgêd his artistry]—would help prejudice Ovid's critical reception down to our own time, as Alison G. Elliott has demonstrated. From a different perspective, the story crystalizes less a frivolous contrariness than a distinctive consciousness, anxious to maintain artistic and textual integrity against the encroachments of forces (hostile or benign) that endanger it. Ovid's deep attentiveness to his audience imparts an uncanny ability to read them and anticipate their reactions.

We have seen this sensibility distilled in the *Amores'* inaugural epigram. No text argues more relentlessly against the prospect of obliteration: this poet will undertake whatever may forestall his words from being carried off upon the winds—an image that scores the elegies throughout. Yet no one betrays more ironically than Ovid's persona an awareness of wit's stunted and even self-destructive potential: "contra te sollers, hominum natura, fuisti / et nimium damnis ingeniosa tuis" [*Am.* 3.8.45–46: your skill works against you, human nature, and your losses show too much cleverness]. This paradox presses beyond the unexceptional erotic entrapment it also mirrors, expressed for example at 2.4.5's "odi, nec possum cupiens non esse, quod odi" [I hate it, but am unable (though willing) not to be what I hate]. Ovid's scattered vignettes of abuse and suffering illustrate most disturbingly the violent folly he dreads. They will also mark the terminus of a frustration presaged in the *amator*'s complicated response to an array of prohibitive boundaries, unfolded in the twin clusters of poems at *Amores* 1.4–6 and 3.6–8.

Almost more than the women he ostensibly courts, blocking situations enthrall Ovid's speaker's imagination. In 1.4, the poet's initial word, *uir*, identifies the barrier he and his mistress must overcome if they are to enjoy one another's company at an upcoming *coena* or symposium: the "man" (either husband or patron) in attendance excites erotic ingenuity just so much as he obstructs their opportunity for a tryst. The lovers' union thrives upon conspiracy, wherein complicity reassures the speaker of his lady's genuine affections. A private language of inscriptions blotted on the table, discreet gestures alive with sexual innuendo, and judiciously prescribed responses will arouse everything except the *uir*'s suspicion. Anticipating 2.19's insistence upon danger's aphrodisiac effect, the agitated lover finds stimulation in his discourse's covert triumph over the inhibiting social dictates it subverts. Their liaison navigates skillfully around the language barrier by means of a scripted silence whose alternative to *uerba* itself further thrills him:

> me specta nutusque meos uultumque loquacem:
> excipe furtiuas et refer ipsa notas.
> uerba superciliis sine uoce loquentia dicam;
> uerba leges digitis, uerba notata mero.
>
> (17–20)

[Watch for my expressions' speaking signs and subtle indications, and send them back. I'll speak silent words with my brows, and you can read my fingers' words—words inscribed with wine.]

Taking liberties with convention, however, also relies in 1.4 upon the poem's own fantasy of control. Driven from the start to choreograph every movement of their evening, the poet can even get ahead of himself, crafting plans that seem to have no object: "ante ueni quam uir; nec quid, si ueneris ante, / possit agi uideo, sed tamen ante ueni" [13–14: Get here before he does. I don't see exactly what this will accomplish, but just do it anyway]. Any sign of explicit disfavor his mistress shows toward her *uir* delights the speaker; but allowing her only enough leverage to keep the husband blinded, he warns that so much as a kiss willingly offered to her mate would provoke his own angry intervention and public appropriation of what he claims exclusively: "dicam 'mea sunt' iniciamque manum" [40: "All mine," I would say, and would take you in hand].

Though he brags that they are both capable of improvising all "resque locusque" to their own advantage, the *amator* himself clearly stakes out new limits within which his mistress must carry on their game. Defensive anxiety about his mistress's proximity to her man unleashes apprehensions that the subterfuge he so confidently exploits can also be turned against him. In any case, his victory is as temporary as his ability to circumvent restrictive obstacles. All fantasy shatters against the *qua licet* represented by the literal boundary of the household's unyielding *fores*:

> me miserum! monui, paucas quod prosit in horas;
>   separor a domina nocte iubente mea.
> nocte uir includet; lacrimis ego maestus obortis,
>   qua licet, ad saeuas prosequar usque fores.
> oscula iam sumet, iam non tantum oscula sumet:
>   quod mihi das furtim, iure coacta dabis.
>
> (59–64)

[I'm a fool. I have masterminded what a few brief hours will dissipate. Night will enforce a separation from my lady; come night, your man owns you. I'll follow, dejected and weeping, as far as I'm allowed—to the wicked doors. Then he will claim your kisses, and more: what I must steal, the law grants to him.]

However far his game displaces the *uir*, the poet must inevitably revert after their evening adventure to his own *exclusus amator* status.

Moreover, the same rich imagination that inspires his illicit plot also torments the poet with thoughts of the pleasures his mistress's *uir* legitimately claims—*iura coacta dabis*—and (even worse) whatever enjoyment she may herself find in the other's embrace. Vainly wishing a morbid silence upon the bedroom into which his words cannot enter, the poet feels his tactical cunning undergo an embarrassing attrition or anticlimax. His devices to cheat her husband began with a plea that the mistress not let his commands slip away ("quae tibi sint facienda tamen cognosce, nec Euris / da mea nec tepidis uerba ferenda Notis" [11–12: understand what I have designed for you to do, and don't let the warm north or south winds carry off my words]), only to conclude with a plea that she manipulate the truth to keep *him* blind to what transpires behind closed doors ("sed quaecumque tamen noctem fortuna sequetur, / cras mihi constanti uoce dedisse nega" [69–70: but whatever should happen tonight, keep swearing to me tomorrow that it didn't]). Though he still presumes to dictate her responses, his sense of control has itself been compromised into absurdity. What had seemed so vital precisely because it was shrewdly concealed from public scrutiny finally begs denial, since (he now suggests) what is not publicly acknowledged does not exist. In the end, circumstances—especially socially defined circumstances—clearly determine this would-be master of *resque locusque*.

Ovid factors out the complex of intimacy and exclusion that 1.4 dramatizes over the two ensuing poems. Elegy 1.5, one of the *Amores'* most striking, recalls a sexual encounter whose very spontaneity offsets 1.4's elaborate machinations. Everything about the poem contributes to an ambience of erotic uncertainty, of things only partially revealed. Its action takes place in a provocative midday twilight:

> Aestus erat, mediamque dies exegerat horam;
>   adposui medio membra leuanda toro.
> pars adaperta fuit, pars altera clausa fenestrae,
>   quale fere siluae lumen habere solent,
> qualia sublucent fugiente crepuscula Phoebo
>   aut ubi nox abiit nec tamen orta dies.
>   (1.4.1–6)

> [It was hot, just past noon, and I had collapsed on the middle of my bed. One of the shutters was open and the other closed, so that the light filtered in as through a forest glade, or like at Phoebus's dusky departure, or when night first gives way to dawn.]

When the thinly clad Corinna suddenly intrudes into this scene, her surprised lover's disorientation corresponds to the setting's ambivalence: he cannot determine whether to compare her with Semiramis or Lais, queen or prostitute. This dreamlike situation poses the perplexing question of access. If Corinna's purpose is evident, her means of arrival is not. The "domestic arrangements" her appearance requires have suggested to some readers that Ovid models Corinna upon his first wife. The speaker seems to be at home, and a mistress's ability to enter his house—let alone his bedroom—unarrested seems rather implausible; they must, therefore, be married.[26] Such speculation misses the real point, which involves exactly her mysterious presence. Unlike the poet, who suffers exclusion in the two surrounding elegies, Corinna enjoys free passage, crossing thresholds unhindered. Her shadowy advent unsettles her lover almost as much as the sensuality that she exudes arouses him.

Corinna's mobility opens questions of volition and command that inflect the more blatant issue of dominance disturbing 1.5. The violent excitement to which Ovid's speaker instantly gives rein transforms the episode into a masculine fantasy of conquest:

> deripui tunicam; nec multum rara nocebat,
>   pugnabat tunica sed tamen illa tegi;
> quae, cum ita pugnaret tamquam quae uincere nollet,
>   uicta est non aegre proditione sua.
>   (13–16)

[I tore off her garment; and while its transparency had not posed much of a problem anyway, she nonetheless fought to keep it on—fought like a woman who did not wish to win, whose self-betrayal forced a not unwilling submission.]

His brutality (itself transparently veiled), coupled with the woman's alleged "self-betrayal," seriously complicates the characterization. The poem discreetly betrays the male lover's own lack of control, figured not only in the unchecked lust he indulges but also by the fact that Corinna is the one who has evidently chosen the time and place for their encounter. Where the previous poem had attempted to script all feminine response, Corinna is here described as feigning a vulnerability that mocks her paramour's illusion of command while it entices his desire. His failure to describe the woman's face when surveying her nakedness implicitly gives away the empowerment he relishes: anyone may gaze upon Corinna's face, but he witnesses a more exclusive spectacle; yet neither his own cunning nor his seductive skill has secured this private audience. The sudden meeting interestingly forecloses all verbal exchange, and though he breaks off his reverie with a flippant "cetera quis nescit?" [who doesn't know the rest?], the poet intimates an awareness that mysteries left unspoken continue both to arouse and frustrate. What erotic success he claims, however immediately pleasurable, arrives on terms not his own.

The *amator*'s small measure of control over his experience leaves dubious the fulfillment of 1.5's casual closing prayer, "proueniant medii sic mihi saepe dies" [26: May my afternoons often turn out like this], a point borne out immediately as the next poem returns us to a circumstance of mournful exclusion. From the heights of his afternoon tryst with Corinna the poet resumes his evidently more routine station, bargaining with the household door's lowly guardian. As he enacts the displacement only contemplated in 1.4's *denouement*, his rhetoric shifts from the earlier dinner party's sensual gourmandizing to an emphasis on physical and argumentative emaciation. The slave need only leave the door partially open, he negotiates, since "longus amor tales corpus tenuauit in usus / aptaque subducto corpore membra dedit" [5–6: Love's ardors waste a body thoroughly, suiting its members to such narrow entries]. Ovid's novel emphasis on the doorkeeper (rather than on classical *paraclausithyron*'s normal addressee, the door itself[27]) further reinforces 1.6's symmetry with 1.4: the amator had earlier lamented being shut out by the *uir* who exercised authority over his lover, but is now kept at bay by one whom she rules. His eventual threat to assert *amor*'s claim violently again rings hollow—the slave responds neither to entreaties nor curses (*precibusque minisque*), and the *fores* remain securely fastened. Quite unlike Corinna, who can transgress unimpeded upon his daytime slumbers, the *amator* petitions sleeplessly throughout the night upon her threshold. She knows, in short, an independence about which he only brags.

The inefficacious designs haunting 1.4–6 are rehearsed in a similar progression occupying book 3's middle, where the poet's desire meets yet another set of barriers. Now, the frustrations are no longer "spousal"—determined by the *uir* or his household— but natural, physical and more broadly societal. The movement impresses upon us brands of separation that refuse to be bargained away.

Amores 3.6 amounts to an essay in futility. The lover's path to his mistress's residence is broken by a stream that has, since his last crossing, swollen into a far less navigable *amnis* or "river." This unexpected impediment seems to ridicule the officiousness he had until now so pointlessly observed, something that exasperates him more than the impasse itself. "Quid properasse iuuat," he asks,

> quid parca dedisse quieti
> tempora, quid nocti conseruisse diem,
> si tamen hic standum est, si non datur artibus ullis
> ulterior nostro ripa premenda pede?
>
> (9–12)

[What good did it do to hurry, without rest, not discriminating day or night, if I have to stop here now, lacking any means to set foot on the other side?]

Not surprisingly, the *carmen* he summons to charm the flood leaves its addressee unimpressed. A poet who discounts such myths as Perseus's magic sandals or

Ceres' chariot early on ("ueterum mendacia uatum: / nec tulit haec umquam nec feret ulla dies" [17–18: lies of the old poets, which never existed and never will]) bears little conviction that flattering legends of watery *eros* might assuage a torrent. Things once benign grow elementally into monstrosities indifferent to lovers and their landscapes, working changes that threaten to render *memoria* inutile. Instead of subsiding, the river swells in response to his entreaties, as if eager to sweep away words all but written on water.

Similar to the way that obstacles to fruition can enhance erotic allure, thwarted aspirations seem to inspire rather than to efface the poetic illusion he doggedly entertains. His stories unfortunately fail to salvage the self-reinforcement that lyric consolation traditionally assays. If anything, as he recalls the success these river deities have known in their amorous pursuits, the speaker is further frustrated by a real *amnis*'s prophylactic barrier. Efforts to quell his rancor yield by the end to an inevitable ceremonial invective against forces curtailing all human endeavor—pastoral, georgic and (most infuriatingly) erotic: "damnosus pecori curris, damnosior agris: / foristan haec alios, me mea damna mouent" [99–100: by your flow flocks are destroyed, and crops as well; perhaps these griefs afflict others, but I have my own worries]. The worst contempt he can express, finally, is a wish that the river come to share the same natural blight afflicting human beings, "sint rapidi soles siccaque semper hiemps" [106: may the sun always parch you and the winter add no moisture].

The discrepancy in 3.6 between a fabulously animated landscape and more recalcitrant realities presages 3.7's arch comedy, where the poet confesses a mortifying incident of sexual impotence. Removal of all external barriers may, sardonically, present no surer guarantee of success, since our bodies can refuse to serve adequately their own appetites. "Optabam certe recipi: sum nempe receptus," he recalls in humiliation, "oscula ferre: tuli;

proximus esse: fui" [47–48: I hoped she would have me, and was welcomed; for kisses, and they were mine; to lie next to her, and so it was], but trains his puzzlement and *pudor* most expressly upon the incommensurate powers of imagination and the flesh:

> at quae non tacita formaui gaudia mente,
>   quos ego non finxi disposuique modos!
> nostra tamen iacuere uelut praemortua membra
>   turpiter hesterna languidiora rosa. . . .
>
> (63–66)

[What silent delights and erotic play hadn't my mind imagined and planned; but at the moment my penis lay, shamefully, as if dead, wilted as yesterday's rose.]

The erection he achieves belatedly following his cataloging of her beauties and the intimacies of their failed encounter, itself stimulated by this very imagination, compounds his exasperation. What the woman's charms and even her language—ranging from words of adulation ("et mihi blanditias dixit dominumque uocauit") to "common" obscenities ("publica uerba iuuant")—could not excite, fantasy supplies *post facto*.

His recovery by poem's end mollifies this lover's passing terror of permanent disfunction, but the episode's inexplicability shadows his relief with an unsettling cognizance of potential breakdown. None of the many possible explanations offered—from his own suspicion that he has suffered enchantment to the woman's more pointedly rational thought that another lover has already spent him —justifies to him the experience. Down to its final comic twist, where the mistress goes through the postcoital, contraceptive washing to keep the servants from realizing that nothing has transpired (rather than the usual ploy of suborning them into keeping from the other mate that something has), the poem threads its way through reversals that recall how little control he may claim over even the most promising situations. Awareness of an ability to transform, instantly, into *truncus iners* keeps the contingency he has come to know in ludicrous perspective.

At last, the poet steps from private embarrassment's confines onto the public stage of social outrage. *Amores* 3.8 vituperates against the devaluation of poetry's worth by a current mercenary greed. Now wealth alone rules, "dat census honores" (56). His talent, though still acknowledged, no longer earns him immediate practical benefits: "cum pulchre dominae nostri placuere libelli, / quo licuit libris, non licet ire mihi; / cum bene laudauit, laudato ianua clausa est" [5–7: Even when my books please my mistress, they get to go where I'm not allowed; though well praised, I remain shut out]. The closed door well known by the *amator* has come to signify a much broader malaise than conventional sexual frustration—what he diagnoses as a vulgar obsession with commodities that poetry cannot secure. He cannot expect to win favor without solid financial introduction; demands for presents have clearly not, as he has asserts offhandedly in 1.10, chilled his ardor, but have only exacerbated his longing for that which appears more than ever beyond reach. He remains outside the door, tantalized vicariously by the sights his books alone can witness, strewn amid the traffic of her bedroom. The poet who had earlier fantasized becoming a ring to enjoy the touch of his mistress's flesh now looks on sadly impoverished, anything but made of gold himself, and therefore ostracized. His forlorn threshold vigil gives substance to the early assertion "at nunc barbaria est grandis habere nihil" [4: but now, to have no money is the supreme barbarism], where lack of funds dictates one's standing as, literally, an "outsider."

Amores 3.8 is a poem about money's sexiness in a mercenary setting. As Ovid's speaker unfolds his frustrated protests, he stumbles upon an even uglier psychological insight crucial to the collection's overall vision.

The riches his upstart rival has accumulated were secured through military service, an inviting (if risky) avenue for personal advancement at this time of imperial conquest. Beneath whatever protest Ovid intended his sneer to register, however,[28] resides an uncommonly candid awareness of violence's lurid draw on the human imagination. The poet's outraged effort to dissuade his mistress from this soldierly competitor's embraces envisions the atrocities to which military life is inured. Her new lover has achieved his status *per uulnera* (by wounds), and blood saturates his entire career:

> dextram tange, cruenta fuit.
> qua periit aliquis, potes hanc contingere dextram?
>   heu, ubi mollities pectoris illa tui?
> cerne cicatrices, ueteris uestigia pugnae:
>   quaesitum est illi corpore, quicquid habet.
> forsitan et quotiens hominem iugulauerit ille
>   indicet: hoc fassas tangis, auara, manus?
>
> (16–22)

[Go on and touch his right hand, once dyed in blood. Can you really manage to reach for a hand by which someone has died? My god, what happened to your tender-heartedness? Examine his scars, tokens from past fights. Whatever's his was won with that body. Maybe he can tell you just how many human throats he has slashed: what greed could prompt you to hold such hands?]

Directed at the decadent society that he simultaneously excoriates and inhabits, these admonitions may well prove ironically counterproductive. However terrifying he intends to make his description, the poet lingers over detail with a precision that seems to betray his own begrudging admiration for the rival's brute, soldierly prowess. What has lost him his mistress is not exclusively a lamentable poverty, nor (as Green suggests) 3.7's genital impotence, nor the exhaustion of his poetic gift (which the mistress, decidedly no philistine, still admires). An unreadiness to practice a more "virile" *ars* also implicitly discounts his sexual attractiveness, in this economy where might makes more than right.[29]

An enhanced sensitivity to violence's subtle and overt role in the sexual relationships that Ovid portrays has helped to revise significantly the way recent critics read the *Amores*. Despite 1.9's definitive "pacifist" boast that, unlike military duty, sexual warfare is conducted *sine caede* (bloodlessly), his conquests entail plenty of coercion, brutality and even bloodshed.[30] What breaks down the celebrated image of love as a battlefield is the absence of the mortal risk that warriors literally take. The poet's confession that he was indigent until drafted into Amor's service transforms militarism into a joke. At the same time, erotic passion sparks the epic aggression and self-destruction his allusions recall. Behind the banner of 1.9's impudent analogy march several of the collection's most disturbing performances. Ovid's *amator*, himself vulnerable to the injurious whims he ponders, mingles consternation with fascination to realize a stunningly complex voice.

Of this, *Amores* 1.7 affords an exemplary case. The poet has, in rage, attacked his mistress. Now awed by the incriminating silence of her horrified gaze, he laments his act. Since Hermann Fränkel first admired the repentant lover's sympathetic stance, this poem has received considerable attention, largely in rebuttal to the "sincerity" such a reading advocates.[31] Like most of the collection, 1.7 is for these critics all rhetorical posture, intentionally funny in its glib overstatement.[32] In his notes to the *Amores*' most recent edition, J. C. McKeown maintains their view: "The tone of the poem is distinctly humorous. Ovid prevents us from taking him seriously by exaggerating the enormity of his offence."[33] Mistress-beating (so it goes) is a matter that hardly sustains such highly wrought response; this all must be a joke.

These critics' reflex to ameliorate or discount the

violence is in one sense understandable, influenced by the speaker's own desperate wish to dodge the issue. Insisting that we cannot responsibly mute the poem's emotional impact with appeals to literary convention, Cahoon martials a compelling revision of their approach, though at the expense of the psychological depth Ovid brilliantly manages. What distinguishes his persona is neither Fränkel's "proto-Christian" sympathy nor the viciousness Cahoon feels Ovid intended us to damn, but the speaker's troubled awareness that he enjoyed the crime he indicts. His multivalent rhetoric profoundly enriches the performance: on one level, he strives, through recourse to mythical precedent and profuse expressions of shocked self-loathing at what his hands have wrought, to mitigate his action to both himself and his victim; deeper still, these very efforts disclose to him the tawdry eroticism inhering in such exercises of violent power.

We first detect movement between these registers at lines 7–18. By way of self-justification, he cites first Ajax's and Orestes' violent losses of control, then drifts from this lame apology into a darker utterance: "ergo ego digestos potui laniare capillos? / nec dominam motae dedecuere comae: / sic formosa fuit" [11–18: Was I on this account justified in tearing her neatly styled hair? Even though the disordered locks by no means disgraced her—she was so beautiful that way]. Her disheveled appearance reminds him first of Atalanta's wild handsomeness when outrun by Milanion, then of Ariadne in her moment of terrified discovery that Theseus has abandoned her, and finally of Cassandra's pathetic splendor at the moment of her enslavement. The impulse is neither ludicrous nor unfeeling, but mortifying—the speaker suddenly coming to terms with the sinister aesthetic and sexual sensation his cruelty discovers. He cancels the reverie abruptly, reverting to a flurry of self-deprecating insults; but upon returning to his mistress's wounded image, he cannot mask the flush of desire he experiences once again:

> exanimis artus et membra trementia uidi,
>   ut cum populeas uentilat aura comas,
> ut leni Zephyro gracilis uibratur harundo
>   summaue cum tepido stringitur unda Noto;
> suspensaeque diu lacrimae fluxere per ora,
>   qualiter abiecta de niue manat aqua.
> tunc ego me primum coepi sentire nocentem;
>   sanguis erat lacrimae, quas dabat illa, meus.
>
>   (53–60)
>
> [I saw her weakened frame and limbs tremble, like poplar leaves disturbed by a breeze, or a reed softly swayed by the gentle west wind, or water's surface brushed by the mild south wind; her tears held in check then flowed down her face like the trickle from a sorry snowdrift. It was then that I began to sense my wickedness. What she wept was my own life's blood.]

Lovingly crafted descriptions capture the scene's pathos while betraying the poet's *nocentiae* to himself. His request that she rearrange her tresses at the end simultaneously pleads for pardon and reminds us that these may forcibly be undone once again. The exercise of violent force holds too great an allure for the embarrassed speaker to make credible his assurance that the event will not be repeated.

    The poet who leaves much unsaid—like what sparked his rage to begin with—now begs the mistress to nullify his deed by striking back at his own unguarded face. The *tristia signa* are not so systematically erased. Against her fearsome silence he translates a newfound appetite for destruction into the self-incriminating poem. Her pain and terror belatedly inspire his own grief, and he now feels a new sense of shame: "in mea uesanas habui dispendia uires / et ualui poenam fortis in ipse meam" [25–26: I have made use of this furious virility to my own cost, have inflicted this punishment upon myself]. Another's tears distill pain that really becomes one's own; to deny either the thrill or the odium Ovid's *amator* finds in his act, any more than the crime's severity itself, is to obscure the poet's achievement. However often he rearranges these *signa* of degradation, there endures an intuition that he only sets himself and others up for yet another fall. Private acts, which look for sanction in the violence of honored communal myths and epics, manifest the destructive core of a subtly terrifying *eros*.

Aggression and self-abuse are further scrutinized in 1.14's dark comedy, where the poet chides a mistress whose cosmetic obsessions have resulted in the loss of her once glorious hair. Now verbal rather than physical, his intense hostility compares to that displayed in 1.7: he will badger the mistress's folly and vanity until she is reduced from distraught consternation to almost tearful breakdown, at which point he relents. Again, the overall tone is neither gloating nor facetious, so much as abusive and melancholy. Ovid fleshes out his persona further with this image of one who, in his eagerness to persecute another for pursuing novelty over natural favor, discovers an even more pernicious brand of self-indulgence.

What especially infuriates the speaker is that the damage his mistress sustains was self-inflicted. Despite its confirmed beauty—sufficiently luxuriant (he attests) to outstrip anything a poet could attribute to the gods—she could not resist the urge to "torment" her hair with harsh cosmetic procedures: "facta manu culpaque tua dispendia sentis; / ipsa dabas capiti mixta uenena tuo" [43–44: You worked the loss you now feel with your own guilty hand; you yourself poured the toxic mixture over your head]. The horror with which he looked upon his own *manus sacrilegae* in 1.7 he now directs toward her hands, inviting her to examine herself with the same critical eye. A wig woven from the hair of German captives, like his extended encomium of her former splendor, will substitute poorly for her incomparable, lost ornament.

His imprecation's tactless, unrelenting severity opens

to question the character's motives, as does the closing about-face (Douglas Parker's prime example of the peculiar Ovidian "coda"[34]). Savage righteousness often shelters ugly self-recrimination; and the *Amores'* speaker, in context, has much to repress. He curses a lust for fashionable variety that recalls his own erotic fickleness: 1.3's disclaimer that he is no *desultor amoris* or "sexual circus rider" in Green's felicitous translation fails to hold up against (for instance) 2.4's professedly omnivorous tastes ("omnibus historiis se meus aptat amor"). Moreover, it is a bruised vanity that strikes out at the woman's alleged narcissism. When Propertius indicts his mistress's cosmetic obsessions, he does so out of jealous fear that she seeks to attract other paramours. Though Ovid's *amator* avoids this direct charge, the convention, along with a more audible pique at her indifference to his counsels and pleas, stands behind his rancor.

Obnoxious self-vindication nonetheless falls silent before the ruinous spectacle to which his harangue finally returns. His awareness that he is vulnerable to the immoderation he immoderately condemns is belatedly exposed in a tactless effort to ameliorate everything. This delivers Ovid's speaker from a charge of total moral blindness even if it cannot unwrite his brutal proclivities. The diversionary exercise of ridiculing another's folly only places him at the center of a more embracing personal guilt. Something beyond patronizing mollification is at stake in the final "collige cum uultu mentem: reparabile damnum est: / postmodo natiua conspiciere coma" [55-56: Collect yourself with other thoughts: the loss isn't irreparable, and in a while, your own hair will again be seen]: the comfort he sheepishly offers is also a brand of self-consolation, an attempt to reassure himself that his own error can be redeemed. The damage she has worked upon her appearance is superseded by the pain he inflicts on her, focusing ultimately for the speaker and his audience the "unnatural" destructive tendencies he displays even as he condemns these.

Regarding this crucial matter of repair, we may put to 1.14 the same question asked of 1.7: will repentance guard against repetition of the abuse, or will reversal also occasion forgetfulness of past failure? *Amores* 1.14 yields a similarly bleak prospect. Occupying the frustratingly paradoxical station of one sensitive to his own insensitivity, Ovid's *amator* learns that scars never fully mend because we will not let them. Hair will grow back, just as it had been rent earlier, and he will find the chance sooner or later to replay the scene: 1.14's opening word, the imperfect *dicebam* ("I always said . . . "), can extend infinitely, given our natural inclination to grow bored and end up mistreating what we hold most precious. Every moment of human regeneration harbors for Ovid the seed of a subsequent return to misery. It is the same notion stitching together the *Metamorphoses*, and threading ultimately through *Ex Ponto*'s confidences:

> saucius eiurat pugnam gladiator, et idem
>   inmemor antiqui uulneris arma capit.
> nil sibi cum pelagi dicit fore naufragus undis,
>   et ducit remos qua modo nauit aqua.
>   (*Ex Pont.* 1.5.37–40)[35]

[When hurt, the gladiator abjures fighting, only to take up arms as soon as he forgets his wounds. The shipwreck victim swears he'll have nothing further to do with the sea, but is out there on the same water again in no time.]

Ovid depicts a perpetual series of promised reversals, coterminous only with perplexed human existence itself.

Somber though the speaker's complexity grows in 1.7 and 14, Ovid trains no harsher light on the work of "blind hands" than in 2.13–14, the traumatic account of Corinna's abortion. The lover's dismayed realizations of how much pain he is capable of inflicting yields, before a supreme vision of unwitting self-destruction, to an agony of terrified powerlessness. Enfeebled justification and empty recrimination dissolve into the frenzy channeling his purposeful language and gestures. The dire circumstance—Corinna has almost killed herself attempting to terminate a pregnancy, precipitating the collection's sole life-and-death crisis—renders these poems the *Amores'* riskiest performances. Ovid must craft a response that captures his speaker's disorientation while it believably complements and amplifies the temperament elaborated elsewhere.

Critical preconceptions have baffled appreciation of the remarkable poise with which Ovid maintains the poem's balance. The same nervousness besetting other approaches to the *Amores'* eccentric tableaux has worked more strenuously than ever to discount this poem's sincerity; and though most have found the *amator*'s posture offensive, at least one reader is not beyond detecting in the incident described some preposterous rhetorical comedy.[36] Even Mary-Kay Gamel, whose understanding of 2.13-14 as challenges to "the *amator*'s male vision of love, politics, and poetry" identifies her as the foremost champion of the poem's sophistication and urgency, must cast the speaker as a ruthless narcissist interested only in collapsing Corinna's misery into yet another occasion to "show off his talents."[37] Again, a deeper complexity is available, wherein desperation rather than the decadence of cynical exploitation serves as keynote: where a friend's death may (we shall see) later in the collection reconfirm his suspicion that there are no gods, his lover's uncertain fate compels the poet all the more fervently to pray that there are. Outrage wrestles with distraught consternation—"illa quidem clam me tantum molita pericli / ira digna mea, sed cadit ira metu" [13.3-4: Her attempting something so dangerous without consulting me surely justifies my wrath; but fear cancels this anger]—in his sudden compulsion to bargain for a life that he cares more about than he previously realized.[38]

Lack of control becomes for the speaker in these

elegies a central issue. The bleak mockery of his own presumption at 13.5–6 ["sed tamen aut ex me conceperat, aut ego credo: / est mihi pro facto saepe, quod esse potest," I was after all the one who got her pregnant—or so I believe (I often mistake the merely possible for fact)] acknowledges the independence Corinna finally maintains, recalling something he would perhaps just as soon suppress: that the child she has aborted was not necessarily his. So recently as the previous poem he had celebrated his intimacy with her, despite all obstacles, only to find himself "excluded" again all the more demeaningly in his view. Circumstance leaves no time, however, for these considerations, eclipsed by the prayer he urgently formulates. His petition's relatively stock rhetorical patterning signals not a glib indifference to her fate, but rather the charged concern of one who speaks formulaically because frantically. In need, he resorts indiscriminately to any goddess—hence the awkward appeal to Ilithyra, the guardian of childbirth, in lines 19–22—and even offers himself as votary. The same urgency propels the most desperate bargain he advances, with expressed trepidation, at the close of 2.14: "di, faciles peccasse semel concedite tuto; / et satis est: poenam culpa secunda ferat" [43–44: Gods, mercifully pardon her this one trespass, and that will suffice; exact a penalty upon a subsequent lapse]. The caution prefacing these words—"ista sed aetherias uanescant dicta per auras, / et sint omnibus pondera nulla meis" [41–42: But may the winds dissipate all my words, so they may all come to nothing]—aims apotropaically to substitute his own blustering severity for the vastly more potent rancor he anticipates any presiding deity might vent. He wishes upon the curse itself, at last, a fate that he everywhere else prays his words might be spared.

Et satis est: both poems conclude with similar pleas, first that Corinna herself swear never to try this again, and second that the gods themselves grant her the opportunity to make good her promise. His willingness to sacrifice her upon further transgression is anything but dismissive or cruel, especially given the way his previous utterance had linked their fates ("huc adhibe uultus et in una parce duobus: / nam uitam dominae tu dabis, illa mihi" [2.13.15–16: Turn this way, and rescue both of us; for if you restore my lady's wellbeing, she'll restore mine]). The gamble is, in any case, doubly chancy, given the melancholy awareness infusing the *Amores*, that we prove all too often our own worst enemies. Cursing abortion specifically, the speaker places our broader potential for annihilation in the "blind hands" his splendid synesthesia identifies:

> Quid iuuat inmunes belli cessare puellas
>   nec fera peltatas agmina uelle sequi,
> si sine Marte suis patiuntur uulnera telis
>   et caecas armant in sua fata manus?
>
> (2.14.1–4)

[What good is it for girls to stay behind at leisure, excluded from martial duty, not to carry a shield among the savage troops, if without Mars's provocation they by their own weapons suffer wounds, and self-destructively equip their blind hands.]

Freed from the enforced cruelty of military service, *caecae manus* turn violently upon themselves, in a paradigmatic gesture focusing the subtle, pervasive awareness that unnerves the poet even more than the immediate mortal plight he addresses.

From the *sacrilegae manus* worthy of chains in 1.7 to 1.14's busy, culpable *manus*, and from the *centimanus* giants of his abandoned epic to the bloodied warrior-*amator*'s *manus* in 3.8, hands figure as grimly officious agents of the violence that traffics on every social register of the world Ovid depicts. Random suffering inflicted within the lovers' leisured class reaches out with equal severity to those serving this stratum of society. In 1.14, the poet remembers in passing that his lady's hair was so easily managed, without frustration, that she was never driven to wound her attendants' arms with needles (17–18), alluding to what was evidently a common practice. In the first book's *paraclausithyron*, he reminds the now recalcitrant *ianitor* of the flogging from which he had once preserved him (1.6.19–20). His abhorrence of the eunuch's plight echoes 2.14's fevered verdict against abortion: "qui primus pueris genitalia membra recidit, / uulnera quae fecit debuit ipse pati" [2.3.3–4: The one who first castrated a boy ought to have suffered the same wound himself]. All we learn about the physical appearance of Cypassis, the maid blackmailed into an ongoing affair with her mistress's lover in 2.7–8, is her lash-scarred back, inscribed with testimony of the lady's temper. They stand exposed, mere victims in the petty intrigues of the gentry. The pain he witnesses, experiences and helps to perpetuate offers little hope for the realization of an overriding sympathy that can rescue Ovid's subjects from one another or from themselves. These privileged figures are all, in his pattern, authors of their own *nequitiae*.

Ovid's speaker had originally studied to write about *uiolentia*, as the work's first line let us know; his preparation has not, evidently, gone to waste. The poet has ironically gotten what he wanted after all, something Cupid's laugh in 1.1 had perhaps anticipated. What animates the *Amores* is an idea that *animus*—the willpower or self-government Seneca would fault their author for lacking—mounts a feeble defense against the term's alternative, conflicting sense of less tractable passions, an innate spirit that may, by turns, incline one to tear down a life's work or breathe life into an undertaking like the *Metamorphoses* ("In noua fert animus mutatas dicere forma / corpora..."). We struggle fiercely to maintain control, Ovid suggests, precisely because we infer just how little of this we actually claim over experience, environment and self. Neither language's inadequacy, nor the baleful misogyny his *amator* indulges along with many other sins, shadows the work so much as a more profound blindness shared by lover and society, author and audience, that encompasses all these component perils. The conviction is sufficiently firm and ranging both to integrate the early collection and to bridge these elegies with the *Tristia*, performances from exile in which the early work's fears, as I have pursued them, are finally and bitterly rehearsed.

Survival and the Imperial Audience

Eros's irrational and often violent potential renders it a traditional vehicle for the poetic exploration of self-destructive appetites. The Augustan elegists all portray love as "a fault which destroys the reason and perverts the will, but a power which the lover is helpless to control and from which he can find no release."[39] Many have found their attitude a deliberate reaction to Lucretius, whose efforts in *De rerum natura* to play against passion's madness a more measured or *sôphrôn* ideal of love established a legacy exploited most thoroughly by Virgil and Horace.[40] Ovid resisted the Lucretian split most boldly, deriding at every opportunity "the assumption that one might, if only he is clear-sighted enough, elude the snares of Venus."[41] In the gleam of Augustus's traditionalist conviction that "there was no greater service that a man could render to Rome than to instruct and train youth, especially in view of the fact that young people had gone so far astray because of moral laxity,"[42] erotic love's reflexes also shade frequently for Ovid into specific literary concerns. The generic anxieties and self-destructive impulses discussed in the previous sections integrate. Awareness that a recusant literary stance can prove professionally unhealthy never seems to defeat the compulsion. Later, speaking in his own person from the premature and grimly unerotic twilight of Tomis, Ovid drew the parallel explicitly:

sentit amans sua damna fere, tamen haeret in illis,
   materiam culpae persequiturque suae.
nos quoque delectant, quamuis nocuere, libelli,
   quodque mihi telum uulnera fecit, amo.
                                    (*Tristia* 4.1.33–36)

[The lover well aware of his folly nonetheless clings tightly to it, returning to the source of his vice; so do I enjoy my books, however much damage they've done me, and love the weapon responsible for my calamity.]

The *Tristia*'s lines reprise the *Amores*' ironic lessons, freshly nourished in the embittered conviction of experience. Neither self-pity nor pleading flattery can persuasively hide Ovid's sensitivity to the risks inscribed in the amatory poet's enterprise. Since the *amator*'s earlier assessments of self and public resonate intriguingly with the author's own desperately purposeful exercises in his exilic work, I want to turn to a brief consideration of the way banishment inflects Ovid's attitude toward literary immortality, before returning to the *Amores*' urgent revaluation of poetic accomplishment and survival in 3.9's Tibullus elegy. In the face of the political removal that he privately suffers, or the personal mortality we all ultimately share, artistic celebrity comes to seem a brittle and inadequate recompense.

One of the poets welcoming Tibullus to Elysium in *Amores* 3.9 is Cornelius Gallus, whom we heard Ovid daringly honor at 1.15. Reputedly Rome's earliest exponent of love elegy, Gallus had abused Augustus's friendship and possibly the political office this had won for him; when punitive ostracism was followed by charges of corruption, suicide appeared the best way out, an option he exercised in 27 or 26 B.C.[43] Writing from Tomis in A.D. 9, Ovid once again remembered Gallus, whose demise early in the emperor's reign must now have seemed a bitter, inverted complement to his own predicament. He insinuates the ironic symmetry in *Tristia* 2: protesting in conventional fashion that his life has been respectable though his muse playful (354), Ovid goes on to observe how Gallus's poetry had not been faulted despite his public misdeeds ("non fuit opprobrio celebrasse Lycorida Gallo, / sed linguam nimio non tenuisse mero" [445–46: Gallus won condemnation not for his praise of Lycoris, but because he could not restrain his tongue when drunk]). Latin literature's triumph under the *princeps*'s alleged auspices would stand neatly bounded by sobering images of imperial power.

Ovid himself informs us that his exile had as much to do with some unspeakable *error* as with the subversive *carmen* (*Tristia* 2.207), certainly a plausible admission given that his *Ars amatoria* had been in circulation since A.D. 1 or 2.[44] His emphasis upon this literary offense throughout the poems from Tomis, however, betrays the writer's fears for his poetic *corpus*. The spirited defense of his art filling out *Tristia* 2 identifies, for one recent commentator, Ovid's drive to reclaim professional turf: "Rather than conceding the emperor's right to pass judgment and to bring the Muses under his sway, Ovid asserts his own right to poetic authority, even over the *princeps*."[45] If this is the case, Ovid nonetheless comprehends the futility of such an impulse. Aesthetic or political judgment, as we all know, too often has little regard for evidence; Augustus, he realizes, may not even have consulted the guilty literature in question (*Tristia* 2.237–38). The circumstance justly inspires dread in one acutely sensitive to the way power determines public taste: "ergo hominum quaesitum odium mihi carmine, quosque / debuit, est uultus turba secuta tuos" [*Tristia* 2.87–88: My poetry has won everybody's disfavor, as was proper, since the people follow the expression on your [the emperor's] face]. The current fame he can still boast elsewhere in the poem (115–20, for example) hangs, after all, by a slim thread indeed.

On the receiving end of the writer's appeal, the emperor seems to have appreciated his advantage. Augustus knew equally well the poet who presumed to see through him. As Peter Green points out, beyond the "calculated cruelty" of his decision to relegate Ovid, he observed an impeccable justice. Censors may coerce speech as well as silence, and *relegatio*—a form of "tempered" banishment that left open the prospect of recall—virtually insured that its victim (in Green's words) "would continue to bombard the capital with fawning rhetoric, with gross endorsements of the regime he had hitherto treated, in his apolitical way, as a kind of bad joke. As a revenge for all the years of superior private sniping ... this particular punishment fitted the crime with quite horrific aptness."[46] More precisely, Augustus perhaps counted on something politically sweeter than the convicted poet's obsequious expressions of remorse; he sought a retraction that might permanently defuse the satirist's public credibility. The best personal apology Ovid could craft was a literary *apologia*, a confession that all his subversive posturing was a ridiculous fraud without any rebellious conviction, which would make a mockery of the mocking texts. Though stung by an exasperated resentment that his lines barely mask, he came up with the banal self-justification tacitly ordered.

He did not share the official *damnatio memoriae* his predecessor Gallus appears to have suffered, but Ovid at last confronted with brutal immediacy the threat of obliteration his *Amores* had theorized so many years before. His book's vain search for its *fratres* on Roman bookshelves in *Tristia* 3.1 projects an especially dismal outlook. It would take more than his exclusion from a few public libraries to cancel the broad fame that, as the exile elsewhere consoles himself, he presently enjoys. However, at the moment when, in the name of a renewed cultural identity, the literary canon is itself undergoing revision—specifically away from the Hellenistic tastes to which his *leuior* manner is more germaine—Ovid's plight had rendered his poetry doubly vulnerable.[47] From the empire's hostile borderlands, the poet who could not stand to leave his page's margin blank gazes apprehensively on his legacy's cultural marginalization.

Trapped as securely inside this harsh parody of sponsorship devised for him by his imperial *iudex* as he is confined to Tomis, Ovid crafts poems that vacillate between defensive self-assurance and depressed reflections on fame's limitations. For instance, encouraging his stepdaughter Perilla to cultivate the poetic gift she has displayed, Ovid voices from the midst of defeat a stirring testament reminiscent of the *Metamorphoses'* closing passage:

> ingenio tamen ipse meo comitorque fruorque:
>   Caesar in hoc potuit iuris habere nihil.
> quilibet hanc saeuo uitam mihi finiat ense,
>   me tamen extincto fama superstes erit,
> dumque suis uictrix omnem de montibus orbem
>   prospiciet domitum Martia Roma, legar.
>   (*Tristia* 3.7.47–52)

> [My talent remains, however, my comfort and pleasure: Caesar can exercise no rights over this. Let anyone dispatch me with a cruel sword, my fame will survive after death, I shall be read so long as Martian Rome herself shall oversee as master all the world's mountains.]

A "happier" artistic glory (*felicior*) will be hers, he prays, and concludes with the command "effuge uenturos, qua potes, usque rogos!" [54: run, however you can, from the funeral that awaits you]. Flanked by equally loud counsels to flee publicity and the social distinction that tempts fate, his stoic disdain and arch resolve are left deeply ironic. *Tristia* 3.4 substantiates its admonition "uiue tibi, quantumque potes praelustria uita" [5: Live for yourself, and avoid as much notoriety as you're able] with a catalog of mythic characters whose desire for elevated heights proved fatal (17–30). *Tristia* 3.10 opens on a note of uncertainty whether anyone at Rome still even remembers the exiled poet. Caesar may have no power over Ovid's private *ingenio*, but he can place him far from the sight and thus eventually from the minds of others—and this will do. The darker sentiment prevails in *Tristia* 5.12's somber disclaimer: "non adeo est bene nunc ut sit mihi gloria curae: / si liceat, nulli cognitus esse uelim" [41–42: The glory I once coveted no longer entices me very much; if it were possible, I'd wish now to be known by no one].

Quite apart from whatever practical qualification Augustus might pose to his headier claims, Ovid has more abstract concerns—the idea of survival he brings to his reflections on the efficacy of poetic "success"—concerns that return us from Tomis to the *Amores*' complex responses. Though he covets artistic immortality with a defensive ardor, the collection's speaker is too much of a skeptic and sensualist to dismiss indifferently that most uncompromising boundary we know, the physical mortality that mocks all artistic pretense. An ultimate reluctance to grant poetry's triumph over death renders *Amores* 3.9, the funeral song for his colleague Tibullus, one of the work's most crucial and controversial moments.

Ovid's immediate predecessors had conventionally incorporated poignant reflections on death into their books of erotic poetry. Catullus's powerful tribute to his deceased brother, Propertius's sober meditation on war's casualty or his own demise, and Tibullus's recollection of his near-fatal sickness while accompanying Messala on one of the general-patron's excursions (an event Ovid's dirge incorporates) all offered their successor a rich variety of models. Emulating these precedents, the *Amores*' poem ruffles their manner, as most readers have sensed. The lament's conventional structure fails to contain the disruptive, confused emotions surveyed. By comparison, 2.6's trifle on the death of Corinna's parrot organizes its conceits in a "more appropriate, or at least less offensive" manner.[48] Most aggressively, reading 3.9 in the context of her thesis that Ovid filters the *Amores* through the voice of a "heartless" persona he intends to indict, Leslie Cahoon attacks the presentation's *gauche* distortions. Venus's and Cupid's initial mourning, "out of all due proportion for lamenting the loss of so minor a *sacrum* as a *poeta nequitiae*," displays an absurd insensitivity to mythic grandeur. The deceased's subsequent comparison to Homer and Orpheus, and the juxtaposition of Homer's poems with the mistresses who inspired Tibullus's books, excite similar ridicule ("the greatest works of civilization correspond, in the lover's view, with Tibullus' passing whims for two ladies of negligible worth"). The poem's overall "theology" is a mess (the gods "who evince extravagant grief over Tibullus at one point, have their existence questioned and their cruelty denounced a few lines later, only to reappear shortly thereafter, once more with tears of compassion in their eyes"). Finally, the women's argument before the pyre stretches decorum and credulity "to the breaking point."[49]

The Tibullus poem's mythic hyperbole and inconsistency can, however, point elsewhere than in the direction of travesty. Generically, funeral elegy contends with the inherent inadequacies of its own form—the unlikelihood of finding comfort for the loss of a human voice through myth's impersonal and inflated conventions, rendered especially acute when the voice had belonged to a poet. Ovid discovers, in the occasionally self-aggrandizing fantasy that grief desperately evokes, the supreme poignancy of our imagination's futile drive to mitigate death's unavoidable impact. The poet's equivocal regard for the healing gestures that he awkwardly entertains invigorates, rather than weakens, his course.

Although 3.9 opens with an invocation that Elegy mourn her dead *uates* as Memnon's and Achilles' mothers had lamented them, our attention fastens instantly on the gaunt spectacle of Tibullus's burning remains, counterpointing the poetic adornment that surrounds it: "ille tui uates operis, tua fama, Tibullus / ardet in exstructo corpus inane rogo" [3.9.5-6: your celebrant, your glory, Tibullus, lies burning there on the pyre, a useless body]. The speaker, who from his first elegy has "burned" in erotic passion, now looks to more oppressively literal fires. Before the pyre, he notes a few lines later, Cupid's torch is extinguished (*sine luce*). Sorrow no less intense than that suffered at the deaths of Aeneas and Adonis, their mythic relatives and paramours, incapacitates the god and his mother. The poet no sooner assembles this fictional entourage than he matches their swollen grief with a perfunctory, somewhat chilly commonplace, "at sacri uates et diuum cura uocamur, / sunt etiam qui nos numen habere putent" [17-18: We are called poets, holy and divinely favored; some even think the gods inhabit us]. His bitterness further excites the impiety voiced at 35-36: "cum rapiunt mala fata bonos, (ignoscite fasso) / sollicitor nullos esse putare deos" [when such a harsh fate carries off the good, I regret to admit, I'm moved to think that no gods exist]. This signals less the inconsistency Cahoon faults than the speaker's shifting emotions as he struggles vainly to shelter the personal, human vulnerability he rediscovers. Gods exist precisely because poets give them substance; deities reside, perhaps, exclusively "within." In effect, Ovid adopts a Lucretian posture, minus some of the rigor.

The Tibullus elegy, in short, draws its power from the way death exposes the fictionality of our consoling legends while forcing us most desperately to fall back on these. Fear and anger incite the poet to call upon the gods and to celebrate poetry's endurance—equally dubious gestures, in context—as he condemns the futility of all our efforts:

> uiue pius: moriere pius; cole sacra: colentem
>   mors grauis a templis in caua busta trahet.
> carminibus confide bonis: iacet ecce Tibullus;
>   uix manet e toto, parua quod urna capit.
>   (3.9.37–40)

[Live pious, and you will only die that way; observe all the sacred rites, and oppressive death will drag you from temple to open grave in mid-prayer. Look there at Tibullus, laid out, all-powerful, now the contents of a tiny urn.]

Try as he might, he cannot (or will not) redirect his gaze from the *corpus inane*, which somehow renders inane all his pacific gestures.[50] Stern experience—not incredulity—inspires the rhetorical question posed in the next two lines, "tene, sacer uates, flammae rapuere rogales, / pectoribus pasci nec timuere tuis?" [have the funeral flames really claimed you, holy poet, unafraid to consume your breast?]: this corpse *is* Tibullus. And a subtle precision marks his protest that any fire sufficiently impious to consume this body would just as readily destroy temples: he feels his own faith in these deities consumed as he beholds the ashen residue of his comrade's physical existence.

Life knows no substitutes. The poet's move away from Orpheus and Homer to Tibullus's survivors, Delia and Nemesis, enhances this basic awareness. Their confrontation over the corpse plays out an indecorous, urgent need for the living to distance themselves from the dead. The fierce combativeness they embody manifests their consciousness that poetic "immortalization"—for subject as for author—is a weak surrogate for the sheer sensual vitality their lover no longer shares:

Delia discedens "felicius" inquit "amata
  sum tibi: uixisti, dum tuus ignis eram."
cui Nemesis "quid" ait "tibi sunt mea damna dolori?
  me tenuit moriens deficiente manu."

(55–58)

[Delia remarked when departing "I was so happy in your love; you lived, while I was your flame"; to whom Nemesis replied, "Why are my losses painful for you?—I was the one he held to when his hand failed in death."]

To claim the author is to reclaim the self: stylized by Tibullus into literary conventions, the women articulate a grief that salvages them from the art whose source they have outlived. Interestingly, they do not regard their own survival in his verse, but the life he led while in their mortal company, something for which all the representation in the world cannot compensate.

The poem's closing moment remains conditional, looking toward an afterlife, the speaker suggests, that almost advertises itself as fantasy. If anything at all remains beyond *nomen et umbra*, reputation and ghost, Tibullus now enjoys the company not of gods, but of human beings: fellow poets gone before him—Gallus among them—any of whom, like Achilles in the *Odyssey*'s Hades, might share the sense that it is better to live unknown in the upper world's light than to reign among the dead. Ovid winds down quickly:

> his comes umbra tua est, si qua est modo corporis umbra;
>   auxisti numeros, culte Tibulle, pios.
> ossa quieta, precor, tuta requiescite in urna,
>   et sit humus cineri non onerosa tuo.
>
> (65–68)

[Your shade belongs with these poets; if a ghost passes bodily form, you join, nurturing Tibullus, the pious. I pray that your bones rest quietly in the urn, and that earth does not lie heavy on your ashes.]

We are left, at last, with recollections of those who distinguished themselves only to share a common fate—these, and the *urna* the surviving poet now grieves over. The staid dignity of these last lines by itself cautions any inclination to deny the elegy's seriousness. Ovid took nothing more seriously than human strategies of denial, either malicious or benign. Inside death's theater, our defense mechanisms operate with the splendid, moving inefficiency his homage to Tibullus captures.

It is also for this reason that 3.9 suffers, formally, by

comparison to the *epicedion* for Corinna's parrot.[51] Because of its relatively ludic setting, 2.6 can maintain an orderly mock-dignity, unimpeded by the emotional deconstruction powering the later elegy's profound sadness. What works for a pet, however skillfully anthropomorphized, cannot fairly measure situations where no such distance is available. The mock-*epicedion*'s smoothness, and not the Tibullus elegy's irregularity, should serve as a barometer of disingenuity. Other parrots may be trained; human voices are not so easily replaced.

Even the most sophisticated strategies of consolation rarely attain their desired pacific end. Our practical best—*quod licet*—is never quite good enough. Ovid's own literary tactics could not redeem the very real-life predicament of Tomis, and he would probably take cold comfort in the thought closing a recent study of his *Tristia* and *Ex Ponto*: "For Ovid himself, the artistic goals were fulfilled more than the personal. Although he died in exile, he left a poetic corpus well worth studying as Augustan poetic books."[52] Frustration over an inability to realize this "personal" objective provokes his "enraged hand"—recalling the hands that blindly work so much damage throughout the *Amores*—to obliterate its own work.

> cum uice mutata, qui sim fuerimque, recordor,
>   et, tulerit quo me casus et unde, subit,
> saepe manus demens, studiis irata sibique,
>   misit in arsuros carmina nostra focos.
> atque, ea de multis quoniam non multa supersunt,
>   cum uenia facito, quisquis es, ista legas.
>   (*Tristia* 4.1.99-104)

[When I remember capricious destiny, what I've become and what I used to be, both how and where my fate has transported me, often my insane hand, furious with its own work, casts my poems onto the hearthfire. And since not much remains of the many, be generous, whoever you are, when you read this.]

To be a fashioner of *publica carmina* is to remain acutely aware of one's contingency. Whatever escapes the artist's self-destructive *manus* ventures out, ever reliant upon those other hands that determine its ultimate fate: "uos quoque, si fas est, confusa pudore repulsae / sumite plebeiae carmina nostra manus" (*Tristia* 3.1.81–82: Take in, you hands of the people, if you can, my songs broken by rejection's shame).

It was Ovid's peculiar genius to focus the way self-awareness—a commodity he prized—involved primarily a grasp of our vulnerability as well as our willful propensity to suppress this aspect of experience. Outmaneuvered by others' superior craft or undone by self-inflicted harms, *amator* and exile cut sorry profiles, early and late. Playing before an authority such as Augustus, who (Suetonius tells us) took Apollo as his special role model, Ovid's disheartened wish never to have been known eerily echoes Marsyas's shrieks at *Metamorphoses* 6.386, "a! piget, a! non est . . . tibia tanti" [Please have mercy! A pipe is not worth so sharp a price]. Confronting the hazards of taking up instruments in a world where others make the rules and call the songs, Ovid originates the idea recast in this section's epigraph. Song, for him, ended up costing more than he was ready to pay.

Whatever audience he immediately conceived—Corinna, Roman society generally or the emperor who ostensibly directed its tastes, or the posterity in whose grander vista all of these entities blurred—Ovid never lost sight of himself as the able yet vulnerable negotiator sketched so exquisitely in the *Amores*' epigram. The demeanor outlined in this crucial opening statement and elaborated throughout the work's delightful and pained moments fashions the core to which the *Metamorphoses*' swelling final assurances and the exilic poems' punishing self-doubt are satellites. Ovid lost the game he played with contemporary political circumstances, dying far from the urban galleries he regarded so lovingly. His work did survive, dilating its influence across centuries and new cultural contexts that saw fit to adapt his pagan myths to altogether different literary and religious ambiences. Though western lyric also adapts, the basic predicament of the poet's difficult relationship with a wider audience, such as the *Amores* had unfolded, survives as a critical constant.

Twelve centuries after Ovid's death, the troubadours were still actively contending with what Sarah Spence, in her study of the competing rhetorics of reason and desire, has termed "private power, public anxiety." Spence mentions that these poets, enjoying power over their immediate audiences, turn to an abject disenfranchisement before the cruelty of the courtly mistress ostensibly addressed in their songs: "While the poet can control the world of his work...the lover cannot."[53] Although I do not agree with Spence's assumption of these poets' confident dominion over their listeners, her observation highlights the endurance of lyric poetry's *agon* with its public. Among Italian poets of the *dolce stil nuovo*, the animosity toward a broad audience with which Horace had opened his third book of odes, "Odi profanum uulgus et arceo" [I hate and proscribe the ignorant rabble], gained renewed currency. As Lauro Martines points out, "despite their commitment to the vernacular, the *stilnovo* poets found their poetic identity in opposition to the triumphant 'vulgarity' of the *popolo*.... Something, therefore, in the essential makeup of the period's 'high' lyric verse was a passionate and pointed rebuttal to the pretensions of the *popolo*."[54] This hostile pose furnishes a backdrop for the work of that most sensitive conductor of Ovidian influence, Francesco Petrarca. Resting on the doorstep of the era we have come to call the Renaissance, Petrarch's own monumentally influential lyric sequence, the *Canzoniere*, refocuses the vernacular poet's connection with his readership: matters of inclusion and exclusion, command and submission gathered in Ovid's text are here refreshed.

Maintaining an aggressively announced indifference to the *popolo*, Petrarch simultaneously exploits his common ties to them. To reject either is to relax the tension from which, as my next chapter argues, his poetry derives its most significant power.

Two

Un uom del vulgo

The Community of Petrarch's *Canzoniere*

Nos autem ea quae sunt in usu uitaque communi, non ea quae finguntur aut optantur, spectare debemus.

Cicero[1]

So far as Petrarch was concerned, Ovid's downfall had much to do with an excessive love of company, especially the feminine kind. Petrarch observed in *De vita solitaria*—his homage to the withdrawn, contemplative life—that if Ovid "had not been of such morals and such a mind, he would have had a brighter reputation with serious men and he would not have come to his exile in Pontus and the solitudes of the Ister, or he would have borne it with greater composure."[2] This sounds harsh coming from one who had elsewhere admired the Roman poet as "multa iocans." Awareness of having outgrown a similar self-indulgence accounts for some of the vehemence: Petrarch confessed that in his youth Ovid had seemed to him "a more serious authority and incorruptible witness, the more licentious his Muse."[3] Now remote from such youthful whim, the *Vita*'s polemical voice renounces the judgments and demands of a *vulgus* to whom Ovid had played all too cagily. Relentless disdain for a public audience, no less than the radically frustrated sexuality imprinting his vernacular *Canzoniere*, sets Petrarch apart conventionally from the more gregarious Latin forerunner.

Petrarch never bothered to muffle his contempt for the crowd. A letter to Luca da Piacenza announces his indifference to popular approbation most unequivocally:

> I am rather astonished when I hear the public extol me with praises that are unexpected and displeasing. Since the first cause of love is a certain likeness, I have dedicated myself to being as unlike that multitude as possible. If I could ever fully achieve it, then I would at last consider myself most fortunate. How then could I please those whom I have always labored with great zeal to displease.... Why do they involve themselves in the affairs and plans of someone who never thinks, not even once, about their lives or deaths, or about them at all except as one often does with cadavers, not to mention beasts?
> (F 14.4 / B 2:230)

Epistola metrica 2.10 takes stock of the author's vocation in similarly fervent terms:

> And as for me,
> my verses must upraise me; without them
> I shall be nothing. But must they then win
> the vulgar herd's approval? Nay, I'd rather
> forego the name of bard and tear the wreath
> of laurel from my brow and, head uncrowned,
> languish long years, inglorious and unknown.[4]

The *Canzoniere* themselves share this surliness—from his early sneer at "la turba al vil guadagno intesa" [the mob, bent on low gain] in sonnet 7, to Amor's protest in poem 360 that love has, as not the least significant of his favors, rescued the poet from becoming "un uom del vulgo" [one of the mob]—thwarting efforts to reconcile Petrarch with the familiar audience whose enthusiasm bears up his celebrity.[5] As noted in the previous chapter, such outspoken animosity enjoyed both classical and contemporary precedents; yet Petrarch plies his studied snobbery with a consistency and intensity that transcend convention. This excess colors significantly the way that we—always the potential objects of his dismissive scorn—react to his idiosyncratic artistry.

All *petrarchisti* must at some point grapple with their subject's fierce animosity. In his seminal study of the poet, Umberto Bosco devotes an entire chapter to the issue, assembling evidence from across the Latin and Italian *corpus* into an image of the ideal literary life Petrarch would transmit to his humanist heirs: "a sweet withdrawal to a benign natural enclosure, with many books, visited from time to time by choice friends (without whom existence would seem lacking and almost blind), yet free from external stimuli that would compel him to take up anything he did not wish to—that is, without concessions to the 'crowd.'"[6] Although Bosco remarks that the poet was "too acute a self-critic not to be aware that there might be something corrupt about this lifestyle, something that renders it fundamentally insufficient," the qualifier is absorbed and lost amid the critic's larger interests about Petrarch's bookish introversion.[7] Subsequent readers have sought to diagnose more exhaustively the elitist temperament that Bosco catalogues. For Arnaud Tripet, Petrarch's will to detach himself from a quotidian *hinc et nunc* provides a key to the poet's revisionary ethic: "It was not *in conformity with* his historical context that he attempted to define himself, but *against* this external space—in terms of what was *other* than himself. He rejected passionately social entanglement, the burdens of the crowd, all but the most essential engagement; he fled the impersonality, the promiscuity, the regard for others; he sought happiness and health in solitude and the retreat to an inner self."[8] More recently, Thomas Greene assesses what he calls Petrarch's "apprehension of otherness" by invoking the poet's self-defensive needs: "Only thus can he taste without risk that sweetness of the alien that will wither the unguarded and the pallid self."[9]

Petrarch's ego was, as Greene elsewhere asserts, sufficiently massive and guarded to become "an event in European intellectual history."[10] It was, still, beneath the crust a generous ego, anticipating—indeed enforcing—a terrific flexibility of audience as well as author. Petrarch essentially invents the sonnet sequence as a deliberate act of contravention, a conscious disruption of and alternative to Dante's achievement in *La vita nuova*.[11] We know the peculiar poetic form he devises to be a cumulative project, involving the gradual convening and distribution of lyrics over time. Yet the end product presents us with something that looks to have involved more an art of careful omission than collection: by withholding the prose links that might have organized his poems into a coherent narrative, Petrarch tears holes in the Dantesque model's tight fabric. "The extraordinary innovation in the *Canzoniere*," John Freccero has remarked, is found "in what the verses leave unsaid, in the blank spaces separating these lyric 'fragments,' as they were called, from each other."[12] More than just innovative, these conspicuous silences create space in his text for other voices—*our* voices. From the arresting vocative that inaugurates the sequence, Petrarch incorporates his audience in an unprecedentedly direct manner into the work they will ultimately inherit.

Petrarch vigorously denied that envy stood behind his failure to acknowledge Dante. The distortion he watched his senior colleague's verses undergo through popular recitation had led to his own early abandonment of Italian composition, he insisted, and so neutralized the possibility of rivalry. Nonetheless, he worked relentlessly to insure that we should continue to recite his own poems above their author's disapproving murmur.[13] Petrarch's sworn indifference to the lyrics for which he is best remembered collides with our knowledge of his lifelong romance with them, evident in the meticulous rewriting and rearrangement that went on into his last year.[14] His appetite for fame, a drive to engineer his status as nothing less than a "living legend" in Aldo S. Bernardo's view[15], indentured him to his audience with an intimacy that no inventory of querulous disclaimers could obscure. "In justifying a gesture he never made (the abandoning of vernacular lyric), in denying any desire to be as 'popular' as Dante, Petrarch gives voice to the very desire he would negate," Nancy Vickers has summarized: "For if his songs were to rise to the challenge of his rival, they too would require the approbation of a disturbingly popular audience."[16] Our awareness of this unwillingness to relinquish public glory, despite Petrarch's glib pleadings to the contrary, has more than anything else helped nurture his reputation for morose disingenuousness, if not outright hypocrisy.

A more complicated and benign *animus* guides the *Canzoniere* than such suspicions of the poet's integrity allow. It is the work of one who recognized clearly that poetic survival—on at least one crucial register—necessitated dispersal among a multiplicity of voices. For all the layers of protective irony in which he wrapped his sympathies, Petrarch was prepared to join with his reader in these *rime sparse*, scattered lyrics. Few challenges situated his imagination with greater consequence than the absurdities occasioned by oxymoronic desires for exposure and concealment, celebrity and privacy. We need to scrutinize more carefully the subtleties of Petrarch's seminal *favola* to uncover the tragicomic attachments that enable its ultimate eagerness to grant as well as receive both *pietà* and *perdona*.

The lover's cry that fills sonnet 234, "'l vulgo a me

nemico et odioso / (chi 'l pensò mai?) per mio refugio chero, / tal paura ò di ritrovarmi solo" [I seek (whoever thought it?) the mob, inimical and hateful to me, as a refuge: so afraid am I of being alone], articulates an inexorable bond only strengthened by the poet's arch reluctance. Marguerite Waller aptly remarks the awareness at stake in such a passage: "unless this exclusive and difficult discourse becomes a collective language, [Petrarch sees,] the poet will find himself writing to and for no one, or worse, he will find himself isolated in the collective misunderstanding of him.... It would be better to remain entirely within the problematic of *l'usanza pessima et antica* than to achieve such a virulent 'solitude.'"[17] This sense of attachment, however psychically compromising Petrarch otherwise found it, spans the distance separating him spatially and temporally (*seu locurum seu temporum*, as he puts it in his *Seniles* 18) from a "posterity" that he kept in view throughout his long career.

CONSPICUOUS TRIVIALITY

On the return journey from Rome, where in April 1341 he was officially awarded the laurel crown—a meticulously orchestrated event that marked the high point of his professional success and a singlehanded revival of classical custom—Petrarch was unceremoniously mugged by a gang of brigands understandably more interested in the wealth his entourage was transporting than the *privilegium* his coronation had secured. Petrarch's laconic reportage of the experience manages to convey (along with the fear any close encounter with mortality inspires) a sense of the absurd anticlimax it provided to his vain triumph.[18] It surely recalled the dubieties of worldly grandeur to the laureate who had in his acceptance oration quoted Ovid's *Epistulae ex Ponto* in justification of the poet's hunger for fame—if he had not been sensitive to such irony from the beginning.[19]

This ironic self-regard, aggravated by his scrape with death, inflects the recriminations Petrarch voices, both playfully and seriously, throughout the works. In one letter to Giacomo Colonna, for example, the poet wryly shrugs off a query as to why he covets, through his art, a morally suspect goal of earthly distinction, with "those words of that learned Hebrew: 'Vanity of vanities, all is but vanity.' Thus are the ways of men" (F 4.6; B 1: 192). In the *Secretum*'s more sober ambience, no less an authority than St. Augustine indicts the insincerity of Franciscus' posturing: "I have observed that no man more than you abhors the manners and behaviour of the common herd. Now see what perversity is this! You let yourself be charmed with the applause of those whose conduct you abominate; and may Heaven grant you are only charmed, and that you put not in their power your own everlasting welfare!"[20] Parallel to whatever feelings of self-importance Petrarch indulged, runs an equally genuine taste for the inconsequential. He believed firmly that even events of the greatest cultural moment dwindle to nothingness when viewed through the spectacles of piety. He also respected the ludic potential of the folly he identified with any too stringent effort to divorce oneself from a shared humanity.

In a brief reflection on the *Canzoniere* entitled "*Petrarca, o dell'insignificanza*," Guido Almansi has celebrated the distinctiveness of what he calls this *non-libro*, specifically in terms of the deliberate "meaninglessness" that Petrarch crafted into its design. "The *Canzoniere*'s glory is its independence, and its independence is its irrelevance. It is a text *en train de s'escrire* that shuts out all irritating interference by an author's autobiographical inclination or by a reader's desires to empathize: both are banished from the closed circle of its egocentrism.... [P]laced beside the *Canzoniere* all other works seem crude, earthbound, intolerably mundane, obscenely realistic, stinkingly informative."[21] Almansi's urbane assessment captures splendidly the work's ostensible pose, but, in refusing to lift this veil, he leaves an important level of the poetry obscured. Petrarch was enough of a rhetorician to grasp the seductiveness of such an aloof stance, the way any pretense of evasion plays to an audience's curiosity. He was no less at home outside the confines of his ego's barricades, at large in a world of ironic inference where (he knew) if all presumed to know him equally, no one actually knew him well enough to impinge upon the freedom he also prized.

Two documents pertaining to the *Canzoniere*, one early and one late, afford some purchase on this less acknowledged side of Petrarch's character. The first, another letter to Giacomo Colonna, formulates within its playfully ironic performance the poet's regard for irony as a way of life. Responding to Colonna's suspicions that the Laura of his poems was a mere fantasy, devised to figure his own lust for popular acclaim, Petrarch facetiously accuses his friend of deploying "that Socratic playfulness which they call irony" (F 2.9; B 1: 102). After acknowledging how life's "bitter sprinkling of sweetness" only hastens our self-destruction as, "against the advice of Apollo, we toil against knowing ourselves," Petrarch speculates:

> If, therefore, in this dangerous and fleeting and insidious journey anyone whom nature or effort had made so wary that after eluding the deceits of the world he himself managed to deceive the world by showing himself outwardly like the multitude but inwardly being unlike them, what would you say about such a man? Where are we to search for him? In him must be a most excellent nature, a mature and reasonable age, and a solicitous consideration of the misfortunes of others. (B 1: 98–99)

His studied public insularity reinforces the fierce self-allegiance his friend should recognize; but, as the final clause suggests, it is a small step from the notion that outward conformity can mask a deep sense of segregation, to the guise of outward indifference that cloaks a profound sympathy. The detachment he works to maintain sets him apart from the multitude whose words, favorable or adverse, he can never bring himself to trust; at the same time, it does not undermine his sensitivity to a broader plight with which he evidently has no desire to lose touch.

By putting himself at his audience's seeming disposal, the writer paradoxically manages a more thorough self-protectiveness. Thirty years later, Petrarch returns to a similar version of this strategy. Writing to encourage Boccaccio—who, depressed by the grand literary achievements of his fellow countrymen, had resolved to destroy his own vernacular endeavors—the elder colleague impulsively admonishes against any such intention, only to recall his own alleged abandonment of Italian verse. Desire to preserve superior work from profanation by a corrupt society is a noble motive, and thoughts that "I and my work would be torn to shreds by the hands of the mob" had cooled his vernacular ardors. "[A]lthough those brief and scattered vernacular works of my youth are no longer mine," he winds up dismissively, "but have become the multitude's [non mia amplius, sed uulgi potius facta essent], I shall see to it that they do not butcher my major ones."[22] In an interesting progress, condemnation modulates instantly into resignation and a form of calculated concession. The poet ends up essentially bequeathing, to a populace he professes to disdain, a work he is less prepared to abandon than he insists. The *Canzoniere* becomes both an agent of his celebrity among the *populo* and a buffer shielding him from this common lot of admirers, leaving him to attend undistracted the more elite private interests he pursues in old age.

The quotidian world of the *vulgus* is by nature an ironic one, and to submit oneself to summary public evaluation as Petrarch does in this work is to enforce a personal irony—one sufficiently vigorous to provide the

Canzoniere's densely personal drama with a critical source of energy. To keep in check the ego this writer explored in such a novel manner would, he perceived, require an equally potent ironic sensibility. His great vernacular *opus* realizes this temperament with a masterful and wry subtlety that continues to elude us. Dante, the arch-rival, could elevate his *commedia* to a divine register; Petrarch, in deliberate contrast, offers something more absurdly secular in its orientation, and thus "comic" in a more distinctively modern sense of the term.

The palinodic prefix inaugurating his *Canzoniere* enacts a sophisticated balance of competing desires for individuation and incorporation. Conventional piety couples with evasiveness in the statement of a speaker who steps forward to cement and perplex a relationship with his auditors.

> Voi ch' ascoltate in rime sparse il suono
> di quei sospiri ond' io nudriva 'l core
> in sul mio primo giovenile errore,
> quand' era in parte altr' uom da quel ch' i sono:
> del vario stile in ch' io piango et ragiono
> fra le vane speranze e 'l van dolore,
> ove sia chi per prova intenda amore
> spero trovar pietà, non che perdono.
> Ma ben veggio or sì come al popol tutto
> favola fui gran tempo, onde sovente
> di me medesmo meco mi vergogno;
> et del mio vaneggiar vergogna è 'l frutto,
> e 'l pentersi, e 'l conoscer chiaramente
> che quanto piace al mondo è breve sogno.

[You who hear in scattered rhymes the sound of those sighs with which I nourished my heart during my first youthful error, when I was in part another man from what I am now: for the varied style in which I weep and speak between vain hopes and vain sorrow, where there is anyone who understands love through experience, I hope to find pity, not only pardon. But now I see well how for a long time I was the talk of the crowd, for which often I am ashamed of myself within; and of my raving, shame is the fruit, and repentance, and the clear knowledge that whatever pleases in the world is a brief dream.]

We are invited into the sequence as special, sympathetic recipients. In a plea that reverberates through to the closing prayer in 366, the poet urges us to experience vicariously the disorientation his passion excites, to gain the *prova* that will lend our verdicts a legitimacy without which they would remain purblind and dogmatic.

However, this privileged intimacy grants access to a story we supposedly already know, the sonnet's sestet discloses. Almost without realizing it, we find ourselves absorbed into the very audience whose knowledge of his plight had shamed the poet. The disarming vocative first charms readers into passive acceptance as the speaker identifies us as confidants, honored among that elect constellation of patrons, friends and associates explicitly addressed at various points in the sequence. Then, an abrupt recollection of the way this open pronoun equally embraces all the literate who encounter the text rudely alters our perspective: we discover our status as Everyreader. In a seamless transaction, Petrarch's speaker closes the distance between his addressee's present *voi* and the crowd he recalls. To become his private witness is to become suddenly aware of one's membership in the *popol tutto*. For all of the metamorphoses this poet-lover will suffer in the following lyrics, he begins with his own vital act of transformation, turning public condemnation into private sympathy, and this exclusive sympathy back into an awareness of one's broader social vantage.

The urgency of this premier gesture to the *Canzoniere*'s aesthetic or moral design cannot be overestimated. As already suggested, Petrarch conventionally defends his undertakings by appealing to the approval of the "best," the noble and learned circle that humanist poets generally labored to create. Sonnet 1's implicit recourse to this mythic elite helps obscure the poem's collapsed distinctions, for which I argue.[23] Pressing his rhetorical allegiance to the "pochi compagni"—as he does, for example, in sonnet 7—Petrarch also saw the risk of placing one's stock entirely in such a nebulous (though narrowly construed) entity. In this, his prefatory sonnet's *conocer chiaramente* reaches past the final line's moral truth. He instructs his listeners more subtly in a kinship they share with one another: a capacity and willingness to receive the text that will sustain his *favola* beyond the mortal brevity he has come to appreciate.

The *Canzoniere*'s reader is summoned to stand apart only to be incorporated instantly into the backdrop of a general audience. The poet himself emerges both as a distant voice, worthy of the public notice (good or bad) he has garnered, and as little more than the embodiment of a popular myth, one more exemplar of an already aging courtly tradition. His celebrity confirms his novel predicament; yet the experience of prodigality and penitence is sufficiently common for him to ground hopes of sympathy in its expanse—"ove sia chi per prova intenda amore." He prefers this delicate poise of exclusion and belonging. Many have found in the peculiar remark that he was once "*in part* another man" the sign of a failed (because merely partial) conversion[24]; but the admission's ambiguity also insinuates his enduring ties as *un uom*. He has not changed so radically as to lose touch with the concerns his writing and his readership keep before him. In this story, professedly not about a *Vita nuova*, the poet will aim to distinguish himself while dispersing his image through the prismatic lens of a *vario stile* that neatly accommodates his various impulses, however vain, toward celebrity and withdrawal.

Setting himself up specifically as a *favola*, Petrarch's speaker advertises his triviality. The Latin *fabula* from which his word derives suggests a narrative emptied of meaning or consequence, with no basis in reality: so

Augustine uses the term as a pejorative in his *Confessions* when he blasts insubstantial poetic constructs.[25] As "scandal" (the more precise sense intended in the sonnet, available in Ovid's and Horace's lyrics[26]) *favola* conjures an image of one ostracized from a society whose public discourse ironically keeps him alive. Without popular reiteration, his story's subject would cease to exist altogether. The same infamy that goads him to depart a world he loved too much keeps open the chance for reintegration, by means of the sympathy he now aggressively covets from the addressed *voi*.

Petrarch hopes his work will edify the pious reader about worldly transience. Never primarily interested in the obvious, he also wants to explore the as yet uncharted *spazio* separating "le vane speranze e 'l van dolore," not the illuminated factuality of religious truth (which he trusts his readers will have the grace to discern) but the fragmented interiority from which the dreams of this world, along with its spiritual aspirations as he understands them, arise.[27] This life may be no more than a *breve sogno*, but much hangs upon that dream's murky and scattered images. His temporal realization sincerely shames him, though it does not effectively distract his attention from the allure of the "gran tempo" he continues to ponder. The *suono* of his verse, ecstatic and reproachful, will animate the *sogno* in which the poet's mercurial and rich *sono* or selfhood resides. Inside the margins of this space, he will work to secure pity and pardon, but also a popularity that he senses is requisite for these.

Although Petrarch never cancels the severe moral indictment of his first sonnet, it is important to grasp the qualification this charge undergoes from the next poem onward. To isolate ourselves or to ostracize others judgmentally is, in the schema of this *favola*, to court painful disillusionment. We learn in sonnet 2 as he begins to anatomize his *innamoramento*, or moment of erotic revelation, that the lover's primary "giovenile errore" was not his infatuation with Laura, but a vain presumption that such disorienting passions could be kept at bay. The most reliable defenses cannot place him beyond their fire:

> Per fare una leggiadra sua vendetta
> et punire in un dì ben mille offese,
> celatamente Amor l'arco riprese,
> come uom ch' a nocer luogo e tempo aspetta.
> Era la mia virtute al cor ristretta
> per far ivi et negli occhi sue difese
> quando 'l colpo mortal là giù discese
> ove solea spuntarsi ogni saetta. . . .
>
> (1–8)

> [To take a graceful revenge and to punish in one day a thousand offenses, Love took up his bow again secretly, like a man who waits for the time and place to hurt. My vital power was concentrated in my heart, to make there and in my eyes his defense, when the fatal blow fell where every previous arrow had been blunted. . . .]

The caution in these lines lends substance to the initial poem's confession. Love postures as an agent of disorder, a stealthy assassin whose brutal efficiency the writer laments and admires. Amor's command of the moment—*in un dì*—has enabled him to pierce through the poet's *virtute*, distorting any temporal economy the latter may have known. The speaker has, as the next sonnet continues, foolishly trusted an etiquette Amor does not honor: "Tempo non mi parea da far riparo / contr' a' colpi d'Amor; però m'andai / secur, senza sospetto" [5–7: It did not seem to me a time for being on guard against Love's blows; therefore I went confident and without fear]. Shattering this security, Love teaches him the perils of a self-assured elitism. A staple of romantic comedy since its origin, Amor's role as a scourge against presumption afforded Petrarch with a model for his no less conventional entrapment. It is a misplaced self-confidence he is still chiding in sonnet 65:

> Lasso, che mal accorto fui da prima,
> nel giorno ch' a ferir mi venne Amore!
>
> . . .
>
> Io non credea per forza di sua lima
> che punto di fermezza o di valore
> mancasse mai ne l'indurato core,
> ma così va chi sopra 'l ver s'estima.
>
> (1-2, 5-8)

[Alas, I was little wary at first, the day when Love came to wound me.... I did not believe that by the power of his file any bit of strength or worthiness would fail in my hardened heart, but so he goes who esteems himself too highly.]

To expose oneself too fully to communal recognition was to risk losing that very selfhood, a catastrophe Petrarch in his measured isolation—figured ostensibly by the "enclosed valley" toward which the *Canzoniere*'s passionate meditations persistently gravitate[28]—struggled to avoid. Despite the self-protective disposition his letters assume, Petrarch discerned in his troubled relationship with a popular following something more than either a professional annoyance or (alternately) the shameful vice of an ambitious man: something actually redemptive. The recognition informs one of his sequence's supremely ironic moments, the speaker's direct confrontation with *la volgar gente* in sonnet 99. The poem, a righteous and intimate plea that the reader accompany him in flight from ephemeral worldly concerns, for the sake of "quel sommo ben che mai non spiace" [3: that highest good which never fails], abruptly undermines its counsel midway through the sestet:

> Voi dunque, se cercate aver la mente
> anzi l'estremo dì queta giamai,
> seguite i pochi et non la volgar gente.
> Ben si può dire a me: "Frate, tu vai
> mostrando altrui la via dove sovente
> fosti smarrito et or se' più che mai."

[You, therefore, if you seek ever to have quiet minds before the last day, follow the few and not the crowd. Someone could very well say to me: "Brother, you keep showing others the way, where you have often been astray and are now, more than ever."]

Amid the pomposity of his homiletic seriousness, the speaker has forsaken a vital sensitivity to his own limitations, an understanding enabled chiefly by the social context he entreats us to flee. However urgent it may be to overcome common appetites, segregation from the crowd can always render one vulnerable to an equally pernicious vanity. The hypocrisy and self-delusion of which he accuses the multitude are discovered, through the agency of this very company, to be his own: outwardly unlike them, the poet understands himself to be inwardly the same. Petrarch transforms the embarrassing circumstance into a comic lesson. Without community, the healthy self-irony on which balance and perspective depend degenerates into a stiffness that (in turn) compromises the very selfhood he had set out to fortify in the first place.

Posing as one ferociously jealous of the privacy into which he nonetheless invites us, Petrarch orchestrates a deliberately oxymoronic game of concealment and disclosure to knit his work together. He enlists our notice in order to betray what he purportedly does not want us to know. Laura's lover flees the populace, sonnet 35 specifies, because "Altro schermo non trovo che mi scampi / dal manifesto accorger de le genti" [5–6: No other shield do I find to protect me from people's open knowing], but he polishes a transparency that uncovers the ludic and potentially ludicrous quality of mythic inflation and self-conscious excess of his poetry. He required no "anti-Petrarchan" backlash to instruct him how well the stance he had perfected courted parody. Sonnet 67's image of a lover stumbling absently into a stream while distracted by a vision of his lady, or 74's reflection on the way "Io son già stanco di pensar sì come / i miei pensier in voi stanchi non sono" [1–2: I am already weary of thinking how my thoughts of you are weariless] offer examples of the way this poet appreciated the comic dimension of erotic impulse. But apart from these isolated instances, a gentle humor also deflates the pretentiousness of several grander moments. Such is the case with one of the *Canzoniere*'s most frequently addressed and longest performances, poem 23, whose puzzling quirks become more comprehensible once we acknowledge the ironic light in which the poet casts his infatuated speaker.

Mythic retribution fills out the canzone that, as Petrarch took the trouble to note in his manuscript, predates all the other lyrics included in the sequence. Recounting the genesis of his obsession with Laura as a series of dark Ovidian metamorphoses, the poet eludes our clear perceptions as competently and obstinately as she resists his heartsick petitions. The speaker at first suffers a Daphne-like transformation, subsequently experiences liquefaction and petrifaction (twice) and ends up an Actaeon figure, running for his life. Prevailing interpretations have emphasized the psychic pain which its pattern of horrific changes is supposed to project. William Kerrigan and Gordon Braden, in a recent exemplary reading, accent our grim impression of the poem's nervous flux, when in the final snarl of the pursuing dogs sounds "the plaintive song whose development the *canzone* has narrated, returning to its now speechless creator.... Petrarch's lover flees from the sound of his own poetic voice, echoing murderously in the bell jar."[29] Even Marco Santagata, who detects an occasional facetiousness beneath the surface melodrama, hesitates to press the notion.[30] Though never obtrusive, the humor is of greater consequence than we have acknowledged. It provides not a casual ornament, but an essential balance to the speaker's headier responses: a fondness or folly that gathers his cluttered metaphors back to *terra firma*.

From the opening lines, Petrarch situates us amid a play between the commonplace and the distinctive. The queer adjectival precision with which the poet isolates his poem's narrative moment—"la prima etade, / che nascer vide et *ancor quasi in erba* / la fera voglia" [my first age, which saw born and *still almost unripe* the fierce desire (my emphasis)]—is buttressed by an uncharacteristically stilted specification of just what he will undertake in the following verses. It endows the opening movement with a certain awkwardness. The redundancy threatened by such a lyric "prologue" is compounded, moreover, by his assertion that we have probably heard it all before:

> poi seguirò sì come a lui ne 'ncrebbe
> troppo altamente e che di ciò m'avenne,
> di ch' io son fatto a molta gente esempio;
> ben che 'l mio duro scempio
> sia scritto altrove, sì che mille penne
> ne son già stanche, et quasi in ogni valle
> rimbombi il suon de' miei gravi sospiri,
> ch' acquistan fede a la penosa vita.
>
> (7–14)

[then I shall pursue how that chagrined him too deeply, and what happened to me for that, by which I have become an example for many people; although my harsh undoing is written elsewhere so that a thousand pens are already tired by it, and almost every valley echoes to the sound of my heavy sighs which prove how painful my life is.]

Is it that his love has become so well publicized that other poets (the *mille penne*) have taken up his story, or is it that his story recapitulates an experience available, under various guises, to all?—the latter would appreciably defuse the exclusivity he affects. This ambiguity overshadows his progress from one who (recalling the second sonnet) presumed immunity to love's powers, to one who must discover his commonality and finally to one whose ability to poeticize love's turmoil in turn distinguishes him, "a molta gente esempio." These are the transformations which take place even before metamorphosis as a subject *per se* sets in. Moreover, the speaker's self-professed unreliability further undercuts his preface's scrambled formality: "E se qui la memoria non m'aita / come suol fare, iscusilla i martiri" [15–16: And if here my memory does not aid me as it is wont to do, let my torments excuse it]. Its assertions unclear and its credibility compromised, poem 23's introduction postures between pomposity and incompetence, in what Almansi might identify as a supremely "insignificant" gesture.

Petrarch further tempers his speaker's mythic stature when he disrupts his catalogue of wonders to interject that we are only getting a selected list:

> Ma perché 'l tempo è corto
> la penna al buon voler non po gir presso,
> onde più cose ne la mente scritte
> vo trapassando, et sol d'alcune parlo
> che meraviglia fanno a chi l'ascolta.
>
> (90–94)

> [But because time is short, my pen cannot follow closely my good will; wherefore I pass over many things written in my mind and speak only of some, which make those who hear them marvel.]

There is something about an edited description of the calamitous metamorphoses he has suffered ("So these are just a few of the changes I've known") that leaves his already incredible lament hard to take altogether seriously. His earnest exactness prompts him to anticipate our disbelief, occasioning the rhetorical comedy of lines 119–20: "Chi udì mai d'uom vero nascer fonte? / e parlo cose manifeste et conte" [Who ever heard of a spring being born from a real man? And I am saying things obvious and known]. The question both emphasizes the experience's wonder and sounds a more pragmatic, skeptical note, recalling to us the absurdity of his exaggeration, a reservation the subsequent reassurance only amplifies. The miracles he speaks of are neither "manifeste" nor "conte," and his words do little to assuage the doubts his excess inspires.

At the forefront of Petrarch's lyric exercise, canzone 23 does, on the other hand, deal with "things known," by subtly taking to task the marvellous expansiveness it addresses. Accelerating Ovid's pace, Petrarch's lover runs together stories of change at a dizzying rate in what becomes a poem essentially about imagination, and the way desire compels the poet to envision himself as an endless array of figures. Petrarch's ability to capture the vitality and absurdity of this drive authenticates the poem's Ovidian texture more completely than the pointedness with which he describes his speaker's metamorphoses. The changes experienced in the canzone bespeak not merely a sense of victimization, but a remarkably adaptive poetic facility. Transformed into a laurel, he identifies himself as one "che per fredda stagion foglia non perde" [40: that loses no leaf for all the cold season]. He cannot be silenced by his mistress's strongest injunctions: "le vive voci m'erano interditte, / ond' io gridai con carta et con incostro" [98–99: Words spoken aloud were forbidden me; so I cried out with paper and ink]. Even the threatened eclipse of his own voice by the hounds' "belling" in his penultimate stanza will give way to a calmer, more measured conclusion:

> Canzon, i' non fu' mai quel nuvol d'oro
> che poi discese in preziosa pioggia
> sì che 'l foco di Giove in parte spense;
> ma fui ben fiamma ch' un bel guardo accense,
> et fui l'uccel che più per l'aere poggia
> alzando lei che ne' miei detti onoro;
> né per nova figura il primo alloro
> seppi lassar, ché pur la sua dolce ombra
> ogni men bel piacer del cor mi sgombra.
>
> (161–69)

[Song, I was never the cloud of gold that once descended in a precious rain so that it partly quenched the fire of Jove; but I have certainly been a flame lit by a lovely glance and I have been the bird that rises highest in the air raising her whom in my words I honor; nor for any new shape could I leave the first laurel, for still its sweet shade turns away from my heart any less beautiful pleasure.]

Taking the trouble at last to tell us what he is *not*, the poet tempers his claim to suggest that nothing really has changed: desire for the original laurel has rescued him from the prospect of any "nova figura." As his imagination settles into a quieter reckoning with his desire, his ultimate attitude recommends that not all visions are equally trustworthy. Just as Laura had previously addressed him, "I' non son forse chi tu credi" [83: I am not perhaps who you think I am], so Petrarch modestly invites his audience to take his love's uniqueness more lightly than the poem outwardly begs.

The speaker's remark that his story has wearied a "thousand pens" captures the exhausted yet somehow inexhaustible capacity of love poetry. Continuing receptivity to his genre relies, however, upon the audience's willingness to recognize the lover and his utterance as bound by an emotion available to all. The recollection that his dismissive attitude towards Amor's victims before Laura's advent had left him vulnerable and ridiculous closes with his admission that "quel che in me non era / mi pareva un miracolo in altrui" [28–29: what was not in me seemed to me a miracle in others]. The statement encapsulates how perspectives are conditioned: experience has enabled a sympathy previously beyond him and has in retrospect rendered the "miracle" beheld at that time now less remote; so it is up to the audience to find "within" a shared vulnerability that humanizes his mythic transformations, translating his hyperbole into something more mundanely familiar and accessible. In such sympathetic appreciation of amorous folly, Petrarch intimates, the *miracoli* actually reside.

It is to this canzone, appropriately, that he will revert at the end of his great "citation" poem, which closes with a reiteration of the earlier lyric's first line. Canzone 70 offsets the seriousness of its opening fear—that the lover's cries may no longer enjoy a responsive audience—with a litany of quotations imported from other love poets, echoes of a shared experience intended to reassure the poet and his listeners of the love lyric's enduring reception. His self-incorporation into this society signals the privilege his artistry has secured for him, but it conversely points out that his own experience and consequent stance are not as novel as his rhetoric would otherwise have us believe. It is a notion, confirmed in poem 94's description of the "miraculous" effect that love works on his own visage, which discloses in its final lines that the speaker realizes these symptoms: "ch' i' vidi duo amanti trasformare / et far qual io mi soglio in vista fare" [13–14: when I saw two lovers be transformed and become in their faces what I often become]. Within the dilated boundaries of Amor's dominion, embracing the poets he revered and the *amanti* he casually observes, he locates a community at once humbling and reassuring, demanding the ironic temperament that stands behind some of his most extravagant claims.

"Nel dolce tempo de la prima etade" sets the pace for the sequence that would eventually emerge from its preliminary experiment. The comic strain I identify in its image of the poet-lover survives to inform with quiet intensity two other critical moments in the *Canzoniere*'s setup. Where 23's radical metamorphoses subtly isolate the commonality that grounds his obsession, the radical obscurity of canzone 105 also wryly comments upon the surface eccentricities of its performance, shattering in like fashion whatever pretensions the speaker may adopt. The poem again combines the *Canzoniere*'s various and competing concerns—erotic and political, melancholic and satiric—into a strange mixture through which we have difficulty seeing clearly. The opacity (as might be expected) has since the earliest commentaries elicited responses ranging from frank perplexity to equally frank irritation. Compare Pietro Bembo's conclusion that the poem "seems to say nothing, but is rather a series of proverbs swept together,"[31] with P. J. Klemp's attack on 105's narrator: "He taunts the narratee ... by ridiculing the listener's supposed inadequacy as an audience.... [T]his poem's meaning lies both in the narrator's show of domination, which leads him to create an apparently meaningless poem to mock a listener who assumes that poetry has a clear meaning, and in the listener's inability to locate the meaning that resides in his interpretive frustration and the narrator's artistic slyness...."[32] Despite all the confusion, enough humor does get through to identify the performance as a caricature of the obscurity it sports. The darkness here does not mock its audience without extending its indictment to the poet as well, whose hermetic affectation collapses upon itself.[33]

The poem begins as a confession, the speaker's confrontation with his own potential for artistic failure: "Mai non vo' più cantar com' io soleva, / ch' altri no m'intendeva, ond' ebbi scorno, / et puossi in bel soggiorno esser molesto" [1–3: I never wish to sing again as I used to, for I was not understood, wherefore I was scorned, and one can be miserable in a pleasant place]. These lines voice a sense of inadequacy as strongly as they betray resentment toward an unresponsive audience. His upset at the interpretive impasse he has encountered is never fully muted by the bravado of his subsequent dismissals, such as line 17: "intendami chi po, ch' i' m'intend' io" [understand me who can, for I understand myself]. His withdrawal into a deeper obscurity, and petulant refusal to elucidate his verse for the public who takes issue with it, projects a sufficiently arch self-irony to contrast the blind hostility that Klemp assails.

To so antagonize one's readers is to court disaster. His knowledge of this point turns the canzone from an assault upon the ignorant audience to a playful admonition of his own indulgence: "Forse ch' ogni uom che legge non s'intende, / et la rete tal tende che non piglia; / et chi troppo assottiglia si scavezza" [46–48: Perhaps not everyone who can read can understand, and he who sets up the net does not always catch, and he who is too subtle breaks his own neck]. As these lines demonstrate, any impulse to condemn the auditor also implicates the poet. The artist knows his liberty's limits.

Bembo correctly asserts that it would be folly to attempt decoding the canzone's individual cryptic statements: the poem takes as its subject and self-satirizing manner the folly of writing in this esoteric vein. Just as 23's metamorphic "wonders" veil emotions that are less exclusive than the lover would insist, so here the fascination with hermetic meaning rapidly dwindles to a more pedestrian indifference with which he must, as an artist, finally reckon: "Tal par gran meraviglia et poi si sprezza" [51: a thing seems a great marvel but then is despised].

Whatever disgust cuts through 105's fogbound surface, in other words, is neither so outwardly directed nor so somber as has been suspected. For all the extremes to which it goes, the poem's sententious rhetoric returns constantly to notions of temperance and accommodation. Whether speaking of love or politics or art (we are never quite sure), the same ethic applies:

> Chi smarrita à la strada, torni indietro;
> chi non à albergo, posisi in sul verde;
> chi non à l'auro o 'l perde,
> spenga la sete sua con un bel vetro.
>
> (12–15)

[He who has lost his way, let him turn back; he who has no dwelling, let him sleep on the grass; he who has no gold or loses it, let him quench his thirst from a glass.]

The poet who offers a dryly qualified boast of independence—"*Quanto posso* mi spetro et sol mi sto" [19: *As much as I can*, I disentangle myself and stand free (my emphasis)]—will repeatedly cite the hazards of presumptuous ambition, from Phaeton's demise at line 20, to the flat counsel "a me pur pare / senno a non cominciar tropp' alte imprese" [35–36: it seems to me prudent not to begin undertakings that are too difficult], to line 78's strikingly balanced affirmation, "del presente mi godo et meglio aspetto" [I enjoy the present and expect better]. Through the fissures in the lyric's dense walls, we catch sight of warnings not to exceed our means. Otherwise, author and audience remain sequestered. In the midst of the verses' irresponsibility sounds a call for an accommodating temperament, which alone can secure a response critical to his ongoing poetic activity and survival. The poem ends up, in short, very close to the sensibility displayed in sonnet 234, the speaker keenly aware of his dependence and belying his initial anguish.

Canzone 105 recovers a balance that anticipates the final representative performance I wish to consider in this section. Almost one hundred poems later, Petrarch devises for his speaker yet another cranky self-confrontation, once more lightened by the poet's marked powers of adaptation. Like its companion canzoni, 207 will delineate the resources that enable the embittered speaker continually to adjust. The canzone trades the sense of failure opening 105 for an exasperation that will stimulate the very ingenuity whose necessity he laments: "Ben mi credea passar mio tempo omai / come passato avea quest'anni a dietro, / senz' altro studio et senza novi ingegni..." [1–3: I believed that by now I could live as I have lived these past years, without new studies and without new stratagems]. As the lyric proceeds, we come to understand that an inexhaustible supply of these *novi ingegni* remains at his disposal. His lady's early favor, though meager, had provided a base whereupon he might enjoy his small recompense. Her late standoffishness, however, commands new strategies:

> Or, ben ch' a me ne pesi,
> divento ingiurioso et importuno;
> ché 'l poverel digiuno
> ven ad atto talor che 'n miglior stato
> avria in altrui biasmato.
>
> (20–24)

[Now, although it pains me, I become annoying and importunate; for a wretch who is starving sometimes commits actions which, in a better state, he would have blamed in someone else.]

Alongside his capacity and will to formulate these actions, the poet-speaker also confesses an enfeebled desire to proclaim himself above these manners: desperation necessitates the "common" ploys for favor that he now braces to undertake.

The notion of his love as a common plight is reprised in the fourth stanza:

> Di mia morte mi pasco et vivo in fiamme,
> stranio cibo et mirabil salamandra!
> ma miracol non è, da tal si vole.
> Felice agnello a la penosa mandra
> mi giacqui un tempo; or a l'estremo famme
> et Fortuna et Amor pur come sòle:
>   così rose et viole
> à primavera, e 'l verno à neve et ghiaccio.
>
> (40–47)

[I feed on my death and live in flames: strange food and a wondrous salamander! But it is no miracle, it is willed by such a one. I lay in his sorrowing flock like a happy lamb for a time; now at the end Love and Fortune treat me as they do the rest: thus spring has roses and violets, winter has snow and ice.]

The presumably marvelous state of personal distinction (yet again) turns out abruptly not to be one. In a kind of momentary respite, the oxymoronic complication melts away into the acknowledgement of seasonal process, to which Love and Fortune tend in his presentation with a distressing regularity. As he reconfirms in the poem's final movement, a quick death at Amor's hands would, given the commonplace predicament he confronts, seem blessed, "non essendo ei disposto / a far altro di me che quel che soglia" [89–90: since he is not disposed to make of me anything but what he usually does].

When the poet inquires rhetorically "Chi nol sa di ch' io vivo" [53: Who does not know on what I live] since meeting Laura, the expression points at once to the celebrity of his verse—his pain has made him famous—and to what he recognizes as the familiarity of the malady he experiences. Duplicity rounds out the canzone, reinforcing once more the speaker's seeming wonder at the resilience he discovers: "Servo d'Amor che queste rime leggi: / ben non à 'l mondo che 'l mio mal pareggi" [97–98: Servant of Love who read these lines, there is no good in the world that is equal to my ills], suggesting both that nothing, at least in this world, could possibly compensate the kind of suffering he has known, and that nothing could possibly dissuade him from his present course of action. The deliberate ambivalence of his resolution hints at the speaker's capacity to do anything, to find always another maneuver that will enable him to stand his ground, *fermo in campo stare*. A security that "Love's servants" will continue to find in his distress and endurance a mirror of their own woes supports his gestures here and throughout. When all else is filtered away, his membership in this community—whose stratagems and language he knows—provides a reassuring constant. Beneath all the embellishment, Petrarch suggests, the love he portrays speaks a common dialect.

Nel commune dolor: Death's Witness

An ironic subtext lines canzone 23's surface narrative, rooted in what Petrarch cast as a comic excess typical of Amor's traumatized victims. Subtle disclosure organizes more directly—and to different effect—the sequence's fifth sonnet. An elegant and witty embellishment of his mistress's name, the poem also proclaims in its octave the speaker's sly victory over restriction.

> Quando io movo i sospiri a chiamar voi
> e 'l nome che nel cor mi scrisse Amore,
> LAU-dando s'incomincia udir di fore
> il suon de' primi dolci accenti suoi;
> vostro stato RE-al che 'ncontro poi
> raddoppia a l'alta impresa il mio valore;
> ma "TA-ci," grida il fin, "ché farle onore
> è d'altri omeri soma che da' tuoi."
>
> (1–8)

> [When I move my sighs to call you and the name that Love wrote on my heart, the sound of its first sweet accents is heard without in LAU-ds. Your RE-gal state, which I meet next, redoubles my strength for the high enterprise; but "TA-lk no more!" cries the ending, "for to do her honor is a burden for other shoulders than yours."]

Encoding his lady's name, the verses unravel all that *Lau-re-ta* enfolds, only to learn that its self-contained richness exceeds his grasp. The poet's design to appropriate the office of "other shoulders" (and the pun on *omeri* / Omeri [= "Homers"], implying that only the greatest of singers may do her justice, sits well in this sonnet of camouflaged identity) opens him to charges of blasphemy. Regardless, a crucial point of his rhetorical game is his ability to outrun the final syllable's injunction to silence. By the time "TA-ci" sounds in his setup, the name has already emerged, and the work it forbids is, of necessity, already behind him. The belated interdiction's impotence mocks discreetly an authority that would presume to narrow the encomiastic scope of this author, whose "redoubled" poetic range evidently leaves him feeling equal to the exalted task. We come away from the skillfully executed maneuver with a sense that, if (as he professes) the sonnet merely garnishes Laureta's substantiating syllables, the name (from another perspective) relies for its very articulation upon this diminutive lyric vehicle.

His resourceful confidence will nonetheless contrast the sestet's more sobering recollection. The second time around, his attempt to augment "Laureta" seems less secure of its capacity to dodge the fate now discerned in the ultimate syllable. Condemnation of the poet's own guilty "lingua mor-TA-l" plays against the laurel's "sempre verdi rami":

> Così LAU-dare et RE-verire insegna
> la voce stessa, pur ch' altri vi chiami,
> o d'ogni reverenza et d'onor degna;
> se non che forse Apollo si disdegna
> ch'a parlar de' suoi sempre verdi rami
> lingua mor-TA-l presuntuosa vegna.
>
> (9–14)

[Thus the word itself teaches LAU-d and RE-verence, whenever anyone calls you, O Lady worthy of all reverence and honor; except that perhaps Apollo is incensed that any mor-TA-l tongue should come presumptuous to speak of his eternally green boughs.]

Whatever price the speaker might have to pay for his transgression, his betrayal of Laura's name has in fact put them both at risk. "Presumptuous" disclosure may incite Apollo to reassert private dominion over his sacred tree, and the hint of mortality that concludes her name is a nervous glance toward the mythic destiny of all those who are beloved by divinity. Laura is no sooner identified—even in this cryptic, broken manner[34]—than her death is presaged. His poem has by the end worked a kind of reverse charm: intended to uncase the lady from her static though splendid Daphnean enclosure, it only renders her vulnerable, once again, to a god's requisition.

In a discussion of Shakespeare and death, James Calderwood has teased out a predicament that the Renaissance cult of fame entertained with unique fervor, that "to have an identity, a face, and especially a name, is to leave Death your address."[35] Petrarch's intuition of this point inflects the lifelong preoccupation with mortality—fueled on one side by the *Vita nuova*'s precedent of the dying mistress and (eventually) on another by the plague's very real killing time—that imprinted itself so deeply on his lyric sequence.[36] Where Laura's transcendent virtue endangers her earthly wellbeing, the literary selfhood her poet gains in her service paradoxically does not cost him a similar misfortune. Rather, even as the *Canzoniere* draws to a close, the lover gains assurance of another "twenty or thirty years" of life (sonnet 362). His lady never manages to embody the spiritual salvation that Dante's Beatrice had promised. Instead, Laura binds him after her death ever more firmly to this now depleted world. The turn forms a grimly ironic codicil to the literary immortality he craved.

Whatever else it might be, the poet's obsession with Laura is an indisputably predatory one. She is doomed so that the artist may endure professionally; she dies for them both, after a fashion.[37] Alongside apprehension about her premature demise, voiced throughout the *In vita* poems, runs a strange eagerness for this event. Even before 1348, when the malady that would ostensibly claim Laura's life had struck, evidence suggests that Petrarch had all but scripted her death into his work's schema. Although the lover's grief becomes such an integral part of the *Canzoniere* that we take it for granted, one important aspect of the self-discovery Petrarch's speaker undergoes involves the vanity of the *vanitas* topos itself: without a primary understanding of what it means actually to suffer the pain of survival—to live on as others die, and so to perceive oneself not as Death's victim but rather as Death's audience—acknowledgement of human mortality becomes facile and insubstantial.

It is this experience that Laura's lover must come to terms with in the *Canzoniere*. His love had begun on Good Friday, sonnet 3 recounts, in the midst of the "universal woe," *nel commune dolor,* and his initial focus on this most terrifying image of finitude available to the Christian audience—the figure of *Cristo moro,* dead god rather than risen savior—directs our attention to the darker bond he will need to confront. If Amor's effects prevent the poet from maintaining the pose of exclusivity he struggles to assume, as argued in our previous section, the refinement of his sensitivity to what loss actually entails will keep the notion of a common mortal lot before him no less emphatically.

The hazards of distinction adumbrated in sonnet 5 arch across the *Canzoniere*'s broad first sector to touch down firmly in 254, an equally revealing moment for the speaker. As the poems move inexorably toward word of Laura's early fate, her lover is compelled to take stock of the premature conclusion that this news should entail for his own *favola*. The recurrence of the term *favola* itself here (its only appearance outside the first sonnet), coupled with the initial clause's *ascoltate,* suggests a reprise of the sequence's opening:

> I' pur ascolto, et non odo novella
> de la dolce et amata mia nemica,
> né so ch' i' me ne pensi o ch' i' mi dica,
> sì 'l cor tema e speranza mi puntella.
> Nocque ad alcuna già l'esser sì bella,
> questa più d'altra è bella et più pudica:
> forse vuol Dio tal di vertute amica
> torre a la terra e 'n ciel farne una stella,
> anzi un sole. Et se questo è, la mia vita,

i miei corti riposi e i lunghi affanni
son giunti al fine. O dura dipartita,
perché lontan m'ài fatto da' miei danni?
La mia favola breve è già compita,
et fornito il mio tempo a mezzo gli anni.

[I still listen, and I hear no news of my sweet and beloved enemy, nor do I know what to think or to say to myself, fear and hope so pierce my heart. To be so beautiful has harmed some in the past; this one is more beautiful than any other and more chaste: perhaps God wishes to take such a friend of virtue away from earth and make her a star in Heaven, rather a sun. And if this is so, my life, my short reposes, and my long troubles have come to an end. O harsh parting, why have you put me so far from my misfortunes? My brief tale is already told and my time filled up in the middle of my years.]

What sets the later poem apart most decisively is the way that Petrarch's speaker has by this turn himself become a listener, who in a moment of strained audition finds himself unable either to receive or transmit adequately. He feels his discourse breaking down, as line 3 reveals, coterminous with the lady's physical existence. He continues to listen, but all is drowned out by the sound of his own fears, an internal dictation that seems to have been prescribed—already *compita*—by the very splendor reiterated in lines 5–8.

The ambiguity with which Petrarch clouds his speaker's expression renders the remorse problematic. The simultaneous "tema e speranza" which he claims animate him may point to nothing more than the fact that he fears the worst while still hoping for the best. His rhetoric, however, also enables the unsettling possibility that he hopes for the fearsome event itself, Laura's convenient willingness to comply with literary convention and thereby to legitimize the prolongation of his lyric grief. Despite his claims, these lines harbor an intimation that the woman's death will not terminate his own story. The "dura partita" he apostrophizes ostensibly curses the literal distance separating him from Laura and news of her condition; yet (again), insofar as the expression addresses the "harsh parting" that her death occasions, it betrays his awareness that he will not soon follow her with the speed he promises—a point the reader easily discerns from the poem's placement, two-thirds of the way through the sequence. By the final line, we are wary of the lament that his life is over at midday, knowing as we do that Laura's death indeed "furnishes" (*fornito*) his creative prime. There is something tragically naive about the lover's enthusiastic regret. He does not yet grasp adequately, amid his inspired melancholy, that the event he alleges would "fill up" his time will actually leave him staring into the void Laura leaves behind. He will feel death's genuine emotional impact only when he discovers himself both emptied and somehow alive.

Though proleptic, the fear voiced in 254 is itself premature. The sequence does not shift *In morte* for another ten poems, and not until sonnet 267 do we know for certain that Laura has died. The poet's reference to Laura as if she were alive in those poems immediately following the break—which Petrarch explicitly authorizes—seems in this regard purposeful, an ironic reversal of the lover's tendency to imagine her dead. Displayed early (from sonnets 31 to 33) and late (the series leading up to poem 254—what Teodolinda Barolini has called the "death sequence"[38]) in the *Canzoniere*'s first movement, the reflex traces a revealing counterimage of Petrarch's persona. The same speaker who impulsively mythologizes love's consequences in 23 is elsewhere prone to underrate death's impact.

Sonnet 31 abruptly summons a vision of Laura's departure from this world "anzi tempo" as a basis for another hyperbolic meditation on her glory:

Questa anima gentil che si diparte
anzi tempo chiamata a l'altra vita,
se lassuso è quanto esser de' gradita,
terrà del ciel la più beata parte. . . .

(1–4)

[This noble soul that departs, called before its time to the other life, if up there it is prized as much as it should be, will hold of heaven the most blessed part. . . .]

The risky gesture of presuming to measure heavenly values with earthly judgments—the inflection picked up in Durling's translation of the third line—discounts both realms, as his tour through the celestial spheres her soul should occupy devolves into a trivial game of encomiastic speculation. Even before arriving at the subversive implications in which his lines culminate, where he conjectures that "se vola più alto, assai mi fido / che con Giove sia vinta ogni altra stella" [13–14: if it (i. e. her soul) flies higher, I am sure that Jove and every other star will be vanquished], we sense how remote we are from any sort of Dantesque transcendence, or even the ethical seriousness of Scipio's dream in Cicero's *De re publica*, which the ascent also recalls. Mortality is, on the contrary, rather crudely exploited for the sake of rhetorical compliment, however graceful the intention.

The moral direction of Scipio's dream, especially as amplified through Macrobius's seminal commentary, congealed one of the classical world's most potent and influential instances of the *contemptus mundi* motif. From the sublime perspective of the afterlife, Cicero's hero surveys the ridiculous insignificance of all earthly ambition and accomplishment. In the following sonnet, which turns from 31's triviality to an indictment of the trivial, Petrarch's lover takes up this motif in a homiletic performance at once generic and unconvincing. Thoughts of death's approach now spur him to put all the delights he knows aside, against the time that he will be able to discern true worth: "sì vedrem chiaro poi come sovente / per le cose dubbiose altri s'avanza, / et come spesso indarno si sospira" [12–14: we shall see clearly then how often people put themselves forward for uncertain things and how often they sigh in vain]. The *altri* of his reflection, "others," more precisely than Durling's collective "people," is telling: he eagerly anticipates a time when the Scipionic vista will segregate him completely from *other* fools. So to speak, he cherishes death for the condescending perspective it will enable. The earlier response to Laura's alleged demise has blurred immediately into a formulaic discourse on the lessons death will provide for him, satisfied with never having to press very deeply into mortality's emotional consequences.

The progression from earth to heaven traced through these sonnets arrives just as suddenly in 33's unexpected reprimand. In a dream, Laura chastises the poet's over-eagerness to credit intimations of her death: "Perché tuo valor perde?," she demands, "Veder quest'occhi ancor non ti si tolle" [13–14: Why does your worth languish? Seeing these eyes is not yet taken from you]. This is the upshot of his very un-Ciceronian dream: not transcendent contempt, but a re-awakening to the "worth" (*valor*) of a temporal existence that it is folly to think one may relinquish so casually. The return to this realm, which his lady forces in the closing lines, connects with those images adduced earlier in the poem, his seemingly eclectic vignettes of dawn's arrival:

> levata era a filar la vecchiarella
> discinta et scalza, et desto avea 'l carbone,
> et gli amanti pungea quella stagione
> che per usanza a lagrimar gli appella . . . .
>
> (5–8)

[the frail old woman, ungirt and barefoot, had already arisen to spin and had awakened the coals; and that time was piercing lovers which by custom calls them to lament . . . .]

Their juxtaposition effectively spans a social spectrum, from the quiet hardship of aged servitude down to youth's pampered (though no less intense) melancholy. Both *vecchiarella* and *amanti* react to the circumstances of their quotidian lives *per usanza*; and in this very "custom" resides a will to maintain one's existence—again, a *valor*—that merits much more than disdain. These *altri*, in their poverty or pleasure, counter his pretensions as effectively as do Laura's words.

Little maturation occurs, however, in this brief series. Near the end of the *Canzoniere*'s movement treating Laura *In vita* we find her lover still focusing his anger upon a world that fails to value (and hence deserve) the woman he celebrates so tirelessly. An assertion of the way Laura's beauty inspires ecstasy in all her beholders ("fa con sue viste leggiadrette et nove / l'anima da' lor corpi pellegrine" [with sights new and charming makes souls wander from their bodies]) prompts thoughts of a more literal departure of souls in sonnet 246. He casts the prospect of Laura's death here specifically as "il gran publico danno," that great public loss, only to encounter in the succeeding poem the skeptical resistance of this very public to his extravagant claims:

> Parrà forse ad alcun che 'n lodar quella
> ch' i' adoro in terra, errante sia 'l mio stile
> faccendo lei sovr' ogni altra gentile,
> santa, saggia, leggiadra, onesta et bella.
>
> (1–4)

[It will perhaps seem to someone that, in my praise of her whom I adore on earth, my style errs in making her noble beyond all others, holy, wise, charming, chaste, and beautiful.]

This, in turn, inspires the harsh, defensive disgust "al mondo cieco che vertù non cura" [for the blind world, which does not care for virtue] in 248. And as the fearsome vision of her death comes to haunt him ever more fiercely by 251, he is astonished that public channels ("altri messi") have not officially reported such a great calamity. But the indifference he encounters ironically mirrors his own unwillingness, caught inside his egocentric obsession, to reciprocate the sympathy he invokes. Since Petrarch makes explicit within the sequence the year of Laura's death (in sonnet 336) as 1348, he deliberately contextualizes the event within a moment of pandemic, catastrophic mortality. The lover's bizarre silence about the plague seems in this regard equally deliberate, betraying his own insensitivity to the fate of a society whose attention he nonetheless demands. Eclipsing all other cares, concern for Laura's wellbeing disrupts a system of reciprocal sympathies of which he might otherwise partake.

Apart from this civic shortsightedness, a more disturbing selfishness infects sonnet 249's recollection of the last day the poet saw his mistress alive. The speaker's admission that, although the memory fills him with apprehensive fear, "non è cosa / che sì volentier pensi et sì sovente" [3-4: there is nothing I more gladly think of or more often], sounds unsettlingly predatory. Her departure may not be wholly disadvantageous to the fate of his own work. If her death removes the only chance of corroborating the accuracy of his encomia—he has challenged those who suspect his extreme praises to gaze upon her, "venga a mirar," in 247 and 248—it will simultaneously withdraw the living evidence of his poetic inadequacy, also feared in 247. Not insensitive to the liberation awaiting him, he idealizes Laura as an exemplar of goodness in a world where, he confirms, "Morte fura / prima i migliori" [248.5-6: Death steals first the best]. To confirm her status and fund her poet's reputation, all Laura needs to do is die.

Overall, Petrarch's lover seems to betray little awareness of death's force, outside its usefulness as a prop for his rhetorical posture throughout the *In vita* segment. His prayer in 146, that he be permitted to die before Laura, translates with relative ease to 251's hopes, when it looks as if she might have preceded him, that "non tardi il mio ultimo giorno" [14: my last day may not be tardy]. Much relies upon her continued existence, according to his hyperbolic claim: "A me pur giova di sperare ancora / la dolce vista del bel viso adorno / che me mantene e 'l secol nostro onora" [9–11: I must still hope for the sweet sight of her lovely face, which keeps me alive and gives honor to our world]. That he finds himself sufficiently alive to pray for death after her feared lapse qualifies all this assurance, and by extension proposes that the world will also find other ways to sustain its *onore*. Not until his lady's death is realized as an uncontrovertable fact in the *Canzoniere*'s second part, rather than the idle speculation and trope it has proved for him up to now, will he arrive at 271's sobering and poignant admission, "né credo ch' uom di dolor mora" [4: nor do I now believe that one can die of grief].

Although the lover is himself slow to discover death's human cost, the woman with whom he is enraptured is not immune to this myopia. The *contemptus mundi* pose indeed unites them perhaps more immediately than anything else we discern in the sequence. Laura's rigor emerges forcefully in the peculiar dialogue sonnet 262, the only poem in which she gets to speak in her own person. Grounding its scenario in Laura's correction of her mother's "reversed" priorities, the poem depicts an oddly inverted image of moral counsel where youth instructs age.

"Cara la vita, et dopo lei mi pare
vera onestà che 'n bella donna sia."
"L'ordine volgi; e' non fur, madre mia,
senza onestà mai cose belle o care,
et qual si lascia di suo onor privare
né donna è più, né viva; et se qual pria

appare in vista, è tal vita aspra et ria
via più che morte et di più pene amare.
Nè di Lucrezia mi meravigliai,
se non come a morir le bisognasse
ferro et non le bastasse il dolor solo."
Vengan quanti filosofi fur mai
a dir di ciò, tutte lor vie fien basse,
et quest'una vedremo alzarsi a volo!

["Life is most dear, it seems to me, and after that, true virtue in a beautiful woman." "You reverse the order! There never were, mother, things lovely or dear without virtue, and whoever lets herself be deprived of honor is no longer a lady and no longer alive; and if she appears the same to sight, her life is much more harsh and cruel than death, and more bitter with sorrow. Nor did I ever marvel at Lucretia, except that she needed the steel to die and that her sorrow alone did not suffice." Let all philosophers of all times come and speak about this: all their ways will be low, and her alone we shall see mount up in flight!]

The tableau readily conforms to the surrounding poems' celebration of her moral insight. Sonnet 260 promotes Laura's "eccellenzia" above that of antiquity's heroines; 261 defines her as the example of all "senno," "valor" and "cortesia" and 263 apostrophises her as "Vera Donna, et a cui di nulla cale / se non d'onor che sovr' ogni altra mieti" [5–6: True Lady, concerned for naught but honor, which above all others you harvest]. Despite 262's enthusiastic postscript, however, the severity of Laura's stern didacticism also steers perilously close to the vain self-righteousness that always threatens to snare the truly pious. Laura's extreme vision of feminine honor may have appealed as deeply to a large sector of Petrarch's audience as it clearly does to her lover, but the harsh assessment of Lucretia—humanism's arch paradigm of female nobility—stiffens precocity into something more symptomatic of naiveté, the piety of inexperience. Even the obsessed poet thinks, however offhandedly, to qualify the hyperbole of his enthusiastic reverence with an interjected "s' i' non erro" [if I do not err (260.12)]. Her unyielding conviction, by contrast, admits no such rhetorical tempering. While the encomiastic fervor of the adjacent sonnets may muffle this objection, the agonized soul-searching of canzone 264 justifies our reservations.

Perhaps inspired by his lady's disdain for all things worldly, he indicts his vanity in recriminations that, subtly though powerfully, implicate her as well. Seemingly on reflex, he refers to Laura as one who "a me troppo *et a se stessa* piacque" [108: pleased me *and herself* too much (my emphasis)]. As they will both soon discover, there are other ways to die than by either "steel" or shame. In a time of epidemic mortality, such a pose is not to be adopted lightly. A great deal must be comprehended by these parties if the moral message of worldly abnegation is to have genuine substance. A franker confrontation with death will soon enable such understanding.

Designated as the opening poem of the *Canzoniere*'s second movement, stationed on the cusp joining *In vita* to *In morte*, 264 justly enjoys distinction as one of the sequence's pivotal performances. Petrarch's lover confronts most starkly in this supreme confessional moment his undeniable ties to his life. This linkage exposes the pomposity or (more threateningly) mortal *superbia* latent in his pose of moral superiority. Bound only by two intertwined threads, his hunger for fame and passion for Laura, he intimates that at least the nobility of these dangerous longings surely elevates him above the common lot: "Tu che dagli altri ch 'n diversi modi / legano 'l mondo in tutto mi disciogli," he prays, "ché non togli / omai dal volto mio questa vergogna?" [84–87: You who entirely free me from all the other knots which in different ways bind the world...why do you not finally take from my brow this shame?]. The filaments are sufficiently strong to anchor him. Before conversion's more exacting imperatives, his divorce from the world *in parte* defends him not at all. Soul-searching turns up only "un piacer per usanza in me sì forte / ch'a patteggiar n'ardisce co la Morte" [125–26: a pleasure so strong in me by habit that it dares to bargain with Death], the spiritual hazard Augustine especially excoriates.[39] The ardent desire to live on renders the contempt he voices, either for " 'l latino e 'l greco" in whose ranks he wishes to enroll, or for the *vulgus* who will presumably entertain his image in these poems, never fully convincing. At this turning point, the poet's intense introversion pointedly reemphasizes his social context: others' examples, "gli altrui esempli," have helped guide him to this crucial pass, which culminates finally in a painful admission of his deep attachment to a world of deliberation, struggle and becoming that he shares with its other inhabitants. He sees all this as *peggiar*, but nonetheless holds tightly as death closes in.

Exacerbated by the shock of Laura's death a few poems later, canzone 264's guilty anguish will inform the balance of Petrarch's sequence. The poet's anticipation of his own death continues to animate the *In morte* poems; but, in contrast to the earlier pieces surveyed, his lament over death's delay becomes more subdued and poignant, less given to the glib posturing that had characterized his original stance. We can chart a path from 268's numbed recognition following news of Laura's death that "Tempo è ben di morire, / ed ò tardato più ch' i' non vorrei" [1–2: It is surely time to die, and I have delayed more than I would wish], to his pained recollection in the anniversary sonnet 278, "O che bel morir era, oggi è terzo anno!" [14: Oh what a beautiful death that would have been, three years ago today!], to those regrets disclosed more quietly as time proceeds. Sonnet 292 dwells sorrowfully upon how Laura "m'avean sì da me stesso diviso / et fatto singular da l'altra gente" [3–4: had so estranged me from myself and isolated me from other people]. The following poem acknowledges the poet's desire to please his audience, whose approval he enjoys:

> S'io avesse pensato che sì care
> fossin le voci de' sospir miei in rima,
> fatte l'avrei dal sospirar mio prima
> in numero più spesse, in stil più rare.
>
> (293.1-4)

[If I had thought that the sound of my sighs in rhyme
would be so pleasing, from the time of my first sighs I
would have made them in number more frequent, in
style more rare.]

His belated awareness comes, he suggests, as a product of the poverty Laura's demise has left him to mourn: "or vorrei ben piacer, ma quella altera tacito stanco dopo sé mi chiama" [13-14: now I am willing to please, but that high one calls me, silent and weary, after her].

Laura's death unquestionably has given him much to sing about, something his more exploitative literary instincts had greedily anticipated in earlier days. Now, standing outside all such artificial prospects, he imagines in 304 what he might have accomplished had her living presence endured to inspire his maturity:

> Quel foco è morto e 'l copre un picciol marmo
> che se col tempo fossi ito avanzando
> (come già in altri) infino a la vecchiezza,
> di rime armato ond' oggi mi disarmo,
> con stil canuto, avrei fatto parlando
> romper le pietre et pianger di dolcezza.
>
> (9-14)

[That fire is dead and a little marble covers it: if it had
gone on growing with time, as it does in others, into old
age, armed with the rhymes of which today I am
disarmed, with a mature style I would speaking have
made the very stones break and weep with sweetness.]

Envy now touches his regard for the *altri* whose experience he would rather enjoy. The self-condemnation of 311, likewise, echoes his earlier "knowledge" of beauty and virtue's fragility with the renewed conviction of experience, which if anything further points up the hollowness of his original assertion. "[C]h' altri che me non ò di chi mi lagne, / che 'n dee non credev' io regnasse Morte," he confirms, spurring him to recall "O che lieve è inganar chi s'assecura!" [7–9: I have no one to complain of save myself, who did not believe that Death reigns over goddesses. Oh how easy it is to deceive one who is confident!]. Although he has won the audience he desired even as he pretended to despise them, he is at last left with the grim silence occasioned by one conspicuously absent addressee: Laura has left behind "con gravi accenti / è ancor chi chiami, et non è chi responda" [318.13–14: one who calls out with heavy accents, but there is no one to answer]. Only irrevocable loss can transform his pretensions in a manner more genuine than all the fanciful metamorphoses his mythic sensibilities had envisioned in his lady's lifetime. "Or cognosco io che mia fera ventura / vuol che vivendo et lagrimando impari / come nulla qua giù diletta et dura" [Now I know that my fierce destiny wishes me to learn, living and weeping, how nothing down here both pleases and endures], he concludes in 311. The *cognizione* has been dearly purchased.

The poet's experience of having lost Laura as a prospective audience is complemented by his fuller discovery of what it means to occupy the space of an audience himself. He assumes this station memorably in the *Canzoniere*'s most relentless depiction of mortal transience, canzone 323. Like its counterpart canzone 23, with which it has been paired to form "those two structural columns of the *Fragmenta*"[40], 323 plays out in its series of allegorical vignettes a vision of worldly impermanence that no capacity for adaptation can at last defer. Death as the great equalizer shadows the erotic commonality playfully intimated in the earlier poem, as myths of transformation yield to ones of termination. Mythological attributes themselves fall victim in the poem's visionary sweep.[41] He has over the course of his sequence enshrined his now deceased mistress securely within the Ovidian Daphne legend, sheltering himself throughout in the tree's umbrage, only to shatter this refuge in what amounts to the tree's unnatural destruction. Recalling his wonder at the laurel's beauty, the speaker witnesses the sudden cancellation not merely of personal security, but of all conventional presupposition:

> Et mirandol io fiso,
> cangiossi 'l cielo intorno, et tinto in vista
> folgorando 'l percosse et da radice
> quella pianta felice
> subito svelse, onde mia vita è trista,
> che simile ombra mai non si racquista.
>
> (31–36)

[And as I gazed on it fixedly the sky around was changed and, dark to sight, struck with lightning and suddenly tore up by the roots that happy plant, whereat my life is sorrowful, for such shade is never regained.]

Petrarch had remarked publicly in his coronation speech on the Capitoline that "as all agree who have written on natural history, the laurel is immune to lightning.... Rightly, therefore, since the laurel fears not the thunderbolt, is a crown of laurel given to those whose glory fears not the ages that like a thunderbolt lay all things low."[42] He had confessed privately to St. Augustine in the *Secretum* that "one of the chief reasons why I love the laurel is because it is said that thunder will not strike this tree."[43] The *Canzoniere* will forsake even this mythic consolation in an effort to strip away all assurance of privilege or preservation. Like the grim splendor of all he beholds "solo a la finestra," the vision excites his pity and dismay, but also seems to leave him one exposed and alone, standing nervously by his open window of vulnerability.

The canzone's concluding self-address drives home the ostensible lesson of mortality that the tragedies he has witnessed firsthand have taught the poet: "Canzon, tu puoi ben dire: / 'Queste sei visioni al signor mio / àn fatto un dolce di morir desio'" [73–75: Song, you may well say: "These six visions have given my lord a sweet desire for death"]. Poised against the vivid, kinetic images of wonder preceding it, the closing sounds strangely anticlimactic. But in its otherwise flat morality (death is transformed from the source of depression to the implied escape from all futile worldly contingency), we are also brought back around to the chief point of discrimination between the two canzoni: where the speaker was himself a spectacle in the earlier poem, he stands apart now as a witness—an *audience*—passively contemplating what moves in such disastrous sequence before him. The chronicler of destruction himself passes unscathed, physically if not emotionally. Rather than go down with the magnificent, the speaker will linger on with the quotidian. At once, the poem reinforces the hazards of distinction while illuminating the poet's profound awareness that, in order to prevent his acknowledgement of personal mortality from being anything more than hollow piety, he must understand what it feels like to assume the spectator's role, to watch others die. For this speaker, apprehension of mortality's crisis will involve a crisis of witness.[44]

The *Canzoniere*, in other words, insists finally that experience must substantiate piety. Petrarch's lover must undergo actual deprivation—"Or conosco i miei danni" [Now I know my losses], he admits in 329—before he can begin to impart any real conviction to his expressions of world-weariness. By 331, his contention that, aside from Laura, "Mai questa mortal vita a me non piacque" [Never did this mortal life please me], requires a franker recognition of the "altro consiglio" that is now his:

> Ma da dolermi ò ben sempre, perch' io
> fui mal accorto a proveder mio stato
> ch' Amor mostrommi sotto quel bel ciglio

per darmi altro consiglio:
ché tal morì già tristo et sconsolato
cui poco inanzi era 'l morir beato.

(31-36)

[But I must always grieve that I was unskilled to foresee my state, which Love showed me beneath that lovely brow in order to give me other counsel, for many a one has died sorrowful and unconsoled who might earlier have died happy.]

He closes the same canzone with a wish that other lovers be spared his expensive education:

Canzon, s' uom trovi in suo amor viver queto,
dí: "Muor mentre se' lieto,
ché morte al tempo è non duol ma refugio,
et chi ben po morir non cerchi indugio."

(61-64)

[Song, if you find anyone living peacefully in love, say to him: "Die while you are happy, for timely death is no grief but a refuge; let him who can die well not seek delay."]

There is no earthly compensation for so great a loss, his anguish forces him to cry out in 344 ("Ogni mio ben crudel Morte m'à tolto, / né gran prosperità il mio stato avverso / po consolar di quel bel spirto sciolto" [9-11: Cruel Death has taken away my every treasure, nor can great good fortune console my adversities for having lost that lovely soul]). He rejoins this evaluation in the following sonnet, recalling how her place, "con li angeli la veggio alzata a volo / a pie' del suo et mio Signore eterno" [13-14: risen in flight with the angels to the feet of her and my eternal Lord], should afford transcendent consolation. At this remove, he can appreciate that for which his *Signore* submitted himself to the *commune dolor*. He is able at last to see through "L' inganni del mondo," the deceits of the world (357), especially those by which he had earlier deluded himself, thinking that he was remote from such worldly attachment.

Such a reading of the poet's shifting response to mortality—which he comes to appreciate only through a more intricate and honest attachment to this world—tends to reinforce rather than impugn a piety which, as Charles Trinkaus reminds us, was "proverbial." We need not attack Trinkaus's opinion that "never in his entire life does [Petrarch] waver in thinking himself the most orthodox of Christians"[45] to understand how faith was for the poet too fragile and urgent a matter to entrust to an unexamined acquiescence. In the *Secretum*, significantly, Augustinus can effectively parry Franciscus's vocal resistance to his admonitions, but he is far more wary of his antagonist's passages of easy deference: points too quickly granted are either not sincerely appreciated, Augustinus seems to fear, or have not claimed an essential emotional purchase on their object of conversion. That Franciscus remains wavering and hesitant at the work's unresolved conclusion, in this respect, constitutes one of its more promising features. Formulaic closure might well compromise more than affirm the *pietas* he ardently sought. Lip service to the doctrinal truths of religion, or to Amor's conventions, is bound eventually to prove hollow. The poet settles finally for no less than a commitment determined by the experience of social witness and engagement, in secular as in sacred affairs.

The Appeal of Mortal Things

In the course of the *De remediis utriusque fortunae*, his massive effort to counsel a Senecan conquest of human vulnerability to the passions, Petrarch at one point proclaims "Non est serendus, qui sui generis sortem luget" [I cannot stand people who despise their own nature].[46] The remark comes in response to an expression of despair that we must die. Mocking this anxiety by means of a stoic resolve that we should all accept natural limitation, the answer also recalls just how naturally human beings grieve over their mortality. The ambiguity typifies much of the treatise's dialogic exchange. In its project to carve out a balanced response to Fortune's hardships and blandishments, the *De remediis* works by interrogative challenges similar to the ones that enliven the *Secretum* or the *Canzoniere*. The obduracy of those personifications whom Reason attempts to comfort or reprimand affords the author a chance to enlarge his copious arguments. Simultaneously, their continued recalcitrance exposes the potential poverty of such advice in an emotionally charged, practical setting. Before the spectacle of human ecstasy or anguish, all the available argumentation he can summon rarely seems even to budge the interlocutor, who tends to reiterate the contentment or suffering under consideration, as if deaf to his counselor's urgings. As James D. Folts has remarked, "the modern reader ... is impressed by the equally relentless power, if not the eloquence, of the human emotions ... which are given voice in the work."[47]

Though one could hear these voices of resistance as Petrarch's caricature of ignorant, "vulgar" opinion, to do so lessens considerably the *De remediis*'s effect. So in the *Canzoniere*, the poet's incorporation of himself among the *popolo*, even as he insists on his distance, further enhances his character's appeal. Petrarch, as he instinctively addressed "human nature," was sufficiently attentive to recognize the self-importance inherent in this authoritarian posture. The insensitivity it sponsors can render one all the more prone to those comic and tragic follies we have so far considered. To extract oneself from a social context may refresh the selfhood his critics consistently celebrate, but such a move also risks nurturing a false sense of superiority, priming that self for a fall.

In response to the numerous apologies for Petrarch's elitism, Ugo Dotti more recently has asserted that the writer's withdrawals were undertaken always with an eye to constant reincorporation, and "represented only a condition that would allow him to participate with greater commitment and seriousness in the life and fortunes of a human community."[48] The pliancy that Petrarch's lover exhibits over the course of his experience will, in like manner, enable him to sue more effectively for sympathetic concessions in the worldly forum he occupies. The consequent ability to adapt and appreciate the positive value of those circumstances he confronts grants an undeniable appeal to the *mortale cose* he contemplates.

Apart from Rodolfo de Mattai's more sympathetic evaluation, assessments of Petrarch's political outlook by even the most enthusiastic *petrarchisti* lean toward dismissal of the poet's visionary impracticality.[49] For a revealing example of his sensitivity to more worldly civic realities, we need only glance at the epistolary discourse on statecraft written, during the last year of the author's life, to Francesco da Carrara, Lord of Padua, and preserved as *Seniles* 14.1. We could view this tract as the culmination of Petrarch's humanist dreams integrated with a lifetime's experience. Evidently solicited by his patron for advice on ruling his city, Petrarch's lengthy reply persistently trims the lofty expectations of the classical philosophical models he invokes, to suit a humbler vision of human nature to which the author's observations consistently revert. The letter merits our attention in the present investigation of his sonnet sequence, which also directs its higher aspirations finally to a confrontation with concerns no less mundane.

Although he begins by encouraging Carrara to meet the political ideals he will recommend, Petrarch soon makes clear that his advice will itself keep its standards within reach. After discoursing on the virtues of cultivating love rather than fear among one's subjects and pondering the urgency of a magnanimous justice, he moves toward a more functional insistence: Carrara must undertake what amounts to a program of urban renewal in Padua, repairing the streets and (even more specifically) preventing local swineherds from letting their pigs run freely through the city. In effect, he alternates leadership's loftier goals—always elusive for temperamental as well as for logistical reasons—with banal, pragmatic counsels. We know what we ought to do, he argues, but we do what we can: "Perhaps someone would say that all this is trivial; I contend it is neither trivial nor to be disdained. The majesty of the noble and ancient city must be restored not only in major things but in small ones.... This is what you owe your fatherland, this I consider worthy of you, this above all is yours to do" (S 14.1; B 534).

Similarly, a discussion of those friendships important for the political leader to cultivate comes to echo Cicero's remark from *De amicitia* (my present chapter's epigraph), to the effect that the wisdom enabling true friendships and alliances is of the more common variety: "We are not seeking one that does not exist; we are satisfied with what the human condition affords..." (B 544). As if to reinforce this pragmatic sentiment, he concludes his brief with one last detail, which he hopes will be manageable, if all else is not:

> But I have already said enough, and, I fear, too much. At first I had intended to exhort you at the end to reform your people's ways; now, in reflecting that what I attempt is utterly impossible and could never be done by force of laws or kings, I have changed my mind. To deliberate over the impossible is certainly useless. Yet, there is one custom of your people I cannot overlook, and I not only urge you but adjure you to apply your corrective hand to this public evil.... (B 551)

The "evil" that so annoys him is the raucous public lamentations that accompany public funerals in the city. This practice suggests to Petrarch an impious disregard for the glory available to all Christians upon departure from this life. It no doubt also unnerved someone of his advanced and infirm age. Even here, he clarifies that he seeks to curtail only that which violates a certain decorum: "I am not asking you to forbid this; for it would be futile and perhaps impossible for a man [not to grieve]" (B 552). A tempering of extant evils is the best he might hope for, but this will serve. Like the letter itself, which concludes with the author's statement "I have perhaps said more than I ought, but less than I wished," leadership must observe a proper balance. Never fully commensurate with one's grander conceptions, moderated ambitions nonetheless permit one to succeed in ways that overreaching expectations cannot efficiently grasp.

Even at their most empassioned, Petrarch's political verses recognized the importance of practical delimitation. His great canzone 128, "*Italia mia*," for instance, moves in its first six lines from the opening apostrophe's vast perspective, to what the weary poet hopes is a slightly more functional (because narrower) address to hostile military factions in Rome, Florence and Parma: "piacemi almen che' miei sospir sian quali / spera 'l Tevero et l'Arno, / e 'l Po, dove doglioso et grave or seggio" [I wish at least my sighs to be such as Tiber and Arno hope for, and Po where I now sit sorrowful and sad]. Outside of such overt historical reflections, however, a similar moderating temperament will, over the course of the *Canzoniere*'s progress, peer through the excess, self-absorption and surly resistance clouding the poetry's surface, and it invites us to look more closely into its discreetly politic gestures.

Management of prodigal ambition becomes the topic of sonnet 146, where an acute awareness of limitation informs, qualifies and empowers the performance, in a fashion perhaps paradigmatic for Petrarch's larger sequence. The expansive apostrophe opening this sonnet incorporates his own giddy anticipation of *copia*: "O d'ardente vertute ornata et calda / alma gentil cui tante carte vergo..." [1-2: O noble spirit beauteous and warm with burning virtue, for whom I line so many pages]. His productivity, in the flush of creative inspiration, at first seems to recognize no boundaries, but suddenly contracts into a significantly narrower, yet not unhappy, domain:

> del vostro nome se mie rime intese
> fossin sì lunghe, avrei pien Tyle et Battro,
> la Tana e 'l Nilo, Atlante Olimpo et Calpe.
> Poi che portar nol posso in tutte et quattro
> parti del mondo, udrallo il bel paese
> ch'Appennin parte e 'l mar circonda et l'Alpe.
> (9–14)

[with your name, if my rhymes were understood so far away, I would fill Thule and Bactria, the Don and the Nile, Atlas, Olympus, and Calpe. Since I cannot bear it to all four parts of the world, the lovely country shall hear it that the Apennines divide and the sea and Alps surround.]

Accommodation reinforces rather than compromises his ambition. Settling for what one can embrace—in this case the more constricted circle of his vernacular audience, for whom he "rules" his pages—will have to do, and may even one day approximate the more dilated scope he initially fantasizes. The poet will discover ample space in the verse emanating from Vaucluse, the enclosed valley, couching his reputation as author as well as Laura's glory in an expansive temperance he skillfully exhibits. If the ship of his life is bound fast by the demands of erotic obsession, as he repeatedly asserts, it is also able to tack effectively with the winds speeding him on his course.

Petrarch and his persona circulate within a network of constant adaptation and readjustment. The exercise promotes, alongside a cautious resignation, an eventual respect for those very agents who qualify whatever idealized plans he might at first have entertained. Although modern Petrarch criticism has not by and large sought to displace the author's religious sensibility in favor of an anachronistic secularism, it has defined the author's contribution to his era's intellectual *renovatio* by the way his influential work rethinks the value of "mortal things." The spiritual reorientation that reportedly takes place atop Mount Ventoux (to cite only one famous example) never quite realizes the Augustinian moment of conversion it explicitly pursues.[50] For all his sincere piety, there seems always something "in part" unswayed about the poet's attraction to the world, as expressed in the *Canzoniere*'s initial plea. In its fulness, the sequence's revaluation of *mortale cose* receives a last great hearing in canzone 360, where love will appeal, in Reason's court, the verdict Laura's paramour urges against him. What results is a devastatingly empassioned defense of the spiritual growth one can discover within the boundaries of the temporal world's restrictions. Although the final ruling will remain deferred at the poem's end, the poet's infatuation with the dead mistress is, in progress, recast as a kind of fortunate fall. The move will chasten the speaker's wrongheaded impulse to dissociate himself from those mundane forces that have enhanced, rather than impeded, his moral responsiveness.

The lover's ultimate showdown with his adversary will take place in the intensely ironic context of a courtroom—the very *locus* from which his love for Laura has rescued him, as Amor will instruct him directly. The poet must, in short, regress to this point of origin in order to comprehend his actual success. In ways deeper than even he appears to recognize, the confrontation will prove for him a kind of purification ritual. Describing himself as one "com' oro che nel foco affina" [5: like gold being refined in the fire] initially, he manages by the end to achieve this refinement through what he unwittingly reveals about himself and the emotions behind his prosecutor's stance. Adopting the tone of unyielding religious orthodoxy, the poet mounts a bitter offensive against

"Quel antiquo mio dolce esempio signore" [my old sweet cruel lord] who allegedly "m'à fatto men amare Dio / ch' i' non deveva, et men curar me stesso" [31–32: has made me love God less than I ought and be less concerned for myself]. But by the time it is over, we grasp that the lover actually wants to indict God himself for the pains he has suffered. Since he cannot legitimately do this before Reason's tribunal, he deflects his rancor onto a less potent—and, he deems, a more vulnerable—deity, Love himself. His charges cluster around the central complaint that Amor has thwarted his chances to dissociate himself from the world, something he feels that he once enjoyed the proper virtue to achieve: "che, s' i' non m'inganno, era / disposto a sollevarmi alto da terra" [28–29: For, if I am not deceived, I was of a nature to raise myself high above earth].

The rhetorical advantage Amor enjoys as second speaker is almost inconsequential, given the vulnerability of the poet's position. We had already discerned, even before Amor steps forward, the poet's awareness of his fame, couched in the partially shamed and partially proud reference to "le parole e i sospiri, / di ch' io mi vo stancando et forse altrui" [73–74: my words and my sighs, with which I go wearing myself out and perhaps others]. Inviting Reason to hear "l'altra parte," Amor launches into a counterattack which effectively sets down a case that his challenger's subsequent self-exposure will clinch. Amor's indictment of the poet's earlier days, for instance, is devastating. Where "Questi in sua prima età fu dato a l'arte / da vender parolette (anzi menzogne)" [80–81: In his first age this fellow was given to selling words or rather lies], Love points out, the "puro et netto" [pure and clean] affection for Laura that he has inspired has preserved the poet's otherwise dubious honor, leaving him one "salito in qualche fama / solo per me, che 'l suo intelletto alzai / ov' alzato per sé non fora mai" [88–90: risen to some fame only through me, who have raised up his intellect to where it could never have raised itself]. He completes his sarcastic charge two stanzas on, alleging

> et sì alto salire
> il feci che tra' caldi ingegni ferve
>   il suo nome, et de' suoi detti conserve
> si fanno con diletto in alcun loco;
> ch' or saria forse un roco
> mormorador di corti, un uom del vulgo!
> I' l'esalto et divulgo
> per quel ch' elli 'mparò ne la mia scola
> et da colei che fu nel mondo sola.
>
> (112–120)

[and I made him rise so high that among brilliant wits his name shines, and in some places collections are made of his poems; who now would perhaps be a hoarse murmurer of the courts, one of the mob! I exalt him and make him known by what he learned in my school and from her who was unique in the world.]

In what emerges as his crucial distinction, Amor proposes that through his agency the poet has managed to secure the favor of both God and the populace: "ch' è in grazia, da poi / che ne conobbe, a Dio et a la gente" (133–34). This argument backs his closing statement: "da volar sopra 'l ciel li avea dat' ali / per le cose mortali, / che son scala al Fattor, chi ben l'estima" [137–39: I gave him wings to fly above the heavens through mortal things, which are a ladder to to the Creator, if one judges them rightly]. Sara Sturm–Maddox has targeted this passage as "a perversion of Augustinian doctrine," since "it is not through 'likeness,' however noble or lovely, that the love of the creature rises towards its Creator."[51] The point of Petrarch's invention, however, is not a "perversion" but a serious reworking of Augustine's outlook—an approach he emulated throughout his life, as the correspondence reflects, but one in which he could not manage honestly or fully to invest, as the *Secretum* betrays with equal force. He has avoided both the claustrophobic careers of the public barrister trapped in the noise of the courts as well as the devout isolation of one cut off entirely from the world. Without becoming one of the *vulgus* in any caricatured or dismissive sense, he nurtures the sustaining respect of *la gente* along with a moral rectitude; he thereby enjoys a dual privilege, in both spiritual and secular contexts. Where the poet had presumed to rise above the world in line 29, Amor discovers that he has attained far more than this vain project could ever yield, through the agency of a lady herself "nel mondo sola," unique in this world—where both terms, her individuation and her presence *in* the world, prove equally essential.

What holds the poem together in such profound tension is not just the clash of a repentant, world-weary speaker with the supple rhetorical competence of his opponent's defense, but the fundamental disingenuousness into which the lover must retreat to press his accusations. His intentions become clear in a startling revelation, capping the exchange. Amor has no sooner finished reiterating all the ways in which his accuser's relationship with Laura has enriched this *ingrato*, and has pointed out that the poet in fact knows it ("et ei l'à detto alcuna volta in rima," [144: and he has said it several times in rhyme]), than the lover breaks in to confirm the indictment unwittingly. Acknowledging in "a tearful cry" that Laura has indeed had this effect on him, he reveals that the true source of his resentment is her absence: "Ben me la die', ma tosto la ritolse!" [149: He gave her to me indeed, but he soon took her back!]. We suddenly discover that his mistress's loss, rather than the undermining of his moral wellbeing, motivates his complaint: not erotic impediment, but what he deems the premature removal of this threat. The righteousness he has affected throughout at last discredited, Petrarch's persona stands before the bar a deeply compromised—yet (for this very reason) powerfully humanized—figure.

At the poem's intriguing close, when both parties finally blend their voices, anxious and haughty, as they turn to Reason to decide their case, she demurs, "smiling," *sorridendo*, remarking only "Piacemi aver vostre questioni udite, / ma più tempo bisogna a tanta lite" [156–57: It pleases me to have heard your pleas, but more time is needed for so great a lawsuit]. It is not Cupid who introduces the jocularity here, as he had at the *Amores'* start, but reason herself, at the *Canzoniere*'s twilight moment. Her benign gesture of silence stems from a sense of consummate professional responsibility. The jury remains out in Reason's court because it is posterity, in all its vulgar mutability, that must finally pronounce a verdict. Long after the God to whom he appeals has passed his definitive judgment on the poet's soul in another, transcendent court beyond all secular audience, we are still left to evaluate his literary performance. Petrarch ultimately deals with the need to know who one's supporters are, and by what policy one may deal with them. He works under the vigilance of the God to whom he prays, as well as the audience's gaze to whom he appeals. After all his aggressive and vocal disdain is spent, our presence is, in the end, honored.

In this way, the sequence's final canzone 366 arrives as an aftermath to 360's performance. Whether or not anyone is listening to the prayer, as Mariann S. Regan has questioned,[52] we must recognize his courtroom confrontation with Amor as something more than merely a barrier to be cleared on a progress toward a divine reconciliation. Rather, it opens the way for this possibility. There is no point in escaping the court's noise, Petrarch comes to reveal, if one simply replicates this internally. There must be a measure of compromise to assure both the *pace* with which the work ends and the worldly resolve in one's accomplishment. More is finally at stake than the basic opposition between impiety and salvation. He summons his spectators to reassemble the work for him, and for themselves. There is something therapeutic, moreover, about this reconstruction: if he never really knows Laura, neither do others ever completely fathom him. And perhaps that is most redemptive for both parties. Just as his own shortcomings and strengths become apparent to him through his assembly of Laura's virtuous image, so through their responsiveness to his revisionary stance an audience may discover something about the way it works in conjunction with (as well as in opposition to) his performance. This is poem 30's vision of an audience "che nascerà dopo mill' anni / se tanto viver po ben colto lauro" [35–36: who will be born a thousand years from now—if a well-tended laurel can live so long]. True to his plans, the poetry has been tended and attended by those whom he has (effectively) antagonized and courted. Both text and reader continue, leagued in all the fragility and strength he could imagine.

One of the final letters gathered into the *Seniles* certifies that Petrarch's skeptical outlook toward his contemporary public remained in place to the end of his life. Responding to the insistence of Boccaccio—the student whose adoration for his master never waned—that he is admired as one of the age's most distinguished artists, Petrarch expresses his opinion that "I have really not equaled anyone except the multitude; to them I would much rather be forever unknown than be like them." Specifying the envy and critical hardship his reputation has also brought him, he concludes "I have always had to stand on the battleline with my banners raised, always resisting assailants now on the right, now on the left.... In short, my laurel has afforded me this: to be known and tormented; without it I could have kept quiet and out of the public eye, which *some think* is the best kind of life" (S 17.2; B 652 [my emphasis]). The last clause, "sine qua quod optimum vitae genus, *quidam putant*," is typical: amid the harsh dismissal, he can still not bring himself to commit fully to the renunciation he aims to declare. The *vulgus*, which has kept him embattled as well as famous, has imparted an unspoken benefit important enough even here to insure the author's partiality. The consequences of this relationship were especially significant for the *Canzoniere*, where, freed from the self-conscious seriousness of the Latin works, he could entertain "vulgar" contexts of which he kept always wary, yet to which he was always drawn. The work kept him rooted in the *popolo*, enforcing an ironic awareness of interdependencies between self and other, and enabling a balanced self-criticism more richly humorous and severe than anything his supporters or attackers could put forward. This feature perhaps helps to account for why the *Canzoniere* reached completion and enjoyed a greater impact than the *Africa*, far outside the national borders for which sonnet 146 had settled.

Boccaccio's insistence upon his generation's international respect for the great man was not an exaggeration. Petrarch had, in his lifetime, secured a fame which enabled him to circulate freely among the era's most powerful and prestigious circles, his literary talent his only credential. During the period separating Petrarch from Shakespeare—to whose lyric work we turn next—a novel brand of social concentration takes place. The artist's reliance upon audience, intuited by the Italian poet, became a steadily more pronounced issue, as the court society that came increasingly to dominate Renaissance life grew more self-conscious and openly articulate about matters of social theory. As Frank Whigham has splendidly documented, the age's social transactions are carried out with an ever-vigilant eye to public approval, reaching a point where "Speech and other significations reveal not power but powerlessness, a pleading with the audience for a hearing, for recognition, for ratification." By the time we reach Shakespeare's London, Whigham asserts, "For established and mobile Elizabethans alike, public life at court was governed by a rhetorical imperative of performance (*esse sequitur operare*: identity derived from behavior)."[53] I find this hunger for "audience ratification" played out in the *Sonnets*, in an intriguingly dramatic manner directly connecting with the lyric negotiations we have traced so far. Preeminently covetous of public sanction, Shakespeare's persona never locates the viable private space toward which his emotions direct him. The deeply fragmented experience that results will place him, we shall see, beyond even the tenuous stability managed by his amatory predecessors.

Three

And Men's Eyes
Shakespeare's Politic Lover

> ... chi regola el traino del vivere suo non in altro che in sulla speranza d'avere a essere grande col popolo, ha poco giudicio, perché a apporsi è piú ventura che senno.
> — Francesco Guicciardini[1]

Reaching for a compliment, Francis Meres could summon no finer tribute to Shakespeare's poetic capabilities than to remark that "As the soule of *Euphorbus* was thought to liue in *Pythagoras*: so the sweete wittie soule of *Ouid* lives in mellifluous & honytongued *Shakespeare*," backing up the praise with reference to "his *Venus* and *Adonis*, his *Lucrece*, his sugred Sonnets among his priuate friends, &c."[2] Presuming these "priuate" lyrics to be among those that would appear over a decade later as *Shakes-peares Sonnets. Neuer before Imprinted*, we have found it easy to hear in Meres' comment something more than a reference to their unpublished status: "The word 'private' suggests not only that the poems were circulating in manuscript according to the common practice but that Shakespeare may have wished them to be kept like that: they were, perhaps like so many of the Sonnets we know as his, intimate in tone and reference, intended for a few eyes only."[3]

Samuel Johnson's speculation about Shakespeare's evident disregard for fame, an indifference to anything beyond "present popularity and present profit," may well be justified.[4] Such an attitude would not prevent the author of *Venus and Adonis* from striking an Ovidian pose, prefacing his verse narrative, destined for great commercial success, with an epigraph culled from *Amores* 1.15: "Vilia miretur vulgus: mihi flavus Apollo / Pocula Castalia plena ministret aqua" [Let worthless matter impress the mob; may golden Apollo refresh me with cups filled from his Castalian spring].[5] But the playwright, whose vocation exposed him to the applause and hostility of an audience in a manner up close and personal, certainly scrutinized within the plays themselves matters of public reception. The topic is especially pronounced in the earlier comedies—perhaps written contemporaneously with the sonnets—running a gamut from the brutal mockery (not generous, not gentle) that the aristocrats of *Love's Labor's Lost* indulge, to Theseus's benign accommodation of the rustics' dramatic endeavors in *A Midsummer Night's Dream*.[6] The intense interest in fame that the *Sonnets'* speaker overtly displays itself arrives as a product of his instinctual, apprehensive regard for a larger societal context, in these most significant closing moments of the tradition Petrarch had inaugurated over two centuries previously. When in poem 29 he announces himself "in disgrace with fortune and men's eyes," the sonneteer betrays a desire to segregate these two determinate entities, along with an equally revealing inability to do so: although he will boast by sonnet's end of the security he claims to find within the good fortune of a private relationship, he remains, in his own outlook, inevitably answerable to a discerning community.

Although we are no longer so confident the quarto that eventually saw publication was unauthorized, the "privacy" surrounding it has come to govern modern critical response ever more exclusively.[7] For instance, Bruce R. Smith's searching analysis of the various homoerotic mythologies current in Shakespeare's day removes the sonnets from "the public domain," transferring them to "the enlarging sphere of personal privacy and communal intimacy that was being shaped in the sixteenth and seventeenth centuries by several forces...."[8] Thomas P. Roche, Jr., assessing the poetry from an entirely different angle, will translate its central dramatic agon as a psychomachia, recasting the young man as a darker facet of the poet's own embattled temperament.[9] Most controversially, Joel Fineman has gone so far as to assert that, in the *Sonnets*, Shakespeare essentially invents literary subjectivity as it would henceforth be understood. The dissociation between an idealized visual apprehension of truth and poetic language's ironic misrepresentation of this reality, emerging incrementally over the course of these poems, makes way for a new literary self-consciousness. The sonneteer's frustrated hope for perfect union with the object of his desire yields to a pained reconception of selfhood as a function of distance or separateness, aptly figured in 152's final image of the "perjured eye."[10]

We can appreciate the invigorating perspective opened by Fineman's theory without granting his professedly gargantuan claim for the novel brand of individuation that the sequence allegedly discovers. Preoccupation with subjective growth in the *Sonnets*, however well merited, ends up telling only half a story. As the chapter's title anticipates, my own reading aims to supplement Fineman's, significantly qualifying his emphasis. Consideration of the key ingredient that Fineman ignores—the broader "world" to which Shakespeare's distinctively social persona is firmly bound—directs the approach in what follows. Briefly, I propose that whatever self-discovery the sonneteer manages in these poems is rooted primarily in his acute, almost obsessive sensitivity to public witness. For this speaker, all articulation of independent subjectivity itself remains subject to (that is, ironically dependent upon) communal critical approval.

Commentators acknowledging the *Sonnets'* public context have consistently deflected their analyses toward other aspects of the work. For example, Anne Ferry affirms that "Both speaker and subjects are portrayed as living in a public and social world," but chooses to emphasize instead their "simultaneous inward existence distinct from what they show to that world."[11] Heather Dubrow similarly brings up the matter of society only to stress how "the speaker is as alienated from the larger community as from the unfriendly Friend and the Dark Lady."[12] Even Sandra Bermann's view of these poems as "among the most public sonnets ever written," or Gerald Hammond's advocacy of an "audience's" role in poems 1 to 126, turns to matters of rhetorical effect rather than sustained scrutiny of the peculiarly social drama that grounds the sequence's development.[13] The only critic to take up this concern directly is Rosalie Colie, who, in the last book she was to complete, closes a splendid chapter on the *Sonnets* by pinpointing their unusual social temper. Arguing that Shakespeare fruitfully crosses the sonnet's traditional "privacy" with the epigram's generically more gregarious temper, she underlines that "the poet's relation to his friend takes place against the world's audible comment, comment which praises the young man and blames him too, comment which mocks the poet. His affair with the mistress takes place, too, within an acknowledged social context. She is known to his friends, whom he then gives up because they disapprove of her." Colie's understanding that "the poet is never really alone with either beloved," that "Even the triadic connection of poet with friend and mistress is depicted as exceptionally shared," enables her penetrating insight into the way that the persona's "self-explorations are set against social attitudes—approval, disapproval, business, multiple preoccupation and obligation—to open the sequence upon the worldly scene...."[14] Unfortunately, arriving only as an appendix to her main thesis, these observations never find the elaboration they deserve.

Patricia Fumerton's trenchant assessment of how specific historical circumstances in England had, by the late 1500s, impacted deeply upon cultural conceptions of public and private boundaries, further justifies this focus. Drawing her evidence from the analogous "intimate" artistry of miniature portrait and sonnet, she persuasively argues that the "Elizabethans were in the . . . habit of representing private experience as inescapably public."[15] What in my estimation distinguishes Shakespeare's response to the societal ambience Fumerton describes is his persona's rhetorical inability to negotiate either the conjunction or discrimination of public and private voices. Never capable of forsaking one for the other, he remains agonizingly unclear, as well, on how to maintain an effective balance. His confusion results in an oscillation between these poles which, in my reading, graphs the *Sonnets'* underlying rhythm.

Because a sense of *officium* or public duty intrudes even upon the *Sonnets'* most introverted reflections, we must regard closely the way their speaker conceives the unspeaking monitors of all he says and does. I turn first therefore to the problematic assumptions informing the procreation sonnets, whose conservative counsels to the young man set the tone for what follows in the sequence. This initial cluster delineates the civic temperament inspiring the poet's adopted role as spokesman for "the world's due." At the same time, his rigid alignment with a legitimizing community exhausts the technical resources of his discourse as it exposes the emotional sterility of the conventions in which he invests. I then follow the poet's attempted retreat to a supposedly private lyric sanctum, more hospitable to passion's specific, nontransferable demands. At this turn, he finds his efforts to restrict his audience crippled both by an internalized "public" consciousness infecting his verses, and by the more frighteningly tangible incursion, in sonnets 78–86, of rival professional talent into the would-be exclusivity of his relationship with the recalcitrant youth.

Ill at ease in both public and private realms, the poet finally trains his focus on the "dark lady" of his affections, whose casual resistance to public standards exemplifies an admired supersession and mastery of the social contexts he cannot surmount. The ease with which she evidently redefines convention, as expressed in 127, compounds his perplexity, as her success casts his failure in more daunting relief. Examination of several key moments from the poems to his mistress refigures and reinforces my argument for the speaker's dependency upon an object of desire who is also the audience that both establishes standards and refuses to satisfy his needs. At the sequence's close, the relationship chiefly at stake is the one that Shakespeare's poet-lover entertains with a community overseeing (in his view) all commerce, public and private.

My concern for the sonneteer's struggle with feared social disgrace furthermore identifies the argument's sympathy with, but also essential departure from, another provocative trend in recent criticism of these poems. Instanced eloquently in the work of Lars Engle, this approach regards the sonnets with an eye to the privileged status they have attained historically for post-Renaissance culture. Still attending to the "special subjectivity" emergent in Shakespeare's sequence, Engle stresses the poet's "emotional recognition that no ascription of value, even between two intimates defying the rest of the world, is independent of the ever-changing value systems that surround particular acts of assessment."[16] The verse continues to hold our attention as it reflects upon its own survival, grounded not in "monumental resistance" to time, but on "a kind of relative activity" that "manages to keep a space for the beloved and for assertions of his value in the corrosive public gaze...."[17] I differ from such a reading in my emphasis on the way Shakespeare's poet-lover never discovers for himself this crucial sense of adaptability, but instead stumbles over his fixed allegiance to the "corrosive" public agency. While these poems may (as Engle asserts) "argue about and for their own cultural centrality," they intone a pervasive nervousness about their speaker's capacity to suit his audience. Through this vital point of characterization, the *Sonnets'* persona enacts the lyric predicament that places him cleanly in line with Ovid's and Petrarch's formulations.

However we see fit to read the sequence—as a coherent "story" or as discrete poems articulating clusters of issues—it illustrates the complex intersection of realms I observe within the lyric poet's enterprise. Ovid presumes the poet's right to endure, while uncovering public contingencies and self-destructive threats that imperil his endeavor. Petrarch takes the initiative by repudiating a vulgar audience, for whom and through whom he nonetheless crafts the *Rime*'s self-preservative strategies. The *Sonnets'* lack of resolution, in turn, dramatizes a bifurcation of public and private sectors in an especially striking manner. Unable to determine a flexible mean—sobering or enriching—Shakespeare's persona paces awkwardly back and forth between worlds. He conceives a parochial audience in whose service he acts, only to recognize a circle of emotion that his skill cannot accommodate. Whatever subjectivity the speaker may somehow find remains forever contingent upon the external agency that he knew was watching all along.

CHILDREN OF STATE: CONVENTION AND CONSERVATISM IN THE PROCREATION SONNETS

However widely the *Sonnets'* concerns will range as their 1609 order progresses, the opening subsequence of poems forms an undisputed bloc, the "procreation" or (less aptly named) "marriage" group. The common topic linking these 17 lyrics grounds a number of principal motifs—time's ravages, the desire for immortality, the preciousness of human beauty and the like—elaborated throughout the work's less compacted balance. In its almost overbearing unity, the movement formulates a distinctive perspective and mission: adopting the role of a pedagogue, the poet aims to initiate his youthful charge by nurturing an awareness of *officium* or civic responsibility within an adult culture. The education begins with an emphasis on the youth's procreative duty, since herein is figured the perpetuation of society itself, as sonnet 11's attack on celibacy clarifies: "If all were minded so, the times should cease, / And threescore year would make the world away" (7-8). Indictment of what he regards as the youth's unnatural detachment sustains the project of indoctrinating his subject into a fuller community—one whose standards and conventions the poet presumes to embody and advocate.

This ambassadorial role becomes an urgent factor in our understanding of the poet's character. Just as the youth has allegedly "contracted" to the narcissistic scope of his "own bright eyes" in the first sonnet, so the speaker sees himself as one contracted or bound to a social world on whose behalf he initially speaks, and to which he turns a steady though covert backward glance. From the authoritative condescension of his initial arguments in favor of "the world's due," for which he holds the addressee liable, to sonnet 17's anguish over his own credibility to future readers, the speaker betrays a troubled concern with public acceptance. Though he determines ostensibly to win the young man to a more beneficial course of action, he also courts a personal legitimization that can be secured, for one of his temperament, only by means of public sanction. An air of confidence and confidentiality often surrounds these and later sonnets, but it is persistently clouded by an arena ambience which also subtly influences his expression.

Shakespeare's persona approaches the young man in a spirit of collectivity, established with disarming directness in his opening statement: "From fairest creatures we desire increase."[18] The *Canzoniere*'s initial *Voi* had designed to draw an audience into an intimate union with the poet; the *Sonnets*' plural pronoun by contrast announces a public context within which their speaker bases himself in order to redirect his addressee's conduct. An unhesitating voice of definitive membership opens the sequence, authorized primarily by its representative function, self-appointed or otherwise.[19] For Shakespeare's pedagogue, education involves chiefly an induction into a network of social commitment. His gestures consequently adapt generic expectations to stimulate not erotic response but civic responsibility. The youth's "proud livery," specified in the second sonnet, signals less his station in a "natural" order than his enrollment in a public community whose standards have determined and thus enabled the celebration of his beauty. His identity as "the world's fresh ornament" remains contingent upon a larger evaluative agency. Moreover, membership carries duties as well as privileges. The indebted youth is required to replenish the ornamental vitality that so pleases them—the "world's due" whose collection the sonneteer steps forward to recall.

The society this poet conjures is, moreover, an exactingly watchful company. We learn in sonnet 5 that the passing hours "Will play the tyrants" to "The lovely gaze where every eye doth dwell"; but this complimentary vigilance of "every eye" focuses its own implicit brand of tyranny. It takes the primary form of the "all-eating shame" threatened in sonnet 2, an emotion central to the *cursus* promulgated by Shakespeare's persona. Taking for granted that the youth cherishes public attention, the poet warns how eventually his verdant beauty "so gazed on now, / Will be a tottered weed of small worth held" (3–4) by judges who (to make matters worse) compound their frankly brutal dismissal by demanding an "excuse" for the temporal attrition he must inevitably suffer. The mockery of faded beauty reinforcing the worn *carpe diem* convention translates, in this speaker's assertions, to an issue of public scrutiny. The poet insists that his addressee, when interrogated at some future time "where all thy beauty lies— / Where all the treasure of thy lusty days," may redeem himself only "If thou couldst answer, 'This fair child of mine / Shall sum my count'" (5–6, 10–11). What matters in this inquest is the subject's answerability to an audience who officiously quantifies the "forty winters" gauging his decline. Others are counting, the poet warns, and if the young man himself wishes to go on "counting" (so to speak) in their estimate, he must take seriously his responsiveness to those who hold him accountable.

In short, the poet initially conceives his public world exclusively according to a system of *of-ficium* or duty so pervasive that it eclipses all prospect of *bene-ficium*, gifts freely imparted under no weight of obligation. The Nature upon which he erects this public vision emerges, in kind, as an ungenerous and unyielding arbiter: "Nature's bequest gives nothing but doth lend," he points out in 4, and pleads in poem 11 "Let those whom nature hath not made for store, / Harsh, featureless, and rude, barrenly perish" (9–10)—an attitude which Joseph Pequigney suitably refers to as "aesthetic eugenics."[20] "Natural" descriptions of this brand prove more the consequence of his stark ideology than its justification. Before the rigors of a jury that has expressly become second nature to the speaker, he reckons his recalcitrant young man surely must bend.

His addressee's compliance may safely be assumed because, as the "If all were minded so" trope invoked in sonnet 11 also clarifies, the social network he honors can brook no dissent or abstention. The ninth sonnet's attack on "single life" preempts the private scruple that may afford the young man with a legitimate dodge—that he avoids relationships "for fear to wet a widow's eye"—by dislodging personal qualms again with the promise of public shame:

> The world will wail thee like a makeless wife;
> The world will be thy widow and still weep,
> That thou no form of thee hast left behind,
> When every private widow well may keep,
> By children's eyes, her husband's shape in mind.
>
> (4–8)

The very formulation *"every private* widow" discloses the poet's inability at this juncture to conceive individuality in anything but categorical, absorbingly communal terms. "The world"—the abstraction governing his lines from the start—always will step in to supplant whatever emotional reservations he may feign, since (as the couplet intimates) it is the agency that adjudicates what constitutes "love toward others." Its transcendent office, which "weeps" for his misplaced priorities at first, will by the end threaten a somber indictment of his "monstrous shame." So long as the world enjoys its ornaments, at whatever cost to the subjects in question, all is well: "Look what an unthrift in the world doth spend / Shifts but his place, for still the world enjoys it" (9–10). Should this joy of ownership at any time become endangered, however, such indifference is quickly put aside.

The *Sonnets'* earliest depiction of direct public scrutiny comes in poem 7, where the focus trains revealingly not upon the ostensible analogy of the young man to the sun, but on the audience whose evaluative responses he follows:

> Lo, in the orient when the gracious light
> Lifts up his burning head, each under eye
> Doth homage to his new-appearing sight,
> Serving with looks his sacred majesty;
> And having climbed the steep-up heav'nly hill,
> Resembling strong youth in his middle age,
> Yet mortal looks adore his beauty still,
> Attending on his golden pilgrimage.
> But when from highmost pitch, with weary car,
> Like feeble age he reeleth from the day,
> The eyes ('fore duteous) now converted are
> From his low tract and look another way.
>   So thou, thyself outgoing in thy noon,
>   Unlooked on diest unless thou get a son.

In the poem's subtle reversal, "mortal looks" at last attend the great cynosure with what amounts to a magisterial rather than an obsequious gaze. Even the sun, he proposes in his rapture, holds his "sacred majesty" at the bequest of these public eyes, which are apt to devalue whatever slips beyond their ken and therefore beyond the strictly delimited circle of *their* "duty." To be "unlooked on" in such a world is to die, a point that the final line's punning non sequitur awkwardly tries to assuage. Failure to perform or live up to audience expectations courts a deadly ostracism these fearfully mortal looks can manage all too efficiently.

Despite his consideration in sonnet 15 "That this huge stage presenteth nought but shows / Whereon the stars in secret influence comment" (3–4), life presents for Shakespeare's poet a spectacle "Cheered and checked" by a jury less remote and far less celestial, whose influence is anything but secret. Beyond the debts to parents that he urges in poems 3 and 13, lie the even more pressing returns owed to a broad social patronage or sponsorship. The speaker relentlessly hounds his addressee with this awareness, we come to discern, primarily because fear of surveillance is his own distinguishing characteristic. The imagined company overseeing the youth's intransigent behavior also studies closely their mediator's progress. Readers commonly attribute the palpable nervousness of sonnet 10, wherein the poet's "I" debuts, to the awakening of his own passion for the boy, something the abstract "we" prevalent so far can no longer contain: "Make thee another self for love of me," he at last entreats. This is partly the case, but the desperation spurring this direct intrusion has much to do with the poet's anxiety over his own failing embassy. As the youth evidently continues indifferent to his counsels, a fear of inadequacy descends upon the speaker, deriving from his consciousness that he has stepped onto a public stage where he is judged as well as judge. A more important dissociation is underway than Philip Martin recognizes, when he suggests that the "many" of whom the addressee is "beloved" serves only as an abstraction of the couplet's more precise "me."[21] The sonneteer's plea registers his initial inkling that he must escape a servile reverence for public contexts if he is to cement an intimacy with the young antagonist. As yet, however, he remains tightly within the grip of his conservative social commitment.

Sonnet 10 exposes a desire which has blossomed sufficiently by the procreation subsequence's final moments to trouble the author's one confident strategy. The halting resolution that takes tentative shape in the newness of 15's couplet, "And all in war with time for love of you, / As he takes from you, I engraft you new," remains uncertain because of the basic disorientation this dramatic shift occasions for the writer.[22] For the first time, he concedes the possibility of speaking not of the surveillance or recrimination one must suffer at society's hands, but benignly, on one's defensive behalf. The fear of competition that he instantly betrays when he ponders this weak literary alternative to "living flowers" nonetheless colors his reluctance to embrace this novel prospect. Were the youth to get an heir,

> Then the conceit of this inconstant stay
> Sets you most rich in youth before my sight,
> Where wasteful time debateth with decay
> To change your day of youth to sullied night....
> (9–12)

Public eyes demand more than a mere poet can provide. Art can never present an adequate substitute, and his own dubious talents (the pedagogue now finds himself the "pupil") are least likely to make the grade.

His nervous apprehension of public acceptance reasserts itself most forcefully in the subsequence's splendid concluding gesture. Sonnet 17 marks the culmination of this now shaken figure's anxieties, in a crisis moment's contemplation of his own public credibility:

> Who will believe my verse in time to come
> If it were filled with your most high deserts?
> Though yet heav'n knows it is but as a tomb
> Which hides your life, and shows not half your
>   parts.
> If I could write the beauty of your eyes,
> And in fresh numbers number all your graces,
> The age to come would say, "This poet lies—
> Such heav'nly touches ne'er touched earthly faces."
> So should my papers, yellowed with their age,
> Be scorned, like old men of less truth than tongue,
> And your true rights be termed a poet's rage
> And stretched meter of an antique song:
>   But were some child of yours alive that time,
>   You should live twice in it and in my rhyme.

The audience's ferocious power stands before him most blankly. From the opening "Who will believe" to the clipped pronouncement "This poet lies" closing line 7, the poet articulates his own desperate contingency. Grasping fully the inherent distrust of youth for age, he ponders future readers' inclination to misconstrue what is actually understatement for vacuous, disqualified overstatement. The stern "tyranny" described in his efforts to intimidate the youth now overshadows his own poetic performance. In such a vulnerable state, even successful encomium faces potential failure at the whim of a surly, skeptical panel.

This apprehension also yields to a more profound awakening encoded in his lines. Alongside his fear, the poet now verbalizes a certain reliance upon the youth, who is capable of rescuing him from scorn in the couplet's expected yet suddenly refreshed resonance. What he conceives in the young man's progeny is both the maintenance of beauty and (as importantly) the endurance of a sympathetic enclave within the future audience, able to substantiate his encomiastic efforts by their inherited visage, as well as by their willingness to defend his endeavor. The sonnet fantasizes nothing less than a mutually reinforcing system of assurances, which may serve as a defensive check against the challenges of readership. Should the youth heed his appeal, these lines—otherwise doomed to obsolescence—may continue to circulate, indifferent to whatever cynicism they will inevitably encounter. The sonnet suggests that friend and verse (as well as the versifier's reputation) will support one another, but it goes much further by positing their solidarity against a larger public that the poet has up to this point advertised as dauntingly unassailable. It manages all this while also giving the public what they want.

Drawing himself fully into this renewed perspective proves an arduous task for the poet. Although his pose is unsettled progressively over the course of this introductory movement—from 10's appeal, to 13's address to the youth as "Dear my love," on to the closing impulses just surveyed that presage the less inhibited confessions of poems like 20—the erotic stirrings he experiences never completely dislodge him from his duty-bound vantage. The difficulty derives mainly from the way his fundamentally conservative disposition has evidently hardened into something unthinking. A good many presumptions and prescriptions must be shattered before he can ever hope to regain some leverage within a world that suddenly no longer appears so safely familiar. He must, in other words, resist the temptation to retreat into a conveniently patterned view of the world, symptomatic of his wish to shelter himself from experience's trials. One of the most glaring and integral manifestations of this conservative stamp is the copious style with which we, in turn, must contend in this early movement.

While the procreation subsequence's tight focus insures coherence, it simultaneously threatens a monotony that has also taken its toll on the poetry's modern audience. Even Wordsworth, who found the young man sonnets admirable enough, was put off by a general "sameness," a feature most damagingly concentrated in this introductory series.[23] Despite Colie's point that generically the sonnet sequence "seems to be an invitation to repetitiousness—or, if one prefers the term, to *copia*,"[24] even sympathetic readers often emerge from an unbroken tour through these 17 poems impressed with the technical splendors of individual sonnets, but numbed by the speaker's monotonous (not to mention dubious) assertion that beauty naturally can, and therefore must, perpetuate itself. Nor does John Kerrigan's straightforward diagnosis that "The trouble is, we have lost touch with the ideal of copiousness so dear to the Elizabethans" adequately address this feature.[25] Though it suits Shakespeare's purpose that we initially account for his sequence's early repetition as conventional rhetorical practice, he is chiefly interested in what this practice comes to imply about the practitioner. It is not the "ideal of copiousness" that occasions the problem, but the persona's failure to examine his technique self-consciously.

Systematized and sanctioned by Erasmus's seminal handbook, *copia* or the "abundant style" was honored in the sixteenth century as a hallmark of Latin eloquence.

The rhetor's capacity to work endless variations on a theme legitimized his verbal skill and keen wit. "If properly done," Marion Trousdale observes, "such amplitude was to the age its own aesthetic justification. Something equated with both wisdom and pleasure could hardly be otherwise, and it is important to realize the extent to which copiousness was admired for its own sake."[26] In his vigorous promotion of the technique, Erasmus had, as Terence Cave emphasizes, adopted the natural world itself, which "proliferates without repeating itself," for his supporting paradigm.[27] On the most practical level for the humanist, mastery of *copia* served to protect speakers from a redundancy bound to alienate the easily distracted audience: "This disorder can easily be avoided by someone who has it at his fingertips to turn one idea into more shapes than Proteus himself is supposed to have turned into."[28]

Due to its potential for abuse, the practice required some careful policing. Recognizing the inherent risks, Erasmus introduces his text with a disclaimer: "As the proverb says, 'Not every man has the means to visit the city of Corinth.' We find that a good many mortal men who make great efforts to achieve this godlike power of speech fall instead into mere glibness.... They pile up a meaningless heap of words and expressions without any discrimination, and thus obscure the subject they are talking about, as well as belabouring the ears of their unfortunate audience." The "unskilled practitioners of the full style chatter on without restraint, and yet say far too little, omitting a good many of the things that need to be said."[29] Used without discretion, *copia* hazards collapsing the world into a false sense of variety, where both speaker and listener are frozen into a frustrating stasis of virtually unlimited alternatives. Further along in the century, Roger Ascham found it necessary to reemphasize this caution against abuse, indicting "that *Nimium*" or excess which even the more learned had come to indulge, recommending the exercise of *epitome* or condensation as an antidote. Ascham goes on to elaborate (in a passage particularly relevant to the present analysis) how *copia* can prove especially unseemly in mature speakers: "This fulnes as it is not to be misliked in a yong man, so in farder aige, in greater skill, and weightier affaires, it is to be temperated, or else discretion and iudgement shall seeme to be wanting in him."[30]

Shakespeare delighted in baiting such figures of pedantry and dullness, with Holofernes and (later) Polonius as his two most memorable victims. Though his sonneteer will never fade into this kind of caricature, his copious enlargement on how "as the riper should by time decease, / His tender heir might bear his memory" (1.3–4) displays him as just such a faulty manager, one who packs relatively little substance behind the shimmering exterior of his words. His repetitiveness serves as a critical feature of the persona's character-fabric. The eloquence which preserves the sonneteer from Holofernes' absurdity, despite the redundancy of his initial assault, also opens a way for more insidious, self-deluded failure. After a fashion, his rhetorical flash masks the actual poverty of his discourse: the collective performances by which he thinks to draw out the youth never get very far beyond the tenuous commonplace that beautiful people beget their kind. His apparent unwillingness to exploit even the shopworn riches of the *encomium matrimonii* tradition betrays a shallowness of conception that dooms him to the facile posturing Erasmus condemns. Commenting on the general peculiarity of his approach, Judith Kegan Gardiner has pointed out that "Shakespeare's arguments in behalf of marriage are unusual ... more for what they omit than for what they say. Of the three conventional Renaissance reasons for marriage—legitimate procreation, sinless sexuality, and marital love, Shakespeare stresses only the first."[31] More troublingly, however, the proliferating versions of a single counsel seem intent upon the preservation of a rather narrowly conceived sense of order. The file of poetic "offspring," all cast in the same argumentative mold, all pointed toward the same end, enact a vision of conformity inside of which the speaker feels safe. Asserting that age will "dig deep trenches" in beauty's field, he remains himself entrenched in a solitary line of discourse from which he refuses to emerge.

The force most enervated by the overall "sameness" of these poems is that of erotic passion itself. Fashioning what amounts to a litany of would-be fertility songs, cast in the contemporary form best identified with expressions of highly wrought emotion, Shakespeare's speaker at the outset stands ironically oblivious to the *eros* without which his procreative schemes cannot be realized. The first sonnet's peculiarly dispassionate "desire" never steps beyond the opening line. Lars Engle is right to suggest that the initial quatrain "might be the voice-over of a Sierra Club film in which California condors soar over their eggless nest."[32]

> From fairest creatures we desire increase,
> That thereby beauty's rose might never die,
> But as the riper should by time decease
> His tender heir might bear his memory....
>
> (1–4)

Progressing from the rather broadly construed "creatures," to the next line's symbolic rose, on to the third line where the subject drops out altogether, the poet betrays himself as one uneager to focus on human beings in any precise manner, much less upon the potentially messy emotions which join them to one another. That we are never clear whether the speaker of these poems is encouraging the young man to marry, or simply to copulate, or if it makes any difference to him, says less about the speaker's outlook towards women or marriage than it does about his basic evasiveness. Questions of detail make him nervous, and he would just as soon stick to the homey blur of abstracted tradition.

The small regard for femininity exhibited in this introductory movement offers further insight into the

Children of State 149

speaker's reductive sensibility. When, after being omitted completely from Sonnet 1's scenario, a woman enters the picture in 3, she does so as "some mother" whom it should shame the youth to leave "unblessed": "For where is she so fair," he asks, "whose uneared womb / Disdains the tillage of thy husbandry?" (5-6). By sonnet 6, this anonymous agent loses even the virtue of her humanity: "Make sweet some vial; treasure thou some place / With beauty's treasure ere it be self-killed" (3-4). Finally, he envisions for the youth how the "many maiden gardens" will actually compete to "bear your living flowers, / Much liker than your painted counterfeit" (16.7-8), so much acreage promiscuously eager to take his seed.[33] Even the most traditional traits commonly attributed to a desirable mate—such as exceptional beauty or noble status—are, from his standpoint, immaterial. Women function impersonally, as vehicles to further the objective he has taken upon himself to promote.

If the poet's antifeminism seems any less malignant at this point than in the indictments that will scar later sonnets, it does so mainly because we read it as part of his programmatic tendency to stereotype. Erasmus had expressed, again, a specific need for variety in character: "It is not enough," he insists, "to grasp what is consistent with the character of an old man, a young man, a slave, the head of a house or a pimp. Otherwise representatives of the various types would all be indistinguishable from each other. The comic poets especially seem to have aimed at variety in characters belonging to the same general type,"[34] a point to which our greatest master of dramatic characterization was likely sensitive. At the opposite end of the spectrum, the "tender heir" actually fares little better. Where any "uneared womb" will do for breeding purposes, the offspring themselves enjoy no distinction save as mirrors for the young man. They provide simply, as the poet reassures him, "another thee," "another self." We have seen how his streamlined theory of generation suppresses the less favored by Nature ("Harsh, featureless, and rude"), and clears the way for the youth to multiply his image: Nature "carved thee for her seal, and meant thereby / Thou shouldst print more, not let that copy die" (11.13–14). Paradoxically, the perfect "copy" of his simplistic schema remain featureless, their identities dissolved in their parent's "sweet semblance." Contemplation of such splendid uniformity inspires the excited calculations of 6, where the poet, like some frantic accountant, enumerates offspring with more relish than Catullus counts kisses:

> That use is not forbidden usury
> Which happies those that pay the willing loan;
> That's for thyself to breed another thee,
> Or ten times happier be it ten for one.
> Ten times thyself were happier than thou art,
> If ten of thine ten times refigured thee. . . .
>
> (5–10)

The limitless replication he calls for looks to his wish in sonnet 13 that the youth's beauty should "Find no determination." The remark, which could well serve as the speaker's motto, suggests both endless renewal and the erasure of all distinctions. Throughout this, the poet ironically mires ever more deeply in the vice of one who "confounds in singleness" his world, the very thing with which he charges his recalcitrant addressee in sonnet 8.

Shakespeare's poet takes up quarters in a landscape inhabited by such imaginary projections, pressing his arguments from a protected, naive vantage. By introducing the subject of children into the sonnet tradition, he implicitly directs attention to the physical sexuality that Petrarchism usually neglects; but having done so, he neutralizes erotic attraction, reducing it to a kind of practical social transaction or (more precisely) a mechanical operation, like planting or coining. He designs a neatly compartmentalized world where *eros* plays no significant role in the fashioning of children, where an orderly genealogy unafflicted by the distracting complexities of obsessive, nontransferable passions keeps time at bay. While he indicts the youth's improvidence, the poet, prisoner to the nearsighted perfections of his artificial constructs, seems guilty of an equally destructive version of self-preoccupation.

What most alerts us to the weakness of these idealized claims is the simple point that the speaker's accomplished rhetoric accomplishes nothing. By definition, *copia* "suggests a rich, many faceted discourse springing from a fertile mind and powerfully affecting its recipient."[35] The "effect," Shakespeare makes clear for us, is here painfully absent. As each consecutive lyric aims to demonstrate further the poet's copious abilities, it also signals a continued practical failure to win the young man to his counsels. The mentor, who has refused to acknowledge vital differences which prevent women from being classified as so many "uneared wombs" and set children apart from their parents, himself meets with the youth's casual indifference. Maintaining an unspoken and unspeaking independence, the young man implicitly ignores one who emphasizes ends over means, and who fails to countenance the variety upon which erotic love thrives. Without a clearer sense of specificity, he might readily demote the elder's plea for procreation much as Adonis does Venus's in Shakespeare's epyllion, as an "idle over-handled theme."

The poet's static pursuit seems to confirm an image of the youth as a belligerent spirit of opposition. We get the impression that, should the poet stop urging him to mate, or tell him not to bother, he would take a lover—which is pretty much what will end up happening later in the sequence. The young man will not play the role of "only herald to the gaudy spring" that has been so carefully scripted for him, nor will he be schooled by the complacent wisdom dispensed by his guide. The hostility from broader future audiences, anticipated by the poet in sonnet 17, is merely another version of the rejection these poems already have suffered at the hands of their addressee. The harsh vision of his words "scorned, like old men of less truth than tongue" betrays a tone of personal injury, as well as a growing sense of inadequacy. He will need to do more than position himself in the midst of an inclusive public circle to secure the kind of acceptance he craves. Interrogation of social orthodoxies by defiant younger generations, figuring into 17's imagined agon between the "age to come" and the "antique song," tempts the conservative speaker into the pleasures of contemplating an alternative, "exclusive" perspective. His resources spent, the poet flees backstage, towards the intimate enclosures demarcating sonnet 18's abrupt tonal shift.

Despite his recognized need for a new start, Shakespeare's persona will never manage to stray very far outside the prospect of a public eye that he has essentially internalized. The sonneteer will, over the course of what follows, return sporadically to self-conscious reflections on *copia*'s role, such as in 76's anxious query "Why write I still all one, ever the same" (5), or 105's attempted defense of the way his verse "to constancy confined, / One thing expressing, leaves out difference" (7–8). His most poignant return to a copious exercise occurs, however, in the sequence's last moments. From the present argument's vantage, we are better able to grasp how the maligned sonnets 153 and 154 complete the frame begun in the procreation poems.[36] For all their peculiarly detached, anticlimactic exposition, they function as products of the poet-lover's enduring quest for the security of institution and convention.

Sonnets 153 and 154, paired imitations of an epigram from the Greek Anthology, offer in their transparent reliance on a canonized original a last glimpse of the persona's desire to relax behind the shield of an accepted source. His own experience and expression desperately out of kilter, he belatedly seeks to recover his balance by reproducing versions of another's words, words that enjoy the safe blessing of an "antique" status. The twin variations he undertakes also signal a much-attenuated return to the copious manner inaugurating his work. The redundancy so commonly faulted here only parodies in a more concentrated fashion the brand of reiteration which protracts the initial movement. Lacking the energy bestowed by an earlier, uninterrogated confidence, however, *copia* is now spent after a single, moribund attempt.

The style he tries to recover is not the only significant aspect of his parting gesture. The model which he selects to translate will in his rendition deal fittingly with the founding of a public institution—the "seething bath which yet men prove / Against strange maladies a sovereign cure" (153.7–8), a "healthful remedy / For men diseased" (154.11–12)—following upon a fruitless attempt to disable Cupid. Given the character delineated within the procreation sonnets, we are no more surprised by the poet's efforts to take solace in these medicinal waters than we are by his inability to find what he wants there:

> I sick withal the help of bath desired,
> And thither hied, a sad distempered guest,
>   But found no cure; the bath for my help lies
>   Where Cupid got new fire—my mistress' eyes.
>
> (153.11–14)

Discovering how "Love's fire heats water, water cools not love" (154.14), he departs cleansed (if not cured) of misapprehensions about the easy remedy promised by such attempts to channel Eros's rebellious force. Early on, he had sought comfort in the presumed security of a public role, only to stumble over intimate passion's more constrictive boundaries. So at the end, he sojourns toward a public institution's promised ameliorations, only to be sent back home, to the "strange maladies" simmering at his own hearthside.

The infant invoked in the first moments of Shakespeare's *Sonnets* finally materializes in these derivative verses, not as a figure of the orderly succession which the mentor had there anticipated, but as the "little love-god" who tacitly presides over all intervening turns of passion, unfazed by efforts to quench his destructive and creative capabilities. Within the space separating the opening sonnet's formulaic desire to preserve and enlarge human *forma* from the more ominous "hot desire" whose infant "general" dozes unconcerned, if temporarily disarmed, in the final poem, we trace the poet's unsuccessful endeavors to cope with the tensions inherent in his lyric project. He is more seduced by the fantasy of laying aside all *officium* than he is by the enticements of a relationship which (in Gardiner's words) lacks any "institutional" sanction.[37] As we shall see, the hermetic world he dreams cannot stand impervious to the voices of the broader public sphere which it attempts to close out.

Public Means and Rival Claims

The abstractions deployed in the procreation series consistently serve a collective function, attempting to fuse addressee and poet to a larger societal purposefulness. Those obtaining throughout the *Sonnets'* vast central region, contrarily, pursue a restrictive intent. Hereafter, in poems 18 to 126, the sonneteer concentrates his energies on maintaining boundaries between the youth, around whom he thinks to restructure a cynosure of exclusive poetic intimacy, and the larger society, before whom he feels vulnerable or (in many instances) even persecuted. Escape so clearly becomes the informing motivation, that the strategies of withdrawal he variously entertains commonly organize critical reaction to this movement.[38] Even 116's preeminently famous exposition on "the marriage of true minds"—which, as Jane Roessner points out, eliminates "all traces of real people, in real time, in real space"[39]—designs a "removal" of its own, from accusatory voices whose constant drive to prove one's errors would presumably erect "impediments" to the sublime fidelity that he champions. The vagueness we noted in sonnet 1 returns here, at what most readers regard as the *Sonnets'* crowning moment; only now, it aims not to gather all into the great fold of "the world's due," but rather voices a defiant challenge to all worldly reservation.

Ironically, though not altogether surprisingly, the divorce he tries to effect renders the poet more rather than less sensitive to pressures of public witness. In the opening movement, private sentiments had eroded the confidence of orthodox pronouncements. The balance of the young man poems derives much of its special vigor from the tension generated, inversely, when a lingering public consciousness encroaches upon erotic lyric's mock-seclusion. Shakespeare's poet keeps an eye trained as closely upon what his new perspective excludes as upon what it has selected. As a result, his focused idealizations and resentful condemnations never argue free of the fiercely social temperament that burdens him. Inability to dodge the "mortal looks" that fasten relentlessly upon him intensifies his self-image as "an imperfect actor on the stage" (23.1), whose need to perform overpowers his desperate hunger for retirement.

A number of factors doom to failure this attempted translation of public into private allegiances. Most obviously, the young man's refusal to reciprocate exclusive affections disables the reinforcement that his friend seeks within love's confines. Unresponsiveness to the poet's entreaties in the procreation sonnets galvanizes into the notorious infidelities skewing the sequence from 33 on. Beyond this, more subtle inhibitions invite our analysis—functions of a distinctively professional dilemma, amplified through the peculiar strength of this archly dependent persona's social reflexes. He cannot so easily shed the demeanor shaping his directives in poems 1 through 17, since the "public means" of his poetic vocation have more deeply ingrained in him an attentiveness to public concerns than he seems ready to acknowledge. I turn first to instances of how his internalization of public voices renders ineffectual any move to shelter within a private relationship with his subject. Because the poet's commitment to "eternize" his lover obliges him to continue circulating outside the contracted focus, we look subsequently to the fearsome vista of competitive strife that gradually opens for Shakespeare's persona. Early in this movement, sonnets that skirt the comparative evaluations he sees his verse must undergo pave the way for a darker confluence of public and private in the famed "rival poet" subsequence; here, he at last encounters a foreign encroachment he can no longer keep at bay. The breakdown that this occasions—harsher than any erotic betrayal he has known—issues ultimately in the reflections on "policy" capping the movement; it is to these moments, and the exemplary awkwardness of their attempts to disclaim attentiveness to larger social spheres that intrude upon his devotion, that we finally turn.

Although many of the *Sonnets'* best-known utterances lean heavily upon the trope of poetry's preservative capacity, the prospect of obliteration articulated so splendidly in 17 is never obviated. The abrupt transitional question opening sonnet 18, "Shall I compare thee to a summer's day?," replaces the harshly evaluative public comparisons threatened in the other 17 with self-conscious poetic metaphor, allegedly destined to eternize its subject. However, alongside the discovery of power announced in the couplet's vital hyperbole, "So long as men can breathe or eyes can see, / So long lives this, and this gives life to thee," courses an acknowledged need for external confirmation that will hedge the speaker's enthusiasm. By reintroducing the audience explicitly into the poem's scenario, the speaker implicitly recalls the role of their judgment, which must arbitrate the preceding lines' enamored evaluation: the youth will survive only so long as readers see fit to look into this text or recite these words. This pragmatic concern casts its shadow deeply upon the poet's self-promotion of his "powerful rhyme" over other public monuments in 55, or the victory over Death that 107 claims, "Since spite of him I'll live in this poor rhyme, / While he insults o'er dull and speechless tribes" (11–12). Lacking a commemorative text, members of the speechless mob will lose their places in recorded time; yet his own survival—like that of his cherished subject—depends upon the continuing vocal approbation, literally the reiterations, of this majority. Sonnet 18's subtle awareness of a reliance upon the nameless receivers' remote "breaths" reaches out to qualify the pretensions of this poet's "poor rhyme."[40]

A grim predicament troubles the very foundations of the sonneteer's endeavor in these poems. Even were the youth willing to grant favor undividedly, he can never adequately comfort or refresh his lover, since the older man proves himself incapable of substantiating the object of his affections as an alternative to the imposing world of public intercourse. Instead, the poet regards his addressee as a surrogate for, or virtual metonym of, the society he renounces. What we see as we move beyond 17 is not a genuine reorientation of the speaker's emotional perspective, but merely a transfer of terms. Rather than dispensing altogether with the oppressive duty allegedly owed to worldly arbitrating agencies, on whose behalf he had earlier preached, he deflects this onto his beloved. Writing in 26 "To witness duty, not to show my wit," the poet obsequiously declares his indenture, specifying his abject dependence upon his reader's sympathetic generosity: "Then may I dare to boast how I do love thee; / Till then, not show my head where thou mayst prove me" (13–14). The poet flees from a setting where his inadequacies may forcibly compel his "removal," toward a substitute situation where he does little more than reconstruct the anxieties he had previously renounced. Escape from one register, where he fears he cannot live up to the audience's standards, issues into another where he acknowledges a continuing removal, always contingent upon the recipient's grace. The burden of "proof" dogs him unrelentingly. In 31, moreover, we encounter his bizarre gesture of concentrating "all those friends which I thought buried" in the young man, so "That due of many now is thine alone." The youth comes to embody a dilated cast—"all they"—which essentially countermands the professed contraction to a private world. Without a more complete withdrawal, the promised consolation remains unavailable, drowned out by the sustained echo of public inquiry.

The poet's retrospective gaze toward that public *cursus* from which he claims to depart invariably distracts the efforts at *recusatio* punctuating his sequence. Two illustrations of this—one proud, one wounded—color the movement's beginning, at sonnets 25 and 29. In sonnet 25's forthright declaration of independence, we glimpse a figure who has weighed carefully the advantages of anonymity against those of distinction. His inability to secure "public honour" inspires a statement on how insecure those publicly acclaimed for their success actually must feel, especially in comparison to the more discrete "joy" he has come to know:

> Let those who are in favor with their stars
> Of public honour and proud titles boast,
> Whilst I whom fortune of such triumph bars,
> Unlooked for joy in that I honour most.
> Great princes' favorites their fair leaves spread,
> But as the marigold at the sun's eye,
> And in themselves their pride lies buried,
> For at a frown they in their glory die.
> The painful warrior famoused for fight,
> After a thousand victories once foiled,
> Is from the book of honour razed quite,
> And all the rest forgot for which he toiled.
>   Then happy I that love and am beloved
>   Where I may not remove, nor be removed.

The heady liberty that he suddenly senses in the position of someone "Unlooked for"—a radical break for one who had urged in sonnet 7 the risks of going "Unlooked on"—excites a terrifyingly precise rendition of disgrace's

Public Means and Rival Claims 159

unbending calculation, in the third quatrain's image of the "painful warrior": one failed move renders the account so carefully tabulated in honor's "book" delinquent. Though he celebrates his relationship's privatized context as a haven from this ruthless evaluation, vivid pictures of "removal" still crowd his imagination. His descriptions impart to these defeated figures a tragic vitality that betrays a residual fascination with, and even respect for, their "painful" demise. The poem's advertised wisdom—occasioned by what he identifies as his preliminary exclusion from any race for "public honour"—leaves us with a paradox. The only way to circumvent the courtier's self-interment or the soldier's deletion from honor's book, it would seem, is to supplant reputation's published rolls with love's private tables: to dig one's grave, in other words, on the obscure textual margins of society. From outside the myopia of his newly adopted viewpoint, we recognize that the poet's declared invulnerability rests upon no firmer foundation than did the other parties' "foiled" assumptions of reward or desert. Ill fortune extends to all corners of experience, and the totality of his investment in hands that he will soon find are quite capable of "removal" cannot guarantee the security he boldly claims. The couplet's self-assurance is falsified by its speaker's need to belong, a desire so intense that it rivals his will to displace the entire system.

The inefficacy of sonnet 25's abjuration becomes more clearly evident four poems later. Sonnet 29 will finally recall 25's escape, but it begins as a cancellation of that sonnet's glib dismissal, unveiling the poet's enduring social wishes:

> When in disgrace with fortune and men's eyes,
> I all alone beweep my outcast state,
> And trouble deaf heav'n with my bootless cries,
> And look upon myself and curse my fate,
> Wishing me like to one more rich in hope,

> Featured like him, like him with friends possessed,
> Desiring this man's art, and that man's scope,
> With what I most enjoy contented least;
> Yet in these thoughts myself almost despising,
> Haply I think on thee, and then my state,
> Like to the lark at break of day arising
> From sullen earth, sings hymns at heaven's gate;
>   For thy sweet love rememb'red such wealth brings,
>   That then I scorn to change my state with kings.

Confessing the tormented shame of an outcast who desires to fit in, and who cherishes this relationship as compensation for (rather than negation of) his exile, the poem discovers completely his inability to break from "men's eyes." Ironically, the personal self-scrutiny recalled here knows a rigor far more relentless than the public gaze identified in line 1. The sonnet makes clear that he is by no standards indifferent to the privilege of social prestige, since his longing for reinstatement grows sufficiently strong to eclipse the love he must force himself to "remember." Moreover, the riches, connections, and talents that he covets can help placate the internalized voice of public condemnation which continues to indict his lack of ambition. Without silencing this voice, the poet remains wedged between the fear infecting the public lives of kings and warriors, and a nervous apprehension for the social contempt that his truancy, forced or elected, may summon.

Across the gulf of intervening disillusionment, the poet's efforts to reassess his public role and deny his contingency continue to sound in poems 110–112. Where in 29 the speaker had regarded the youth's love as compensation for the world's oppressive hostility toward him, he here summons his force to foreclose all communion with the realm outside their relationship. Once more, we witness a total inversion of the vigilance and duty urged in the procreation sonnets. Affirming his shamed indenture to the larger society, within which he continues to circulate, the poet disdainfully pronounces in these sonnets his renewed disgust for the audience to whom he has "vulgarly" pandered. Poem 110 refigures the social converse he has known as a kind of prostitution ("Alas 'tis true, I have gone here and there, / And made myself a motley to the view" [1-2]), and its successor elaborates this with an even more memorable fury:

> O for my sake do you wish fortune chide,
> The guilty goddess of my harmful deeds,
> That did not better for my life provide
> Than public means which public manners breeds.
> Thence comes it that my name receives a brand,
> And almost thence my nature is subdued
> To what it works in, like the dyer's hand.
>
> (1-7)

In the speaker's public reckoning, men's eyes—the "public means" lamented here—have themselves become his "fortune." No longer calling upon the young man to breed an enduring community of heirs, he lashes out at the society that, he alleges, "breeds" a commonness he cannot singlehandedly escape. His image of the "dyer's hand" poignantly captures the vocational hazard pondered in these lines. The only way to avoid the stain is to forsake the profession altogether. Once blotted, the poet may not be able to find refuge even in this maneuver. He must wear his office like an indelible brand, identifying him as one whose actions—even his silences—are subject to public review.

Sonnet 111 leaves off with a plea for "pity" and a hope for "cure"; 112 evidently marks the fulfillment of this, accompanied by a deflatingly self-conscious feint at liberation:

> Your love and pity doth th'impression fill,
> Which vulgar scandal stamped upon my brow;
> For what care I who calls me well or ill,
> So you o'er-green my bad, my good allow?

You are my all the world, and I must strive
To know my shames and praises from your tongue;
None else to me, nor I to none alive,
That my steeled sense or changes right or wrong.
In so profound abysm I throw all care
Of others' voices, that my adder's sense
To critic and to flatt'rer stopped are.
Mark how with my neglect I do dispense:
   You are so strongly in my purpose bred,
   That all the world besides me thinks y'are dead.

Stephen Booth's essay-length note to the notorious obscurities of lines 7, 8 and 14, which seem to "call attention to their faultiness," supposes the poem "to be unfinished or abandoned because it is atypical of Shakespeare's sonnets *only* in being incomprehensible."[41] Booth's conjecture overlooks that his unique obscurity is consonant with the poem's announced indifference to our reception. We do not matter, since a sole addressee has displaced "all the world." What compromises this extreme gesture, however, is its very exhibitionism: the twelfth line's awkward advertisement compels us to question its veracity. Can such a psyche really divorce itself from the judges who vindicate or condemn every "purpose"? Again, he has managed only to reconvene a concentrated version of society in the youth himself. If the world is dead to him, he will as surely go ignored by all the world, a scenario he can never (for all his disclaimers) fully bring himself to accept.

Jane Roessner has aptly called attention to the awkward break between the outlook directing these poems, and the vocational emphasis of those sonnets that immediately precede them in the sequence: "in Sonnets 100–108 the speaker is defined as praising poet, the friend as needing, in his decaying beauty and truth, those praises; in Sonnets 109–114, the speaker is defined as the public man, slandered and weary, the friend as the healing lover. It is as if the two halves of the group do not know about each other...."[42] The lyric psychology that Shakespeare develops explains (if it does not repair) this division, as symptomatic of his persona's struggle with competing professional and emotional desires. An audience relies upon its poets for survival, but the poet no less emphatically depends upon his audience. The point Shakespeare incorporates into his sequence is that the "two halves" of this poet's experience are painfully aware of one another, in spite of his prolonged efforts to segregate them. To be a poet is to place oneself before a public that cannot reasonably be brought to heel on a short leash of artistic control. The sonneteer can no more plausibly isolate the poetry from its critical public than he can remove himself utterly from his poem—though fretful and absurd entreaties like 71's "if you read this line, remember not / The hand that writ it" (5–6) attest to this speaker's pressing desire to effect just such a split.

This renegade advocate of societal obligation imports an awareness of public disavowal and shame into the intimate confines of his love. Coping with the internalized voices of censure is one thing; contending with external, actualized challenges to this fragile privacy is quite another. Long recognized as a distinctive feature of Shakespeare's construct, the rival poet sonnets become especially integral when considered in light of the troubled interrelationship of public and private that we trace. Although the *Sonnets*, like all of the major English sequences, were composed against the backdrop of the Tudor court's fiercely competitive society,[43] these poems stress matters of sexual and poetic contest with a special vigor. As deeply as Astrophil may lament the loss of his Stella to a "rich foole" in Sir Philip Sidney's sequence, his quandary seems tame compared to the tangle that results when the young man of the *Sonnets* takes up with his poet's mistress. Interestingly, Shakespeare's persona can salve the blow to his sexual vanity—glossing over his lovers' mutual betrayal with the kind of "Sweet flatt'ry" we find in sonnet 42—or can even face down Time itself, which in Howard Felperin's view also stands forward as a "powerful rival."[44] He cowers only before the intimidating specter of artistic rivalry.

We are primed early on for the distress that will ultimately overwhelm the sonneteer, which throws into sharpest relief his inability successfully to restrict his social context. A poem about poetic competition, sonnet 32 mediates neatly between 17's expressed fears and the complexities encountered in the rival poet subsequence. "If thou survive my well-contented day" momentarily broadens the cast to consider hypothetically those other writers whose accomplishments will, of necessity, influence the youth's long-term judgments. As the poet had likened his subject to a summer's day in sonnet 18, so his subject must inevitably, in time, compare him to other poets:

> If thou survive my well-contented day,
> When that churl death my bones with dust shall cover,
> And shalt by fortune once more re-survey
> These poor rude lines of thy deceased lover,
> Compare them with the bett'ring of the time,
> And though they be outstripped by every pen
> Reserve them for my love, not for their rhyme,
> Exceeded by the height of happier men.
> O then vouchsafe me but this loving thought:
> Had my friend's muse grown with this growing age,
> A dearer birth than this his love had brought
> To march in ranks of better equipage.
>   But since he died, and poets better prove,
>   Theirs for their style I'll read, his for his love.

The "privatization" that becomes the poem's topic fixes its recipient as an ideal audience. Privy to the author's benign intention, the addressee enjoys a privileged critical vantage which promotes his lover's verses beyond what their slight technical merits otherwise warrant. Intimacy seasons judicial objectivity with subjective sympathy. Comparisons, the main stock of a poet's trade, make this writer nervous; he aims here to head off the prospect of dying "unlooked on" by appealing prematurely to his receiver's accommodating spirit, which alone can insure the extension he craves. The policy he takes out is nonetheless a conspicuously limited one. His self-deprecating modesty squares with the general insecurity before public tribunals that we have noted so far, but by anticipating his own *Nachleben* he simultaneously evokes the question, "If you survive me, will my verse survive you?" Those "happier men" to whom he defers derive at least part of their joy from their lack of reliance upon the kind of straitened prospect that he knows. In the poet's publicly conditioned world, "style" can "prove" or speak for itself in a way that love cannot. The reassurance he crafts upon the recipient's critical good will can never exceed these strictly delimited boundaries.

What finally enables 32's relatively easy relaxation is the poet's notion that his reader can observe a casual dichotomy between style and content, leaving ample room for all parties involved to coexist, and thereby heading off a zero-sum contest. In this, the poem also reaches back toward a more general and informative apprehension about rivalry foreshadowed in poems 20 and 21. Sonnet 20 had negotiated the dilemma occasioned by his incipient erotic interest in this male friend: "But since she pricked thee out for women's pleasure, / Mine be thy love, and thy love's use their treasure" (13–14). Such divisions are not so neatly maintained; he no sooner disclaims a rivalrous temperament in these lines than he voices in 21 a ruffled concern for this very possibility. In a gesture reminiscent of Ovid, he anguishes over the idea of being too successful, and tempers his encomium of the youth by refusing to indulge "a couplement of proud compare" so common among contemporary panegyrists. "Let them say more that like of hearsay well," he concludes, "I will not praise that purpose not to sell" (13–14). The public psyche is an embattled one. Those resolutions devised in sonnets such as 20 and 32 are, consequently, dubious at best. In light of this, it seems appropriate that, just as 21 had checked the glib resolve of 20, so 32 issues onto 33's response to the youth's evident betrayal. The shaken speaker must eventually acknowledge how "Suns of the world may stain when heav'n's sun staineth" (14)—a violation of 21's tempered renunciation of "heavenly" comparisons as much as a check to 32's cavalier spirit.

Sonnet 32 offers a pacific version of what will erupt later in the sequence. Its sentiment is reprised as late as 102: "That love is merchandised, whose rich esteeming / The owner's tongue doth publish everywhere." On the eve of the rival subsequence, however, poem 75 graphically anatomizes the poet's appreciation of opposing drives toward exposure and concealment. He recounts the "strife" that he experiences in terms of the relationship between "a miser and his wealth,"

> Now proud as an enjoyer, and anon
> Doubting the filching age will steal his treasure;
> Now counting best to be with you alone,
> Then bettered that the world may see my pleasure....
> (5-8)

Either impulse carries a price. Poetic pride checks the guarded apprehension he feels, while a justified (for soon to be substantiated) fear of appropriation curbs his enthusiasm to publish such wealth. He finds himself, ironically, mimicking the gluttony that he had faulted back in sonnet 1's sermon to the youth. More than just vain ostentation goads him to market his wares before the capricious company he so distrusts. If the praise he heaps upon his lover is to live up to its encomiastic promise, he must reenter the public domain. To hoard his affections privately is to forsake his vocation altogether, thereby abandoning the one virtue which he boasts might keep him attractive to his lover. Though publicity entails clear risk, silence—in his metaphor's setting—identifies the most abject kind of poverty.

Poem 21 signals the paradoxical fear of success resident within the public valorization of any interest that one guards closely. The "rival" sonnets 78–86 reify this nascent anxiety, and in so doing carve out publicity's dilemma most starkly. All affectation of control fades before the threat of "every alien pen" encroaching upon what the poet-lover prizes as his exclusive encomiastic domain. He had vainly striven to restrict his coveted audience, only to have his effort recoil into a celebrity for his subject that now augurs the poet's own displacement. Others are attracted incidentally by his beloved's beauty, but primarily by the poet's public enlargement of this trait. More precisely, they descend upon the artistic success that the writer has enjoyed by means of the youth's inspiration. To step forth as one even—or especially—of modest artistic pretensions is to elicit popular scorn and antagonistic rebuttal from those aggressively jealous of their poetic talent's precincts. What binds these sonnets together most firmly is the sudden, renewed prospect of the youth as a circulating public figure, one not the author's alone to market or conceal, as 21's couplet had implied.[45]

The rival poet sonnets essentially reorient the sequence's focus away from general concerns about reception, toward a precise fear of interception. On the wings of the young man's inspiring beauty and worth, the poet's "heavy ignorance" has risen "As high as learning," we read in 78; in turn, the writer's confessedly inferior and insecure efforts have publicized his "Muse" to a height from which he risks the appropriation of his subject by those very talents he had at last felt able to match. The bitterness with which he regards this ironic progress has much to do with unstated public ambitions that linger behind his self-effacing postures. Quite apart from his jealous hoarding of the young man's affections, he recognizes in this rival a specifically professional threat. In the competitive arena he conceives, an audience economizes its favor tightly. The praise or honor offered by a rival does not enlarge his own contributions, but eclipses them. Despite the characteristically morbid deference to his competition's ability—from his promotion of the "alien pen" in 78 to the "worthier pen" in 79, and both of these finally to 80's "better spirit"—he resents deeply what he perceives as a personal attack:

> O how I faint when I of you do write,
> Knowing a better spirit doth use your name,
> And in the praise thereof spends all his might,
> To make me tounge-tied speaking of your fame.
>
> (1–4)

Silencing an upstart, as much as securing the youth's favor, motivates this rival's incursion, in the speaker's paranoid account. Feelings of intimidation augment his amorous resentment and distress.

By admitting rival claims into their encomiastic enclosure, the recipient allegedly cheapens his own worth; hence the recrimination in 84, which faults the youth for valuing quantity over quality ("Being fond on praise, which makes your praises worse"). "In others' works thou dost but mend the style," the exasperated poet warns in 78: not content to reign as the substantiating element of his lover's intimate verse—"all my art"—the youth lowers himself to serve as the garnish for passing "alien" musings. With this dispersal, however, also comes discovery. Regardless of the accusations, the poet sees that he is the one who has actually been discounted in the exchange. Poetic monopoly has blunted his competitive edge, so that at the moment of encroachment he finds himself a pathetically illiterate accessory to another's wit:

> I think good thoughts, whilst other write good words,
> And like unlettered clerk still cry amen,
> To every hymn that able spirit affords,
> In polished form of well-refined pen.
>
> (85.5–8)

Such enfeebled confirmations count for little outside the private circle of his thoughts, to which he has retreated. Even were he able to find poetic satisfaction within these sheltered limits, his subject would himself demand greater exposure. "Finding thy worth a limit past my praise," the speaker confesses in 82, he fell into a silent admiration which justifies practically his young man's ranging attentions. The privacy which has supposedly nourished the poet's confidence has also threatened to muffle his subject's merit, further smoothing the way for the public incursion he now anxiously reviews.

Striving to attain an erotic and artistic "alone"-ness with his beloved, the poet finds himself the victim of a displacement that now mocks his taste for privacy. The bereaved recollection opening sonnet 79, "Whilst I alone did call upon thy aid, / My verse alone had all thy gentle grace," marks the collapse of a privileged intimacy into a lonely isolation from both the youth's company and men's eyes. Once the circle has been broken—"And my sick Muse doth give another place"—he turns to indict the sterile circulation characterizing his rival's deceptive inventiveness: "what of thee thy poet doth invent / He robs thee of and pays it thee again" (7–8). The terror such ostracism inspires in the speaker nonetheless transcends anger, to prompt 80's atypically "willful" assertion. Scrambling for some sense of reintegration, he envisions a broader communal favor of which he can partake, even if he can no longer boast a privileged status:

> But, since your worth, wide as the ocean is,
> The humble as the proudest sail doth bear,
> My saucy bark, inferior far to his,
> On your broad main doth wilfully appear.
> Your shallowest help will hold me up afloat,
> Whilst he upon your soundless deep doth ride....
> (5–10)

Sharing the metaphorical waterways with his rival, he will effectively resist the danger of himself going "soundless," obscure and lost in his timidity. By effectively tongue-tying him, such rivalry threatens not only to remove the youth from his lover's view, but to obscure the poet from the public gaze he also loves.

The intimidation posed by this rival proves more effective than 80's bravado would advertise: the burden of sonnets 83–86 becomes the speaker's excuse for an evident "silence" into which he has lapsed, confirming in sonnet 85 his "tongue-tied" state. He breaks this silence only to clear his name, in an apologetic rush which also appears dedicated to making up for lost time. Sonnet 86's proud denial that the rival's potency cowed him into reticence closes the series upon a critically dignified note, before the acerbic self-denigration that chokes the ensuing ten sonnets. He reviews, publicly, his own breakdown:

> Was it the proud full sail of his great verse,
> Bound for the prize of all too precious you,
> That did my ripe thoughts in my brain inhearse,
> Making their tomb the womb wherein they grew?
>
> (1–4)

His denial, "No, neither he, nor his compeers by night / Giving him aid, my verse astonished" (7–8), culminates in an admission that what finally substantiates a poet's lines is not an "affable familiar ghost" of inspiration, but the expression of favor from without: "But when your countenance filled up his line, / Then lacked I matter, that enfeebled mine" (13–14). The poetry that he practices proves inescapably an art of "countenance," suggesting not just the comeliness of one's subject, but the sanction of external support.[46] This stands out as the determinate element that alone can "fill up" whatever "intelligence" is supplied by the nocturnal visitations of one's private muses. Even were he able to maintain his fantasy of an audience delimited to this choice recipient, his vulnerability lingers. The "spiritual" reinforcement enjoyed by his rival, which he shoulders aside, must at last connect with the more genuine "matter" of a tightly budgeted approval. Otherwise, a poet finds himself not just enfeebled, but ensepulchered within a collapsed vocation. The youth's wide ocean apparently knows its boundaries after all. This melancholy discovery sounds a fitting coda to the rival subsequence's jarring experience.

Amid this cluster of sonnets, one poem stands out as ostensibly removed from the specific topic of rivalry. Sonnet 81 contracts its focus to the pairing of speaker and subject, in what at first seems a strange competition over who will outlast whom. By the end, it reaches out to define the urgency of a public acknowledgement which consistently defines "immortal life" in this world:

> Or I shall live your epitaph to make,
> Or you survive when I in earth am rotten,
> From hence your memory death cannot take,
> Although in me each part will be forgotten.
> Your name from hence immortal life shall have,
> Though I, once gone, to all the world must die.
> The earth can yield me but a common grave,
> When you entombed in men's eyes shall lie.
> Your monument shall be my gentle verse,
> Which eyes not yet created shall o'er-read,
> And tongues to be your being shall rehearse,
> When all the breathers of this world are dead,
>   You still shall live—such virtue hath my pen—
>   Where breath most breaths, ev'n in the mouths of men.

In context, the author's stated lack of concern for his own achievement looks transparently disingenuous: we know from the larger setting that he cares deeply for what his unique encomia have attained, and line 13's parenthetical brag internally reconfirms this pride. The monument that promises to enshrine the youth "in men's eyes"—even in "eyes not yet created"—stands remote from the silent entombment fraying authorial nerves in 86. The self-effacing "common grave" that the poet allegedly must suffer itself provides a certain comfort, drawing into view the mortal community in which both writer and subject will finally share, in common with each other (as the opening lines propose) and ultimately with the audience as well. Something more complicated than false modesty inheres, however, in his assertion that a public honors the thing praised while forgetting the praiser. Viewed from another angle, the dissociation marks the closest he will come to a resolution, pressured perhaps most intensively by the surrounding emergency circumstances: his subject shall endure in the scrutiny of public eyes, while he may himself relax into a common anonymity. Like all of his fantasies, it nonetheless cannot effectively break the bonds that always implicate the artist in his creative endeavor. Men's eyes will not permit the protected, vicarious pleasures he had first entertained in 36, and to which he still clings in 81.

Whatever else they trace out, the *Sonnets'* middle bloc works through the full range of anxieties attendant upon public exposure. Fears of rejection previewed in the procreation segment give way to terrors of appropriation best figured in the rivalry poems. Alongside all this, the poet's larger audience clearly refuses to countenance uninterrogatively the idealized image of his beloved that he struggles to project: the embarrassment voiced in poems like 69 ("But those same tongues that give thee so thine own, / In other accents do this praise confound / By seeing farther than the eye hath shown" [6–8]) compounds the speaker's discomfort. Resentful of their scrutiny, he also envies the audience's capacity for shrewd discernment, a vision that frustrates his encomiastic efforts while further fueling his wounded emotional outrage. The youth's commonality has reconfirmed that outward appearance and inward dignity need have little in common. The "world's eye" looks down upon the young man's corruption, demanding an integrity the poet's own desperate apologies cannot convincingly salvage. Even in 121's attack upon society's capacity to judge accurately, the independence the speaker again proclaims cannot impart an unqualified security. "'Tis better to be vile than vile esteemed" announces the poet willing to pit his subjective judgments against society's calculations, which he discerns as inconsequential precisely because they are themselves subjectively based. Disgusted that pleasure's worth must be determined "Not by our feeling but by others' seeing" (4), he now indicts an orthodoxy that he finds tarnished by the same prejudice and vanity it is collectively supposed to transcend:

> For why should others' false adulterate eyes
> Give salutation to my sportive blood?
> Or on my frailties why are frailer spies,
> Which in their wills count bad what I think good?
> (5–8)

The entire sonnet dwindles to an elaborate rhetorical trick to preempt the public incrimination of which we know the poet is himself worthy from the previous sonnets' confessions. His freedom is grounded in an implication that the deeds of his own "sportive blood" are commonplace—that no one may judge because everyone is guilty; he in effect partakes of the cynicism the couplet's "All men are bad" attempts to mock. Trying to establish that he is beyond the scope of their authority, the speaker ends up quenching this spark in the communal "badness" of their "reign."

The sonneteer's chore throughout the sequence's central phase is to avoid becoming "mixed with seconds," as 125 puts it: not simply to resist the contamination of his devotedness to the young man by unworthy interests, but to deny any external threat to the exclusivity of their relationship. When the youth proves no more tractable to the poet's desires than the larger society had been, the inefficacy of this private "policy" becomes glaringly evident. Whether the word intends something like "prudence," as in 118's usage, or carries a more pejorative intonation of time-serving cunning, as in 124's harsher inflection, "policy" etymologically suggests a system of negotiation with a *polis* or public context. Any form of policy that seeks to deny a public is doomed to absurdity. The speaker's ultimate description of himself as one who "all alone stands hugely politic" (124.11) imagines an ideal adjustment to meet his predicament; instead, this supreme oxymoron signals only a confusing dividedness—a contradiction that springs from failed compromise.

Of paramount concern for this speaker throughout his relationship with the youth, policy presses more explicitly into the foreground as the young man sonnets draw to a close. It obtrudes, that is, at the moment when his renunciation of those bonds joining him to such an orthodoxy grows the loudest, the poems "essentially protesting" (in Thomas Greene's description) "the poet's freedom from self-interest and the enduring purity of his feelings, which will never flag and can dispense with ostentatious demonstrations."[47] Individually or as a pair, sonnets 124 and 125 mark the dismissal and redefinition of what constitutes policy itself. Articulating his novel formulation of political "aloneness," the poet, to the last, points us toward a public converse from which he cannot divorce himself:

> If my dear love were but the child of state,
> It might for fortune's bastard be unfathered,
> As subject to time's love, or to time's hate,
> Weeds among weeds, or flow'rs with flowers gathered.
> No, it was builded far from accident;
> It suffers not in smiling pomp, nor falls
> Under the blow of thralled discontent,
> Whereto th'inviting time our fashion calls.
> It fears not policy, that heretic
> Which works on leases of short numb'red hours,
> But all alone stands hugely politic,
> That it nor grows with heat, nor drowns with show'rs.
>   To this I witness call the fools of time,
>   Which die for goodness, who have lived for crime.
>   (124)

> Were't ought to me I bore the canopy,
> With my extern the outward honoring,
> Or laid great bases for eternity,
> Which proves more short than waste or ruining?
> Have I not seen dwellers on form and favor
> Lose all and more by paying too much rent
> For compound sweet forgoing simple savor,
> Pitiful thrivers, in their gazing spent?
> No, let me be obsequious in thy heart,
> And take thou my oblation, poor but free,
> Which is not mixed with seconds, knows no art,
> But mutual render, only me for thee.
>   Hence, thou suborned informer! A true soul
>   When most impeached stands least in thy control.
>   (125)

Posing as sonnets about discovery and liberation, these poems are overtaken by a spirit of persecution and resentment. Petulant countercharges now buffer him against the same world of public commerce within which he had at first sought shelter. Unable to temper his responses—because unpracticed in such moderation—he resorts to a fantasy isolation, removed from the social circulation that he associates with a realm of "accident."[48] Assertion is qualified by typical interrogative hesitancy, however ("Were't ought to me...."; "Have I not seen...?"), and his language still cannot close out the existence of those poets who comment on his adopted manners. The controversial identities of the fools and the informer who debut so abruptly are less important than the speaker's awkward compulsion to acknowledge them, against his asserted indifference to such outsiders and all they represent or advocate. Ensnared always in his need for outside confirmation, he betrays his own status as a pathetic "gazer," one who has watched his watchers carefully, and has almost "spent" himself in so doing. He lapses, moreover, by the final couplet's arch renunciation, from anxious vigilance to paranoia: the informer he addresses is "suborned," in the employ of a larger conspiracy that plots his downfall—an agency he has always feared and now appears to hate. We discover by the final lines that all the sonnet's utterances have been made for the benefit of this other party's ears as much as for his beloved's edification. Over one hundred poems after he had first likened himself to an "unperfect actor," the speaker continues to play out an agonized, vulnerable public role.[49]

Lars Engle has proposed that "To be 'hugely politic' is to understand that success in the *longue durée* is the result not of an absolute escape from time's hold but of a more farsighted understanding of contingency and time."[50] But this precious insight seems to be the very thing that remains beyond the preoccupied and biased ken of Shakespeare's speaker. Whatever security one may seek in love's respite is hedged by an exacting public standard that informs—and informs *on*—his vivid imagination. Even at its most generous, this fickle entity is bound one day (always probably soon) to revert back to the harsher verdicts by which it is most commonly identified and represented by the poet—himself forever "a motly to the view," whose nature is subdued with fear of public correction even more strongly than his dyer's hand knowingly would indicate.

Public Manners and Dark Conceits

The Young Man sonnets leave us with a sense that policy is a matter more richly complex than either benumbed conformity or bleak cynicism can encompass, or than the poet-lover appreciates. They do not fully prepare us for what comes hereafter, in the sequence's ultimate phase. If the *Sonnets* tell a story, it is a nonsequential, overlapping one. Behind both the drama of his courtship of the youth, or the closeup account of his relations with the woman we call the Dark Lady, however, "the world" consistently lingers, a feared shadow character. Whatever draws the poet to the young man, the female lover's capacity to reform conventional outlooks influences the disruptive sexual allure she holds for him. At the threshold of yet another compartment of the poet's experience, she represents a unique power over the public he courts and shuns: one who declines to respect society's manners, though they feel compelled, with fascination, to study hers.

Shakespeare's Dark Lady, in other words, embodies a novelty that teases and frustrates her lover. She debuts as a lover-antagonist who is genuinely contraventional, rather than merely unconventional, in her impact. Although conventions, as the word's etymology indicates, intend to serve a unifying function, they manage this by honoring and reaffirming discrete categorical groupings. So, as the poet struggles to argue with the youth's flouting of social expectations in sonnets 1 through 17, he instinctively flees the facile gender taxonomy of 20. His mistress, herself relegated to a final subsequence, impedes his capacity, if not his will, to maintain such preordained divisions. Representing a physical difference from, and temperamental indifference to, the norms he still observes, she even more intensively concentrates his awareness of a discrepancy between personal response and a broader orthodoxy that sanctions the very idea of tradition. The social world on whose behalf he had initially accosted the youth has approved the young man's beauty, just as it has implicitly determined the "sere" ugliness with which the aged poet berates himself. It has not legitimized the woman's darkness in the same way: beheld though unbeholden, she has mastered her context with a finesse that the poet envies. Disturbed by the youth's apparent avoidance of social responsibility at the start, he is terrified by her analogous autarchy, the "will-power" (and power over Will) she exerts.

The Dark Lady sonnets are most commonly associated with the departure from Petrarchan tradition we encounter in 130, "My mistress' eyes are nothing like the sun."

Before the poet honors this inversion, however, the initial compliment of his lover's distinctive virtues in 127 makes clear that this woman has, on her own, managed successfully to reshape public manners. Such liberation exerts an ambivalent attraction for one so deeply enmeshed in webs of social dependency as the speaker has consistently demonstrated himself to be. The resulting agitation leaves its subtle mark upon these lines, and upon what ensues. When he comes to sort out his conflicted reactions, what results is a richly ambivalent moment of revaluation consequent upon societal devaluation, a gesture which celebrates novelty only through valorized "old age":

> In the old age black was not counted fair,
> Or if it were it bore not beauty's name.
> But now is black beauty's successive heir,
> And beauty slandered with a bastard shame;
> For since each hand hath put on nature's pow'r,
> Fairing the foul with art's false borrowed face,
> Sweet beauty hath no name, no holy bow'r,
> But is profaned, if not lives in disgrace.
> Therefore my mistress' eyes are raven black,
> Her eyes so suited, and they mourners seem
> At such who, not born fair, no beauty lack,
> Sland'ring creation with a false esteem.
>   Yet so they mourn becoming of their woe,
>   That every tongue says beauty should look so.

Regardless of the tenth line's assertion, it is actually the poet who mourns here. In ironic contrast to the procreation sonnets' original petition for beauty's sustenance, he realizes in this fresh start only cosmetic parody, in a grim modernity of bastardy and namelessness. Along the twisting pathway to line 9's abrupt and unsequential compliment, we sense a barely subdued, opposing anxiety. The urge to conform to current fashion—itself arbitrarily dictated by society—has destabilized the present by enabling a democratic mobility, offensive to his deeply conservative sensibilities. As Nature's hand had wondrously plucked back the youth in the preceding sonnet, this deity's privilege is now appropriated by and distributed among a populace who no longer needs to remain what birth has ordained.

Amid this discovery, the poet seems equally enthralled by the way he imagines the woman to have secured public admiration precisely by means of her refusal to comply. Nothing so orderly as a legitimate "succession" promotes her; rather, she emerges as one who has possessed enough insight to fill the vacancy opened by "fair" beauty's devaluation. In a move which reaches back to Ovid, he implies that her *probitas* serves as the best cosmetic.[51] The woman's refusal to mask her darkness endows her with an authenticity that she turns to her advantage. The poet finds captivating this artful artlessness which challenges the newfangled drive for uniformity with a paradoxically more conservative novelty. Her resistance itself imparts value, giving a new definition to what he truly finds "becoming," both what is attractive and what is coming-to-be.

The paradoxical complication that she embodies simultaneously occasions an external dilemma for her admiring lover. The same self-assertive refusal to make herself different simply to uphold stock Petrarchan standards, a recusancy that stimulates him sexually, also triggers his poetic impulse to translate her darkness into a new orthodoxy, to endow her with a legitimacy only public officiation can confer. His need for public approval of his attraction to her—as much at stake as her own actual appearance—shines through the couplet's insistence "That every tongue says beauty should look so." However, this woman's indifference to accepted public manners sets her also beyond the reach of his apology on her behalf: an unsettling independence for the poet to contemplate, as he will throughout the succeeding poems. Her freedom from societal restrictions implies a discomforting possibility that she can remain equally aloof from her praiser. Subsequent moments will betray ("some say that thee behold / Thy face hath not the pow'r to make love groan" [131.5–6]) that this sonnet's couplet is not as true as the poet would have it. He is aware that his words are all part of an encomiastic consolation, itself cosmetic and conventional. The broader social appropriation of her beauty for which he presses is a fantasy that her autonomous temperament, we gather, would not condone.

The Dark Lady's real enticement, and threat, is her opacity. She asserts inscrutability's seductiveness against the thinly disguised ugliness that the poet mocks. His nervousness with this suspicious empowerment issues in the poem itself, which delineates less the mistress's beauty—sanctioned or otherwise—than (once again) his own hunger for consensus, acceptance and approval. From here on, his perceptions will be pitted against the world's, and he is never comfortable with this opposition. Enduringly troubled by that which cannot be "counted" or does not compute with public averages, as the first line proposes, he strains to reassure himself by the poem's end with the reconstructed sound of "every tongue."

When we place 130's textbook anti-Petrarchism within this longing for conformity, the poem uncovers a more seriously distressed sensibility. Couched between 129's anguished indictment of lust and 131's disabused protests, it wears its contraventional boldness less lightly than decontextualized readings suggest. On one side, it ironically shares with its predecessor the status of a failed *remedium amoris*. Sonnet 129 had followed lust's vicious progress only to confess in the end that "All this the world well knows, yet none knows well / To shun the heav'n that leads men to this hell." Attending to the same flesh which occasions this desire, 130 catalogues the mistress's less-than-ideal physical attributes in what at first looks like an exercise in self-dissuasion—to degrade and thereby to make possible escape from the object of one's affection—only to falter in the closing admission that "by heav'n I think my love as rare / As any she belied with false compare." Swearing by the same "heaven" earlier defamed as a pathway to certain damnation, the speaker professes his rapture with her more common charms. Cast in the glare of 127's initial predicament and outlook, the couplet discloses an irony apparently unavailable to its speaker. Condemning Petrarchan affectation, his final scoff also covets the idealized model he cannot locate. The poet would prefer to celebrate his woman in conventional terms: when he finds himself unable to do this, he must retreat into an anatomy of those attributes which sounds much like insult (the "reeking" breath, the "wire" hair).[52] He will end up indicting not so much Petrarchism's stale tropes, but rather those other women who, although they also fall short of the ideal, are nonetheless praised falsely in its language. As in 127, the speaker worries mainly over the pollution of an idealized source alongside the ascendency, by default, of his own lady's now "rare" frankness.

On the far side of all this, 131 immediately deflates 130's attempted counterideal by measuring the speaker's insecurities about his troubled relationship against harsher public evaluations. One consolatory advantage for the advocate of the unconventional is the prospective gratitude he might secure as his "due" from the subject. His charge that "Thou art as tyrannous, so as thou art, / As those whose beauties proudly make them cruel" (1–2), alerts us to the speaker's rough willingness to remind his mistress of her inferiority by all traditional standards. He stops just short of stating outrightly that her appearance disqualifies her indulgence in coy games. We are not surprised to find this particular object of affection unprepared to relinquish her pseudo-courtly prerogatives, refusing to admit that her darkness should tame her in the way he implies. In so doing, he unwittingly exposes a psychology that qualifies the preceding sonnet's "earthy" compliment. The second quatrain definitively focuses the public frustration he wrestles with:

> Yet in good faith some say that thee behold
> Thy face hath not the pow'r to make love groan;
> To say they err I dare not be so bold,
> Although I swear it to myself alone.

In contrast to 130's contraventional declaration, we now discern his actual terror of challenging boldly the public eye's consensus, available in the diluted "some say." Unnerved, he must isolate his idiosyncratic verdict—"thy black is fairest in my judgement's place" (12). To the end, he remains frustrated by her evident security not in "fairness" or virtue, on the Petrarchan model, but in her very *darkened* lack of concern for the light of public evaluation: "In nothing art thou black save in thy deeds, / And thence this slander as I think proceeds." Where she "Know'st," he only "thinks" or at best rests upon forced utterances of certainty ("in good faith," "to be sure") that in context ring hollow. He wants, at the start, to remark simply that she is as "tyrannous" as she is *fair*, but she complicates this formula—she is as cruel as *other* "beauties," despite her refusal to assume their prescribed form. The line's awkward confusion intones appropriately and subtly the presumption which is actually his own rather than the lady's, thinking to alert her to a public opinion by which she remains unmoved.

When the mistress's courtly unkindness quickly ignites into the more devastating trauma of her affair with the young man, the poet experiences an even deeper tear in his already badly shredded sensibilities. He labors, on the one hand, to put the best face on his anguish, dismissing her infidelities as the way of the world. On the other, beneath the guise of weary resignation, he is stung into an expression of lonely outrage at the double betrayal. These alternate emotions are figured respectively in sonnets 138 and 144, poems which had appeared a decade before the Q text's publication, in the 1599 anthology *The Passionate Pilgrim*. Even in their preliminary (or corrupt) forms, they presage with intriguing judiciousness the collection which would come before the public intact a decade later.[53] The first poem enacts a politic stance that itself mediates between what would become the *Sonnets'* two most famous postures, 116's empassioned idealism and 129's bitter condemnation of "lust in action."

> When my love swears that she is made of truth,
> I do believe her though I know she lies,
> That she might think me some untutored youth,
> Unlearned in the world's false subtleties.
>
> (1–4)

The quatrain charts an investment and its motive: in a world that regards naiveté as a contemptible vice, the poet celebrates his managerial tact. The discreet negotiation of his mistress's duplicity intends to impress us rather than the woman, who presumably already accepts the adequacy of his savvy performance. He prudently strikes a sexual golden mean, neither too young to appear "Unlearned" (or "Vnskilful" in the earlier version) nor too old for the erotic play he wishes to maintain with the compliantly flattering lover. This public affirmation of the poet's awareness establishes his authority and permits the closing couplet's docility, "Therefore I lie with her, and she with me, / And in our faults by lies we flattered be." Conversely, "Two loves I have of comfort and despair" (144) recasts the poet from 138's knowing and willing participant in a conspiracy against himself to an excluded and marginalized victim, one who professedly shall "ne'er know, but live in doubt" regarding the precise configuration of the alternative society that his friend and mistress together "suggest." He no longer masters his situation, trapped inside the very suspicion that he had proclaimed himself above in the previous poem. Caught up in his misogynistic wrath, the poet is torn by the affair's ambivalent implications. What he understands as her seductive entrapment of the youth at once justifies his own attraction to the woman—the "better angel" to whom he grants authority finds her sexually appealing—while reconfirming his awareness that her unfashionable darkness still affords him no special dominion over her. To confess to the mistress that his friend "is thine," as he had in 134, is to affirm that his own "surety" in this unkind situation is anything but secure. He observes with brutal lucidity how little a purchase he has upon his erotic predicament.

The poet is left infuriated and impotent before his realization that the dark lady's dismissal of society simultaneously dispenses with him. Emptied of at least one form of pretension after his friend's betrayal, the speaker not only confesses but demonstrates himself her poetic fool in the promiscuous wordplay of 135 and 136, the "Will" sonnets. In these poems, his name becomes a toy, as well as a signifier of her volitional power and sexual potency. Even if William Kerrigan is correct that the *Sonnets* express an abhorrence of the female genitalia (the "will" of Elizabethan slang), we have here an awed wonder at the organ's sheer capacity, in Eve Kosofsky Sedgwick's words its "gargantuan, distracted catholicity."[54] His vengefully sardonic compliment of her acquisitive appetite suggests an elemental spaciousness that could serve as the locus for all *copia*. Just as the youth had "embodied" all past friends in sonnet 31, so here the woman hyperbolically takes into her body all of society, the youth just one "member" among these: "Whoever hath her wish, thou hast thy will, / And will to boot, and will in overplus" (135.1–2). These two sonnets consistently tax the patience of most readers; Stephen Booth finds their rhetorical sport "grotesque." For all their playfulness or malignancy, success or failure, they contact a central feature of the sequence overall, namely the human lust for *more*—more beauty, more prestige, more years, more sex, more poems, more ways to say things. Far from the procreation sonnets' original copious procedure, and *en route* to 153 and 154's failed reprise of this, the poet beholds the antagonizing, absurd fecundity that his lover embodies and deploys. She manages her voracity with an expertise that his feeble rationalizations can never approach. Lust's genuine power and horror, expounded in 129, here finds its most proficient practical expression.

These poems' obsession with "will" tends to obscure the point that their chief concern is actually not names, but numbers. Numbers frustrate him, since, despite the woman's alleged promiscuity, he nonetheless finds himself excluded. Her erotic gifts are not distributed indiscriminately. He is displaced deliberately in a demonstration of her "will"-power, a volition she exercises more decisively than those others who exert merely a passive "wish": "If thy soul check thee that I come so near, / Swear to thy blind soul that I was thy will, / And will thy soul knows is admitted there" (136.1–3). Amid so great a sum of sums, the poet himself cannot thrive. His defense, impulsively, is to step back into the anonymity of quantity, to "pass untold" in the excessive accumulation that these poems caricature:

> In things of great receipt with ease we prove,
> Among a number one is reckoned none.
> Then in the number let me pass untold,
> Though in thy store's account I one must be,
> For nothing hold me, so it please thee hold
> That nothing me, a something sweet to thee.
>
> (7–12)

The price of incorporation is the loss of individuality. The passage perfectly enacts his primary tension: aching for individuation on some private plane, he relinquishes this selfhood to the dissolution of a nameless assembly. The name-game struggles to dupe the "blind soul" that nonetheless ostracizes him from the alternative society she all too clearsightedly fashions. The two poems' resolution transports us closer to the silent undercurrents flowing through 138's dry resignation, into the stark, reduced enumeration of 144's opening "Two loves I have," where his exclusion is bitterly signified in the affair's neat triangulation. Hungering for the undivided love of these two paramours, Shakespeare's conformist poet exhibits a pained willingness to compromise and parley for what little he can retain, sheltering in the safety and pleasure of crowds while sensing the emotional and erotic poverty of this escape.

Through all of this, he never forsakes his desperate wishes to forge a much-needed "correspondence," grounded in a co-responsiveness of his lovers to his desires. Agonizing in 148 over the troubling disparity he finds ("O me! what eyes hath love put in my head, / Which have no correspondence with true sight!" [1–2]), he explains his predicament by the exhausted "watching" and accompanying "tears" blinding just vision. The harder one looks, the less one sees. What he watches for is the correspondence that he covets between his own understanding and the world's verdicts. He explicitly defines "true sight" not as an inner judgment, but rather by way of the public approbation pondered in the central quatrain:

> If that be fair whereon my false eyes dote,
> What means the world to say it is not so?
> If it be not, then love doth well denote,
> Love's eye is not so true as all men's: no.
> How can it?

The colon separating the final negation here is contested, since its absence would free the line's initial "eye" for richer punning: all men's "no" opposes the "aye" this "I" asserts.[55] Unable to bridge the gap between his personal claims and the world's opinion, his rationalization grows increasingly frantic and depressed. His negotiations in 140, where, once more following Ovidian precedent, he had counseled the woman to act as if she loves him whether or not this were actually the case, do not hold up. Desperation may drive him to "speak ill" of her, he warns, and "Now this ill-wresting world is grown so bad, / Mad sland'rers by mad ears believed be" (11–12). He promises, in essence, to join the company already predisposed to judge her harshly: a "correspondence" from which he gathers almost as much satisfaction as he does from her private favor, but which he manages to realize with no greater success. Since the woman does not partake of his dependencies, she stands beyond the social threats he marshals. He has sacrificed social approbation for the sake of a woman who flees their ranks, but can discover no community in the fugitive state that he presumes to share. His frustration precipitates 150's sardonic appeal, "O, though I love what others do abhor, / With others thou shouldst not abhor my state" (11–12). The more rigorously he struggles to assemble some form of alternative, replacement community, the more thoroughly and bitterly he finds himself ostracized.

An oath is more than a promise, and perjury more than a lie: both require recourse to a corroborative agency external to the private circle of the word exchanged. The unmooring that goes on in the *Sonnets'* final poem of direct address, 152, dwells explicitly upon this public transgression as the poet tabulates one last melancholy time:

> In loving thee thou know'st I am forsworn,
> But thou art twice forsworn to me love swearing,
> In act thy bed-vow broke and new faith torn
> In vowing new hate after new love bearing.
> But why of two oaths' breach do I accuse thee,
> When I break twenty? I am perjured most,
> For all my vows are oaths but to misuse thee,
> And all my honest faith in thee is lost.
> For I have sworn deep oaths of thy deep kindness,
> Oaths of thy love, thy truth, thy constancy,
> And to enlighten thee gave eyes to blindness,
> Or made them swear against the thing they see,
>   For I have sworn thee fair: more perjured eye,
>   To swear against the truth so foul a lie.

An overzealous devotion to the tribunal of sacred social convention has lapsed into violated faith and fractured custom, leaving him detached from the *polis* (with which he seems doubtful that he can reform his alliance) as well as from his friend and mistress (whose partnership has also left him in darkness). Sonnet 152 takes the poet beyond the self-deluding lies over which he has fretted with ever-increasing intensity, to a more direct confrontation with the violated public trust that "perjury" conveys. The pain of having gambled so much upon this now forsworn company is great: "Of him, myself, and thee, I am forsaken," he had mourned back in 133. By the end, however, the totality of his loss has come home to him. Lines 11 and 12 grieve a "misuse" or misrepresentation that dilates into an attempt to deceive all witnesses: the ocular trickery cheapening his encomia has distorted not merely his own weak vision, biased to begin with, but the "men's eyes" that he knows have never averted their gaze. He finally mouths the words so feared in sonnet 17, "This poet lies," himself. His confession cements his absolute isolation, confirming his guilt of what was—by Renaissance standards—the most contemptible social vice. Leon Battista Alberti's indictment of the dishonest man as "disreputable, despised, and vile," one deservedly cut off from his community, is representative of this commonplace: "Everyone scorns him as a joke. He knows no friendship and enjoys no authority of any kind. No virtue, great as it may be, will win respect or admiration for a liar, so disgusting and ugly is this vice. It stains and dishonors any other splendid honors he may have won."[56] Dreading the "removal" that the "painful warrior" had suffered in 25's contemplations, the poet finds himself facing an analogous societal fate. Ironically, his distortions of truth have abused the very "policie" which, closer to Shakespeare's own day, Pierre de La Primaudaye had expressly identified as "the cause that men do communicate together without fraud or hurt."[57] Buried beneath a heap of violated pledges, he rests "all alone"—no longer "hugely politic," but dwarfed by the overbearing polity that shuts him out. In the regret it voices for a lost sense of membership, sonnet 152 serves as an appropriate closing utterance, sounding the deepest palinodic lament that the speaker can muster.

Anguishing over truths owed not just to one another, but to the court of social mores before which all this company stand perjured, the poet revisits in his final disenchantment a concern for the "world's due" advocated at the start. In the procreation sonnets, an adopted public demeanor had conflicted with lyric intimacy. Subsequently, in sonnets 18 through 126, the poet makes an unsuccessful bid to withdraw from a public to a private focus. The counterexample of an independent woman figured in the Dark Lady poems, surveyed from his dependent perspective, clarifies a pose which Shakespeare's persona longs for, but which remains ever beyond the grasp of his social consciousness. The mistress affords neither the justifying agency presumed in 1 through 17, nor the coveted haven fantasized in the bulk of the Young Man poems. Her sexual acumen awes him and inspires his envy. Things change, as his numerous earlier reflections on time had acknowledged; but those who have the power to change things—such as the woman in all her darkness has done, in his evaluation—truly command our interest. The attempt to emulate such a "manner," poised against a care for the legitimizing nod from an audience of which his "more perjured eye" has (in spite of himself) never lost sight, situates the drama of competing dependencies that the sequence profoundly and tantalizingly unfolds.

The "poetics of vision" employed by Joel Fineman to focus his ambitious analysis of the sequence surely comprehends some of the most vital tropes and levels of discourse that Shakespeare draws upon in the work. Still, any critical attention to the poet's "perjured eye" must take into account that external "eye" to which Shakespeare's poet holds himself perennially answerable, defining this lover's transgression specifically as an act of "perjury." Recent challenges to the extremity of Fineman's claims aside,[58] my own premise looks to align Shakespeare more firmly with a dilemma traditionally faced by lyric poets, as illustrated in the works of Ovid and Petrarch. Outside the poet's carefully ordained subjectivity—however intense—waits the company that will finally assess the distinctive voice itself. The crisis in the *Sonnets* is not, as Fineman has it, the poet's gradually discovered "desire for something he does not admire,"[59] but his protracted awareness of a thralldom to those whom he fears will not prove sympathetic to his talents and needs. Shakespeare's presentation differs in degree—though not in kind—from what we find in Ovid and Petrarch. The nervous temperament with which he endows his poet-lover never allows the fluid (though pricey) maneuverability that the *Amores'* persona masters, nor the wry, seriocomic sensibility animating the *Canzoniere*. The sonneteer is left, consequently, to vacillate between extremes that he can never fairly reconcile into the elusive "policy" he invokes.

At sonnet 118, Shakespeare's poet takes somber inventory of his misdirected attempt to formulate "policy in love." His reflections clarify bitterly the frailty of even the most vigilant human anticipation, and the potential counterproductivity of all efforts at politic "prevention." A compulsion to erect secure bulwarks "against that time" has motivated this poet from the outset of the procreation poems; his rhetoric of sustenance at last refracts into a mockery of foresight. In the manner of those who "sicken to shun sickness," the poet claims to have forsaken the "ne'er-cloying sweetness" of his friend's love in an abortive attempt somehow to avoid suffering:

> Thus policy in love t'anticipate
> The ills that were not grew to faults assured,
> And brought to medicine a healthful state,
> Which rank of goodness would by ill be cured.
>
> (9–12)

An extension of his efforts to rationalize his own faithless transgressions, the specious apology is itself both a confession and an example of the "policy" in question. However disingenuous, the argument registers its speaker's seeming inability either to relinquish his affiliation with a world of policy (as he intends to do) or to maintain a more fluid compatibility between public and private roles. The result is a supremely unhealthy, impolitic maneuver: it is not love that "poisons" the lover, as the couplet laments, but his own duplicitous ingenuity. Less successful than his lyric compatriots in the *Amores* and the *Canzoniere*, the *Sonnets'* protagonist is fleshed out by his very sensitivity to this provoking inadequacy—his failure to shape a plausible policy that might empower him to deal in an efficient manner with the watchful, always ultimately unknown entity that is the audience.

AFTERWORD

The Poetics of Intimacy, and Its Publics

"The moment I cease to believe in him," Borges wrote, "'Averroes' disappears."[1] The point travels close to the authorial concern that Ovid, Petrarch and Shakespeare instance in their poetry. By the close of our study, we might see fit to invert several of the tropes conjured in the Introduction. If we—the present audience—are cast somehow as the poet's fiction, the poet at last becomes our fantasy as well. Moreover, where we are frankly excluded from the intimate poetic circumstances upon which we are simultaneously invited to eavesdrop, neither do these remote authorial voices really belong in our world, although we summon them repeatedly for scrutiny and evaluation. Paul de Man has insisted that

"Our claim to understand a lyric text coincides with the actualization of a speaking voice, be it (monologically) that of the poet or (dialogically) that of the exchange that takes place between author and reader in the process of comprehension."[2] Scrupulously attentive to this point, the authors I have treated in the preceding pages review accommodations that reinforce rather than undermine poetic integrity in the long term. The transactions which further enliven the already charged ambience of their erotic pursuits confirm that, in art, love is never a solitary or private matter, and that an audience's wariness of poetic personae is matched by the artists' own anticipation of and careful regard for this critical inquiry. What these dealings carve out might be termed, in effect, a poetics of intimacy.

Before we presume to depart upon such an assertion, some concluding differentiations are in order, specifically regarding the critical issue of selfhood. Three radically different modalities of poetic self are projected by the authors I have considered. Ovid bases identity upon the Roman citizenship he deeply valued, and whose advantages were traumatically lost to him as the result of his exile. Petrarch spent his career cultivating an ego he examined through the lens of a medieval Christianity that was itself challenged by the incipient humanism for which he stood as the arch-spokesman. Notably nonreligious in the *Sonnets*, Shakespeare casts selfhood in the mold of a communal reputation determined by the workings of the court society dominating his era. Subjectively oriented readers, surveying this diversity, might protest that the audiences to which these artists react are no more than functions of their psychologies—a charge that compromises the distinctiveness of my assertions, by aligning them with the rhetorical or psychological approaches to this poetry that are already well in place.

The poets in question are indeed inclined and compelled to conceive their audiences while shaping private gestures into public works of art. I contend that they do so, however, in response to the genuine promise of promotion or failure at the hands of arbitrating agencies which they cannot ultimately constrain or control, imaginatively or actually. New historicist critics have enabled us to recognize even "self-fashioned" versions of this subjectivity as embattled and vulnerable, the products of shaping social ideologies and pressures.[3] Ovid had the grim spectacle of Gallus's fate, Petrarch's humanism only further sensitized him to the loss of a now-remote classical splendor (a sense of loss honed by the plague's more immediate catastrophe), and the threat of censorship hanging perennially over the careers of London playwrights left Shakespeare similarly aware that texts are every bit as ephemeral as marble or gilded monuments (despite his sonneteering persona's eloquent denial). But the "threat" I elaborate involves something more enduring and pervasive than the temporally specific circumstances attended by the historicists. As exponents of the lyric genre, these poets in some measure all cultivate an "autonomous ego"[4]; but they can do this, I stress, only in conjunction with a careful regard for the public whose presence they outwardly resent. The intimacy that they nurture with a beloved, or even with their own accomplishments, becomes in a determinate way an analogue for another brand of intimacy altogether, one that they paradoxically court with the public who will grant or deny their long-term fame.

The subjective element, in other words, is always a consideration built into the genre, in the broadly formulaic manner of classical *recusatio* or something as monumentally novel as the individuation that Joel Fineman finds in the *Sonnets'* progress. I trust that my approach, in its revaluations, has not slighted or obscured the importance of this component. My own investigation acknowledges issues that have interested other critics of poetry: the identities, moral and psychological, of the poetic speaker and listener construed by the text understood as performance; the character of the speaker's self, understood not as an identity in any positive sense but as desire, lack, or anxiety; and the social, negotiated character of the speaker and the speaker's language understood as a bargain made between the writer and society. I bring these issues variously into play in order to uncover the multiple, contingent aspects of love and writing as the poems present them. Above all, however, I have tried to demonstrate how the consciousness of a heightened vulnerability is also unavoidably consequent in their adopted manner of lyric discourse. The poet cannot forsake the public realm for the private, or *vice-versa*, and he can never rest absolutely secure that whatever balance is achieved can be successfully maintained. As witnesses and judges of their performances, we need to appreciate how they craft their voices against the anticipated public response that will legitimize their boasts of literary-historical endurance, or relegate their efforts to the cultural refuse heap that also smolders, disconcertingly, just below the writer's window.

In his intriguing collection of aphoristic fragments entitled *A Lover's Discourse*, Roland Barthes contests at one point the modern convention that madness is the product of a sense of depersonalization; rather, he proposes, "it is becoming a *subject*, being unable to keep myself from doing so, which drives me mad. *I am not someone else*: that is what I realize with horror."[5] The hyperbole of this pungent remark shocks us into an awareness of the predicament that, in my own argument, authors of recusant poetry perennially confront. Struggling for a selfhood defined through separation, they also must protect themselves from the figurative madness—and actual obliteration—threatened by isolation from a critical, preserving polity.

Notes

Notes to Introduction

1. Text and translation are from Fred J. Nichols, ed. and trans., *An Anthology of Neo-Latin Poetry* (New Haven: Yale University Press, 1979), 486–87.

2. See also the poet's *Basia* 12 and epigram beginning "Dicite Grammatici" for even more aggressively antagonistic instances of this strategy. Additional commentary on Secundus's *recusatio* can be found in David Price, "The Poetics of License in Janus Secundus's *Basia*," Sixteenth Century Journal 23 (1992): 289–301.

3. Writing at another time in sincere praise of his father's legal treatise, the *Topica*, Janus conjures an analogous scene of tutorial misery, playfully though unironically, to stress the elder's enduring accomplishment. See "In commondationem Topicorum Legalium Nicolai Euerardi patris," from the first book of epigrams: "Dum puer, imperio tutoris pressus acerbo, / Damnabit longae tempore lenta morae, / ... / Vsque tuum in toto nomen celebrabitur orbe, / Longaque durabit secula fama recens" [So long as a boy, burdened by the teacher's severe direction, will curse the time squandered in long delay [over his lessons], ... for so long an age will your newfound fame endure, and your name be celebrated throughout the entire world].

4. Cf. Daniel Albright's notion of lyric as "what is left over when all other genres are subtracted from the corpus of literature" (*Lyricality in English Literature* [Lincoln: University of Nebraska Press, 1985], ix).

5. See esp. Werner Jaeger, *Paideia: The Ideals of Greek Culture*, trans. Gilbert Highet, 2nd ed., 3 vols. (1935; New

York: Oxford University Press, 1945), 1:118–19; and Bruno Snell, *The Discovery of the Mind: The Greek Origins of European Thought*, trans. T. G. Rosenmeyer (1953; New York: Harper, 1960), 43–70.

6. Theodor W. Adorno, "On Lyric Poetry and Society," in *Notes to Literature, Volume 1*, ed. Rolfe Tiedemann, trans. Shierry Weber Nicholsen (New York: Columbia University Press, 1991), 37.

7. T. S. Eliot, "The Three Voices of Poetry," in *On Poetry and Poets* (New York: Noonday, 1961), 97.

8. Tony Woodman and Jonathan Powell, eds., *Author and Audience in Latin Literature* (Cambridge: Cambridge University Press, 1992).

9. W. R. Johnson, *The Idea of Lyric: Lyric Modes in Ancient and Modern Poetry* (Berkeley: University of California Press, 1982), 144.

10. William J. Kennedy, *Rhetorical Norms in Renaissance Literature* (New Haven: Yale University Press, 1978), 41.

11. Bruce R. Smith, *Homosexual Desire in Shakespeare's England: A Cultural Poetics* (Chicago: University of Chicago Press, 1991), 241.

12. But for a stimulating reconsideration of the *Canzoniere*'s more pervasive influence, see Roland Greene, *Post-Petrarchism: Origins and Innovations of the Western Lyric Sequence* (Princeton: Princeton University Press, 1991).

13. On Petrarch's familiarity with Ovid, for example, see Jennifer Petrie, *Petrarch: The Augustan Poets, the Italian Tradition, and the* Canzoniere (Dublin: Irish Academic Press, 1983). Ovid's influence on Shakespeare is discussed in J. B. Leishman's classic study, *Themes and Variations in Shakespeare's Sonnets* (New York: Harper, 1961), 27–44. More recently, Jonathan Bate reassesses the matter in *Shakespeare and Ovid* (Oxford: Clarendon Press, 1993): see esp. 83–100 on the *Sonnets*, an expanded version of his earlier "Ovid and the Sonnets; Or, Did Shakespeare Feel the Anxiety of Influence?," *Shakespeare Survey* 42 (1990): 65–76. Leishman also takes up Shakespeare's debt to Petrarch on pp. 44–53 of *Themes and Variations*, and the English poet's mediated reception of his Italian model is freshly addressed in several recent articles by William J. Kennedy: see esp. "'Sweete Theefe': Shakespeare Reading Petrarch," *Annals of Scholarship* 6 (1989): 75–91; and "Commentary into Narrative: Shakespeare's Sonnets and Vellutello's Commentary on Petrarch," *Allegorica* 10 (1989): 119–33. See also Thomas P. Roche, Jr.'s general presentation in *Petrarch and the English Sonnet Sequences* (New York: AMS, 1989).

14. Pierre de La Primaudaye, *The French Academy* (1586), tr. T. Bowes, anthologized in James Winny (ed.), *The Frame of Order* (London: Allen, 1957), 107–8.

15. Walter J. Ong, S. J., "The Writer's Audience Is Always a Fiction," *PMLA* 90 (1975): 17. Speaking specifically of Renaissance love poetry, William Kerrigan and Gordon Braden extend the notion: "Cutting in two the face-to-face encounter that speech, one assumes, originally developed to serve, the skill of writing traffics at both ends in absent presences. A simulacrum of speech, it diverts language from literal to fictive others whose existence depends on the operations of a solitary's fantasy" (William Kerrigan and Gordon Braden, *The Idea of the Renaissance* [Baltimore: Johns Hopkins University Press, 1989], 163). In his discussion of modern dramatic spectacle, Herbert Blau regards the audience as "not so much a mere congregation of people as a body of thought and desire. It does not exist before the play but is *initiated* or precipitated by it; it is not an entity to begin with but a consciousness constructed. The audience is what *happens* when, performing the signs and passwords of a play, something postulates itself and unfolds in response" (*The Audience* [Baltimore: Johns Hopkins University Press, 1980], 25). Blau cites Walter Benjamin's extreme formulation that art "posits man's physical and spiritual existence, but in none of its works is it concerned with his response. No poem is intended for the reader, no picture for the beholder, no symphony for the listener" (36).

16. Ong himself acknowledges this alternative prospect *en route* to his own position: "Practically speaking, of course, . . . [the author] does have to take into consideration the real social, economic, and psychological state of possible readers" (10).

17. For a fine illustration of this rhetorical methodology at work, see for instance Marion Trousdale, *Shakespeare and the Rhetoricians* (Chapel Hill: University of North Carolina Press, 1982).

18. See, for example, Wolfgang Iser's observation that "we react as if we knew how our partners experienced us; we continually form views of their views, and then act as if our views of their views were realities. Contact therefore depends upon our continually filling in a central gap in our experience. Thus, dyadic and dynamic interaction comes about only because we are unable to experience how we experience one another, which in turn proves to be a propellant to interaction. Out of this fact arises the basic need for interpretation, which regulates the whole process of interaction" ("Interaction

between Text and Reader," in *The Reader in the Text: Essays on Audience and Interpretation*, ed. Susan R. Suleiman and Inge Crosman [Princeton: Princeton University Press, 1980], 108). See also Suleiman's introductory essay to the volume, "Varieties of Audience-Oriented Criticism," 3–45.

19. Kennedy, *Rhetorical Norms* (note 10 above), 5. Even earlier, John T. Shawcross urges several vital corrections to rhetorical approaches to poetry in his "The Poet as Orator: One Phase of His Judicial Pose," in *The Rhetoric of Renaissance Poetry: From Wyatt to Milton*, ed. Thomas O. Sloan and Raymond B. Waddington (Berkeley: University of California Press, 1974), 5–36. Of particular interest to the present investigation is his convincing challenge to Earl Miner's dissociation of "public" and "private" technique, 32–33.

Notes to Chapter One

1. *Language and Silence: Essays on Language, Literature, and the Inhuman* (New York: Atheneum, 1967), 38.

2. Against Jasper Griffin's view of Augustan moral policy's general "insincerity" (*Latin Poets and Roman Life* [Chapel Hill: University of North Carolina Press, 1986], 22–24), compare Gordon Williams's point that "There could be no mistaking Augustus' seriousness: he persisted with the idea for thirty-six years and made use of his legislation" (*Change and Decline: Roman Literature in the Early Empire* [Berkeley: University of California Press, 1978], 59). The most comprehensive and convincing assessment of the emperor's enigmatic character remains Ronald Syme's *The Roman Revolution* (Oxford: Oxford University Press, 1939), though see the revaluations in Kurt A. Raaflaub and Mark Toher (eds.), *Between Republic and Empire: Interpretations of Augustus and His Principate* (Berkeley: University of California Press, 1990). On the laws—the substance of which was essentially to render adultery a civil offense—see esp. P. A. Brunt, *Italian Manpower 225 B.C.–A.D. 14* (Oxford: Clarendon Press, 1971), 558–66; Leo Ferrero Radista, "Augustus' Legislation Concerning Marriage, Procreation, Love Affairs and Adultery," *Aufstieg und Niedergang der römischen Welt* [hereafter *ANRW*] 2.13 (1980): 278–339; Richard I. Frank, "Augustus' Legislation on Marriage and Children," *California Studies in Classical Antiquity* 8 (1975): 41–52; and L. R. Lind, "The Tradition of Roman Moral Conservatism," in *Studies in Latin Literature and Roman History I*, ed. Carl Deroux (Brussels: Latomus, 1979), 7–58.

3. Gordon Williams, "Phases in Political Patronage of Literature in Rome," in *Literary and Artistic Patronage in Ancient Rome*, ed. Barbara K. Gold (Austin: University of Texas Press, 1982), 21. See also Williams's *The Nature of Roman Poetry* (Oxford: Oxford University Press, 1970): "The decisive—and original—new feature of Augustan poetry was the success of central authority in engaging the interest of poets in political aspirations and ideals" (10).

4. For a thorough investigation of the available (and inconclusive) theories regarding the poet's "error," see John C. Thibault, *The Mystery of Ovid's Exile* (Berkeley: University of California Press, 1964).

5. W. R. Johnson, "The Problem of the Counter-classical Sensibility and Its Critics," *California Studies in Classical Antiquity* 3 (1970): 143. Andrew Wallace-Hadrill notes that Ovid "reverts to the Golden Age theme more frequently than any other Augustan poet, but always irreverently" ("The Golden Age and Sin in Augustan Ideology," *Past and Present* 95 [1982]: 27), and R. O. A. M. Lyne confirms that "Ovid stands out against the moral earnestness of Augustan Rome; he also stands out against the romantic earnestness of his poetic predecessors. . . . One gets the impression that Ovid would have stood out against anything earnestly uttered or authoritatively imposed" (*The Latin Love Poets: From Catullus to Horace* [Oxford: Clarendon Press, 1980], 283). Jean-Marie André surveys the changing social ambience to which the elegists reacted in his *L'otium dans la vie morale et intellectuelle Romaine des origines à l'époque augustéenne* (Paris: Presses universitaires, 1966), 385–429. On poetic response to the promulgated ethic, see also Richard I. Frank, "Augustan Elegy and Catonism," *ANRW* 2.30.1 (1982): 559–79; Francesco della Corte, "Le *leges Iuliae* e l'elegia romana," *ANRW* 2.30.1 (1982): 539–58; and (for a view generally more sympathetic to the emperor) J. K. Newman, *Augustus and the New Poetry* (Brussels: Latomus, 1967). Ovid's specific reaction is treated by Richard A. Lanham, *The Motives of Eloquence: Literary Rhetoric in the Renaissance* (New Haven: Yale University Press, 1976), 48–64, and Wilfried Stroh, "Ovids Liebeskunst und die Ehegesetze des Augustus," *Gymnasium* 86 (1979): 323–52.

6. For the best sketch of classical prejudices influencing Ovid's reception, see Alison G. Elliott, "Ovid and the Critics: Seneca, Quintilian, and 'Seriousness,'" *Helios* 12 ns (1985): 9–20.

7. Georg Luck, *The Latin Love Elegy*, 2nd ed. (London: Methuen, 1969), 153.

8. Molly Myerowitz, *Ovid's Games of Love* (Detroit: Wayne State University Press, 1985), 105.

9. W. R. Johnson, for instance, finds in the *Amores'* "hollow" protagonist Ovid's renunciation of "a depleted genre" ("Ringing Down the Curtain on Love," *Helios* 12 ns [1985]: 25–26). Compare Brooks Otis's view of the collection as "a *reductio ad absurdum* of the genre as exhibited by Gallus, Tibullus and Propertius" ("Ovid and the Augustans," *Transactions and Proceedings of the American Philological Association* [hereafter *TAPA*] 69 [1938]: 197; and Kenneth Quinn's sense that the poetry entertains, "but it has almost no effect on our opinions, or on our understanding of human relationships" (*Latin Explorations: Critical Studies in Roman Literature* [New York: Humanities Press, 1963], 266). Other representative readings of the work as essentially comic include E. Reitzenstein, "Das neue Kunstwollen in den Amores Ovids," *Rheinisches Museum für Philologie* 89 (1935): 62–88; I. M. LeM. Du Quesnay, "The *Amores,*" in *Ovid*, ed. J. W. Binns (London: Routledge, 1973), 1–48; John T. Davis, "*Risit Amor*: Aspects of Literary Burlesque in Ovid's 'Amores,'" *ANRW* 2.31.4 (1981): 2460–2506; and J. C. McKeown's introduction to his edition of the *Amores* (4 vols.; Liverpool: Cairns, 1987–), 1:11–31.

10. See Mary-Kay Gamel, "*Non Sine Caede*: Abortion Politics and Poetics in Ovid's *Amores,*" *Helios* 16 (1989): 183–206, and Leslie Cahoon's series of articles: "Juno's Chaste Festival and Ovid's Wanton Loves: *Amores* 3.13," *Classical Antiquity* 2 (1983): 1–8; "The Parrot and the Poet: The Function of Ovid's Funeral Elegies," *Classical Journal* 80 (1984): 27–35; "A Program for Betrayal: Ovidian *Nequitia* in *Amores* 1.1, 2.1, and 3.1," *Helios* 12 ns (1985): 29–39; "Raping the Rose: Jean de meun's Reading of Ovid's *Amores,*" *Classical and Modern Literature* 6 (1986): 261–85; and "The Bed as Battlefield: Erotic Conquest and Military Metaphor in Ovid's *Amores,*" *TAPA* 118 (1988): 293–307.

11. McKeown, 1:26.

12. Du Quesnay, 7.

13. Warren Ginsberg treats Ovid's outlook toward audience reception and the artist's contingency in the *Metamorphoses* in his "Ovid's *Metamorphoses* and the Politics of Interpretation," *Classical Journal* 84 (1989): 222–31. Ginsberg discusses specifically the poet's awareness of how little control can be maintained over intended meaning, given his understanding that "all interpretation is an act of appropriation, an imposition finally based on power, nowhere fully sanctioned by the

text, nowhere fully denied by it either" (222).

14. All quotations from the *Amores* refer to E. J. Kenney's edition (Oxford: Clarendon Press, 1961). Translations from Ovid throughout are my own.

15. See *Epistulae ex Ponto* 3.9.17–20.

16. Gian Biagio Conte, *The Rhetoric of Imitation: Genre and Poetic Memory in Virgil and Other Latin Poets*, tr. Charles Segal (Ithaca: Cornell University Press, 1986), 85–87. Conte cites the Virgil on page 85:

> Ille ego qui quondam gracili modulatus avena
> carmen, et egressus silvis vicina coegi
> ut quamvis avido parerent arva colono,
> gratum opus agricolis, at nunc horrentia Martia
> (arma virumque cano ...)

> [I am he who once composed a song on a slender pipe; then, having left the woods, I made the fields nearby obey the settler even if he was very greedy, and the work pleased the farmers; now, however, (I sing of) the fearful (arms) of Mars (and the man).]

See also Antonio La Penna, "Ille ego qui quondam e i raccordi editoriali nell' antichità," *Studi Italiani di filologia classica* 3, 3rd series (1985): 76–91.

17. Commentary on the epigram has almost exclusively turned upon speculation about the first version's makeup. For a catalog of the extensive literature on the subject, see McKeown's notes, 1:74. E. J. Kenney observes in his introduction to A. D. Melville's translation of the *Amores* (Oxford: Oxford University Press, 1990) that individual books of the work likely circulated as Ovid wrote them, and that "there was never an 'edition' in five books" (xiii).

18. Where classical epic was composed in dactylic hexameter, elegy removed one of the six metrical feet from every other line of the form: hence the caricature of elegy as a "crippled" mode.

19. For the immediate Latin models of the speaker's posture here, see Tibullus 1.1 and Propertius 3.2.

20. On this see, for example, D. W. T. Vessey, "Elegy Eternal: Ovid, *Amores*, I, 15," *Latomus* 40 (1981): 616–17.

21. On Gallus, see Cassius Dio, *Historia* 53.23–24. The fullest modern assessment remains Jean-Paul Boucher, *Caius Cornelius Gallus* (Paris: Société d'Edition "Les Belles Lettres," 1966).

22. Peter Green (tr.), *Ovid: The Erotic Poems* (Harmondsworth: Penguin, 1982), 288.
23. Cahoon, "A Program for Betrayal," 33.
24. Quinn, "The Poet and His Audience," 144.
25. For a sensitive assessment of the inadequacies of language pondered in the *Amores*, see Douglas Parker, "The Ovidian Coda," *Arion* 8 (1969): 80–97. Ovid "will build structures and deliberately tear them down, not to demonstrate his superiority as creator, but to show the shortcomings of words themselves.... Life, and particularly love, demands more than words, words which distort them" (96). See also John M. Fyler, "*Omnia Vincit Amor*: Incongruity and the Limitations of Structure in Ovid's Elegiac Poetry," *Classical Journal* 66 (1971): 196–203.
26. Green, 23 and 273–74.
27. See Frank O. Copeley, Exclusus Amator: *A Study in Latin Love Poetry* (Madison: American Philological Association, 1956), esp. 82–90 and 125–40; Francis Cairns, *Generic Composition in Greek and Roman Poetry* (Edinburgh: Edinburgh University Press, 1972), 225; and J. C. Yardley, "The Elegiac Paraclausithyron," *Eranos* 76 (1978): 29–34.
28. See Green's discussion of the poem's politics in his notes, 322–24.
29. At *Ars amatoria* 2.711–16, Ovid again speculates on the sex appeal that soldiers manage to exude. He imagines Briseis not simply enduring the touch of her blood-stained captor Achilles, fresh from battle, but actually being aroused by the violent circumstance: "an fuit hoc ipsum quod te, lasciua, iuuaret, / ad tua uictrices membra uenire manus?"
30. Cahoon, esp. "The Bed as Battlefield," and Gamel.
31. Hermann Fränkel, *Ovid: A Poet between Two Worlds* (Berkeley: University of California Press, 1969), 18–21.
32. See, for example, Akbar H. Khan, "*Ovidius Furens*: A Revaluation of Amores 1, 7," *Latomus* 25 (1966): 880–94; Barbara E. Stirrup, "Irony in Ovid *Amores* 1.7," *Latomus* 32 (1973): 824–31; Peter J. Connor, "His Dupes and Accomplices: A Study of Ovid the Illusionist in the Amores," *Ramus* 3 (1974): 18–40; and Davis.
33. McKeown, 2:164.
34. Parker, 84–87.
35. All quotations from the exilic poems, *Ex Ponto* and *Tristia*, refer to S. G. Owen's edition (Oxford: Clarendon Press, 1915). For the sake of consistency, I have made occasional minor adjustments to the typography.

36. See for instance, besides Cahoon and Gamel, Mario Labate, "Poetica ovidiana dell'elegia: la retorica della città," *Materiali e discussione per l'analisi dei testi classici* 3 (1979): 66–67; Florence Verducci, *Ovid's Toyshop of the Heart: Epistulae Heroides* (Princeton: Princeton University Press, 1985), 214–15; Laurie J. Churchill, "Discourses of Desire: On Ovid's *Amores* and Barthes's *Fragments d'un discours amoureaux*," *Classical and Modern Literature* 8 (1988): 305; and (for the "burlesque" elements) Davis, 2499. A more sympathetic reading is provided by Otto Steen Due, "Amores und Abtreibung: Ov. *Am.* II 13 & 14," *Classica et Mediaevalia* 32 (1971–80): 133–50.

37. Gamel, 197 and 200.

38. My approach risks classification as the kind of "male" reading Gamel opposes. But her unrelenting insistence on the speaker's "exhibitionism" yields too reductive a conclusion to sustain the poetic performance she otherwise assesses so powerfully. I see too little at stake if we do not assent to the lover's investment in the relationship with Corinna. I seek to remedy or avoid the kind of contradiction Gamel's approach finally encounters, as when she faults the *amator* both for presumptuously claiming responsibility for the pregnancy and then later for not acknowledging his "complicity" in the abortion (though how, exactly, he should be complicitous in her expressly independent decision remains unclear). See Gamel, 192.

39. Archibald W. Allen, "Elegy and the Classical Attitude toward Love: Propertius I, 1," *Yale Classical Studies* 11 (1950): 264.

40. On Lucretius's influence, see (besides Allen) Quinn, *Latin Explorations*, 144–48; Jeff Schulman, "*Te Quoque Falle Tamen*: Ovid's Anti-Lucretian Didactics," *Classical Journal* 76 (1981): 242–53; and Irving Singer, *The Nature of Love, Volume 1: From Plato to Luther*, 2nd ed. (Chicago: University of Chicago Press, 1984), 122–46. On the ideal of *sophrosyne*, see Helen North, *Sophrosyne: Self-Knowledge and Self-Restraint in Greek Literature* (Ithaca: Cornell University Press, 1966).

41. Schulman, 243.

42. Zvi Yavetz, "The *Res Gestae* and Augustus' Public Image," in *Caesar Augustus: Seven Aspects*, ed. Fergus Millar and Eric Segal (Oxford: Clarendon Press, 1984), 19.

43. On Gallus, see Boucher, 49–57, and Kurt A. Raaflaub and L. J. Samons II, "Opposition to Augustus," in Raaflaub and Toher, 423–25.

44. On this, see Thibault, 33–36.
45. S. G. Nugent, "*Tristia* 2: Ovid and Augustus," in Raaflaub and Toher, 254.
46. Green, 46–47.
47. On Augustan canon revision and beyond, see H. I. Marrou, *A History of Education in Antiquity*, tr. George Lamb (Madison: University of Wisconsin Press, 1956), 277–78, and esp. the intriguing article by James E. G. Zetel, "Re-creating the Canon: Augustan Poetry and the Alexandrine Past," in *Canons*, ed. Robert von Hallberg (Chicago: University of Chicago Press, 1980), 107–29.
48. Elisabeth Thomas, "A Comparative Analysis of Ovid, 'Amores' II, 6 and III, 9," *Latomus* 29 (1970): 599.
49. Cahoon, "The Parrot and the Poet," 31–33.
50. Since *corpus* in Augustan Latin can mean "book" as well as "body," Ovid suggests a parallel—and not just a contrast—between the writer's corpse and the text that is supposed to "live on."
51. Besides Cahoon and Thomas, see on the parrot poem Barbara Weiden Boyd, "The Death of Corinna's Parrot Reconsidered: Poetry and Ovid's *Amores*," *Classical Journal* 82 (1987): 199–207.
52. Harry B. Evans, *Publica Carmina: Ovid's Books from Exile* (Lincoln: University of Nebraska Press, 1983), 177.
53. Sarah Spence, *Rhetorics of Reason and Desire: Vergil, Augustine, and the Troubadours* (Ithaca: Cornell University Press, 1988), 122.
54. Lauro Martines, *Power and Imagination: City-States in Renaissance Italy* (New York: Vintage, 1979), 66.

Notes to Chapter Two

1. *De amicitia* 5.18: "We, on the other hand, should consider things in terms of common experience, not as they are imagined or wished to be."
2. Petrarch, *The Life of Solitude*, tr. Jacob Zeitlin (Urbana: University of Illinois Press, 1924), 2.7.2, 274.
3. *Letters on Familiar Matters*, tr. Aldo S. Bernardo, 3 vols. (Baltimore: Johns Hopkins University Press, 1975–85), book 24, letter no. 1; 3:309. All further quotations from the *Familiares* refer to this translation: hereafter, I cite in the text both book and letter number (F), followed by the volume and page reference in Bernardo (B).

4. Translation from Thomas G. Bergin's "Petrarch's *Epistola metrica* II.10: An Annotated Translation," in *Dante, Petrarch, Boccaccio: Studies in the Italian Trecento in Honor of Charles S. Singleton*, ed. Aldo S. Bernardo and Anthony L. Pellegrini (Binghamton: Medieval and Renaissance Texts and Studies, 1983), 183–229. Bergin's Latin reads:

> Scriptis ego sum tollendus in altum;
> his sine nullus ero. Nunquid tamen illa probari
> est opus et vulgo? Titulo caruisse poete,
> abiecisse graves spoliato vertice ramos
> maluerim, et longis latuisse inglorius annis. (132–36)

5. All quotations and translations from the *Canzoniere* refer to Robert M. Durling, *Petrarch's Lyric Poems: The Rime sparse and Other Lyrics* (Cambridge MA: Harvard University Press, 1976). Reprinted by permission of the publisher.

6. Umberto Bosco, *Francesco Petrarca*, 2nd ed. (Bari: Laterza, 1961), 110: "un dolce appartarsi in seno a una natura amica, con molti libri, a quando a quando visitato da dolci amici, senza dei quali l'esistenza sembrerebbe manchevole e quasi cieca, senza stimoli esterni che costringano a fare quello che fare non si vorrebbe; senza cioè concessioni al 'volgo.'" For the broader discussion, see 103–17 passim. For other treatments of Petrarch's elitist stance, see Adelia Noferi, "Il canzoniere del Petrarca: scrittura del desiderio e desiderio della scrittura," *Paragone* 296 (1974): 5; Aldo S. Bernardo, "Petrarch and the Art of Literature," in *Petrarch to Pirandello: Studies in Italian Literature in Honour of Beatrice Corrigan*, ed. Julias A. Molinaro (Toronto: University of Toronto Press, 1973), esp. 40; Francisco Rico, "'Rime sparse,' 'Rerum vulgarium fragmenta': Para el titulo y el primer soneto del 'Canzoniere,'" *Medioevo Romanzo* 3 (1976): 122–23; Eugenio N. Frongia, "Creative Leisure and Personal Freedom: The Case for Scholarship in Petrarch's Writings," *Studies in the Italian Renaissance: Essays in Memory of Arnolfo B. Ferruolo*, ed. Gian Paolo Biasin et al. (Naples: Società Editrice Napoletana, 1985), 67–85 passim. Charles Trinkaus discusses the strains this outlook placed upon Petrarch's social ethic in his *The Poet as Philosopher: Petrarch and the Formation of Renaissance Consciousness* (New Haven: Yale University Press, 1979), esp. 52–89.

7. Bosco, p. 111: "troppo acuto autocritico per non avvertire che cosa inquini questo modo di vivere; che cosa faccia sì che nemmeno esso, in fondo, lo soddisfi."

8. Arnaud Tripet, *Pétrarque ou la connaissance de soi* (Geneva: Droz, 1967), 30–31: "Lui-même, ce n'est pas *selon* le contexte historique qu'il entendra se définir, mais *contre* cet espace extérieur, *autre* que lui. Il rejettera avec une passion tout intéressée mais nécessaire, l'instance sociale, le poids du groupe; il fuira l'aliénation, la promiscuité, le regard d'autrui; il cherchera le bonheur et le salut dans la solitude et le retour à l'intériorité." See also 187.

9. Thomas M. Greene, *The Light in Troy: Imitation and Discovery in Renaissance Poetry* (New Haven: Yale University Press, 1982), 97.

10. "The Flexibility of the Self in Renaissance Literature," in *The Disciplines of Criticism: Essays in Literary Theory, Interpretation, and History*, ed. Peter Demetz et al. (New Haven: Yale University Press, 1968), 246.

11. For a potent analysis of the relationship between Dante's and Petrarch's respective poetics, see Robert Pogue Harrison, *The Body of Beatrice* (Baltimore: Johns Hopkins University Press, 1988). The literature on Petrarch's relationship with his great predecessor is massive; for a sample bibliography, see Marco Santagata's recent *Per moderne carte: La Biblioteca volgare di Petrarca* (Bologna: Il Mulino, 1990), and his own chapters on the subject, 25–91.

12. John Freccero, "The Fig Tree and the Laurel: Petrarch's Poetics," *Diacritics* 5 (1975): 34. On Petrarch's invention of the sonnet sequence, see esp. Teodolinda Barolini, "The Making of a Lyric Sequence: Time and Narrative in Petrarch's *Rerum vulgarium fragmenta*," *Modern Language Notes* 104 (1989): 1–38; Gérard Genot, "Strutture narrative della poesia lirica," *Paragone* 212 (1967): 35–52; and Sandra L. Bermann's remarks in her *The Sonnet Over Time: A Study in the Sonnets of Petrarch, Shakespeare, and Baudelaire* (Chapel Hill: University of North Carolina Press, 1988).

13. "Here may be the proper place to mention that this was not the least of my reasons for abandoning his [Dante's] style of composition to which I devoted myself as a young man, for I feared for my writings what I saw happening to the writings of others . . . ; I had no hope, then, that the tongues or minds of the rabble would be any more flexible or kind to my works than they were to those whom long habit and favor had made popular in the theater and public squares. Events have proved my fears well-founded since a few pieces that slipped from my youthful pen are constantly being mangled by the multitude's recitation, something that is so vexing as to make me hate what I once loved" (F 21.15; B 3:205).

14. The authoritative treatment of the *Canzoniere*'s specific evolution remains Ernest H. Wilkins's *The Making of the "Canzoniere" and Other Petrarchan Studies* (Rome: Edizioni di storia e litteratura, 1951), 145–94.

15. Aldo S. Bernardo, "Petrarch's Autobiography: Circularity Revisited," *Annali d'Italianistica* 4 (1986): 48.

16. Nancy J. Vickers, "Vital Signs: Petrarch and Popular Culture," *Romanic Review* 79 (1988): 195.

17. Marguerite Waller, *Petrarch's Poetics and Literary History* (Amherst: University of Massachusetts Press, 1980), 55.

18. The event is noted in F 4.18 (B 1: 96).

19. Wilkins translates the speech in "Petrarch's Coronation Oration," *PMLA* 68 (1953): 1241–50. The Ovid reference is found on 1245. Cf. also the remark of P. J. Klemp: "Perhaps no other writer [than Ovid] equalled Petrarch's awareness that, without an audience, he and his work would cease to exist" ("Narrator and Narratee in Petrarch's *Canzoniere*," *Italian Quarterly* 29/114 [1988]: 11).

20. *Petrarch's Secret*, tr. William H. Draper (London: Chatto and Windus, 1911), 167–68.

21. Guido Almansi, "Petrarca, o dell'insignificanza," *Paragone* 296 (1974): 70. "La gloria del Canzoniere è la sua indipendenza, e la sua indipendenza è la sua irrilevanza. È un testo "en train de s'écrire" che esclude ogni molesta interferenza di un autore con velleità autobiografiche o di un lettore con aspirazioni empatiche: entrambi sono esiliati dal circuito chiuso del suo egocentrismo. Testo eristallino e incontaminato, di fronte al Canzoniere ogni altra opera sembra volgare, legata alla terra, intollerabilmente mondana, sconciamente realistica, turpemente informativa."

22. *Seniles*, book 5, letter no. 2, tr. Aldo S. Bernardo, *Letters of Old Age*, 2 vols. (Baltimore: Johns Hopkins University Press, 1992), 162–63. All further citations from the *Seniles* refer to this translation, following the same convention set for the *Familiares* quotes, using S to designate the work. The interpolated Latin is from the *Opera* (Basel, 1581), part. 1, 795.

23. See A. Noyer-Weidner's representative view of Petrarch's effort "distanziare il 'popol tutto', il 'vulgus' dunque, secondo l'espressione parallela nel *Secretum*, da quell' élite a cui si alludeva con 'voi ch'ascoltate', e poi soprattutto con 'ove sia chi per prova intenda amore'" ("Il Sonetto I," *Lectura Petrarce* 4 [1984]: 346).

24. See, for example, Harrison, 106–7; and Adelia Noferi, "Da un commento al 'Canzoniere' del Petrarca: lettura del sonetto introduttivo," *Lettere Italiane* 24 (1974): 170.

25. See, for example, the passages in *Confessions* 3.6, 4.7, and 5.9. For an indepth discussion of the term, see the monograph by Paule Demats, *Fabula: Trois études de mythographie antique et médiévale* (Geneva: Droz, 1973). For further assessment of the term in Petrarch, see Noferi, "Da un commento": 174, and "Il canzoniere del Petrarca": 21–22; and Noyer-Weidner: 347. For interesting remarks on the "favola" in reference to Boccaccio, see Janet Levarie Smarr, *Boccaccio and Fiammetta: The Narrator as Lover* (Urbana: University of Illinois Press, 1986), 161–62.

26. Tragedy addresses the poet in *Amores* 3.1 for his infamy—"fabula, nec sentis, tota iactaris in Vrbe, / dum tua praeterito facta pudore refers" (21–22)—and Horace poses a similar point of self-recrimination in his Epode 11, "heu me, per Vrbem—nam pudet tanti mali— / fabula quanta fui" [7-8; O what a fable I was all over town—I'm ashamed of such torments].

27. On the import and structure of the *Canzoniere*'s religious concerns, see esp. Marjorie O'Rourke Boyle, *Petrarch's Genius: Pentimento and Prophecy* (Berkeley: University of California Press, 1991), and Thomas P. Roche, Jr., *Petrarch and the English Sonnet Sequences* (New York: AMS Press, 1989), 1–69.

28. For an informative overall treatment of the relation between Petrarch's poetic and the geography of his sequence, see Sara Sturm-Maddox, *Petrarch's Laurels* (University Park: Pennsylvania State University Press, 1992), 63–100.

29. William Kerrigan and Gordon Braden, *The Idea of the Renaissance* (Baltimore: Johns Hopkins University Press, 1989), 167. For a fuller reading of the poem, see Braden's article (from which these remarks originally come), "Love and Fame: The Petrarchan Career," in *Pragmatism's Freud: The Moral Disposition of Psychoanalysis*, ed. William Kerrigan and Joseph Smith (Baltimore: Johns Hopkins University Press, 1986), esp. 147–53. See also Durling's introductory essay to his translation.

30. Santagata, 306–7. Santagata's treatment stands out overall as the best sustained reading of the canzone.

31. As reported in Ludovico Castelvetro's *Le Rime del Petrarca brevemente sposte* (Basel, 1582), part. 1, 193: "che questa canzone non viene a dir nulla, ma che sono proverbi raccolti insieme...."

32. Klemp, 18.

33. For an interesting recent attempt to read the poem in terms of autobiographical allegory, see the work of Frederic J.

Jones: "An Analysis of Petrarch's Eleventh *Canzone*: 'Mai non vo' piú cantar com' io sloeva,'" *Italian Studies* 41 (1986): 24–44; and "Petrarch, Philippe de Vitry, and a Possible Identification of the Mother of Petrarch's children," *Italianistica* 18 (1989): 81–107.

34. Noting that Laura is not even punningly identified in the original cluster of poems which Wilkins isolates as the *Canzoniere*'s nascent form, Sara Sturm-Maddox also observes in the poem's hesitation a "kind of 'failure,'" since "the name *Lauretta* is not directly recorded but syllabically fragmented and concealed among the verses, an anagram to be only phonically revealed." See her discussion in *Petrarch's Metamorphoses: Text and Subtext in the* Rime sparse (Columbia: University of Missouri Press, 1985), 19.

35. James L. Calderwood, *Shakespeare and the Denial of Death* (Amherst: University of Massachusetts Press, 1987), 34.

36. On the Dantesque precedent, see Harrison; on Petrarch's preoccupation with mortality, see Barolini's discussion; on Petrarch's work and the plague, see Renée Neu Watkins, "Petrarch and the Black Death: From Fear to Monuments," *Studies in the Renaissance* 19 (1975): 196–223, though much remains to be done on this particular subject.

37. Cf. Mariann S. Regan: "Perhaps the Poet-Lover of the *Canzoniere* even tries to appropriate Laura's death for his own defensive purposes, another act of distancing.... Of course, she is never by any means so direct and immediate a presence as Beatrice. But still, the poems continue to grow in the space cleared by her death..." (*Love Words: The Self and the Text in Medieval and Renaissance Poetry* [Ithaca: Cornell University Press, 1982], 193).

38. Barolini, 29–30.

39. Cf. esp. *Confessions* 6.12, which recalls Isaiah 28:15.

40. Barolini, 30.

41. For an interpretation of the poem as prophetic vision, see Boyle, 93–112. See also Fredi Chiappelli's extended reading in *Studi sul linguaggio del Petrarca: La canzone delle visioni* (Florence: Leo S. Olschki, 1971).

42. Wilkins, "Petrarch's Coronation Oration," 1250.

43. Draper, *Petrarch's Secret*, 156.

44. The opportunity for such an awareness was ingrained deeply in the poet's own biography. For all the egotism which fills out his works explicitly or impicitly, Petrarch was beset by a sense of personal sinfulness all the more poignant for his efforts at suppression. While he acknowledges and dismisses the lustful appetites that beset him in youth in his "Letter to

Posterity," the unremarked consequences of these—particularly his illegitimate son Giovanni, whose misconduct to the time of his premature death pained his parent greatly—were not so easily bracketed; and see Pierre de Nolhac on the diary entries where he agonizes over his repeated relapses into carnality (*Pétrarque et l'humanisme*, 2nd ed., 2 vols. [1907; Paris: Librarie Honoré Champion, 1965], 2:283–92). His touchiness about how well he actually deserved the laurel given his slender output at the time of his crowning—best available in *Epistola metrica* 2.10's rancor—also manifests his insecurity. But perhaps most emphatically, he encountered an object of contrast in the career of his brother Gherardo, who as a Carthusian monk stood at his monastic post during the plague, a sole survivor left to bury his 34 fellows, as Petrarch reports in *Fam* 16.2. Gherardo's place as a foil to his own spiritual torpor in *Fam* 4.1, the "Mount Ventoux" narrative, extended even further than this famous account suggests.

45. Charles E. Trinkaus, *In Our Image and Likeness: Humanity and Divinity in Italian Humanist Thought*, 2 vols. (Chicago: University of Chicago Press, 1970), 1:3.

46. *De remediis* 2: 119. The Latin refers to Petrarch's *Opera omnia* (Basel, 1581), 208; the translation is Conrad H. Rawski's, *Petrarch's Remedies for Fortune Fair and Foul*, 5 vols. (Bloomington: University of Indiana Press, 1991), 3:299.

47. James D. Folts, Jr., "Senescence and Renascence: Petrarch's Thoughts on Growing Old," *Journal of Medieval and Renaissance Studies* 10 (1980): 237. Much remains to be done on the *De remediis*, which Rawski's impressive achievement should greatly facilitate. Prior to Rawski, the only extended study was Klaus Heitmann's *Fortuna und Virtus: Eine Studie zu Petrarcas Lebensweisheit* (Cologne: Böhlau, 1957). See also the remarks in George W. McClure, *Sorrow and Consolation in Italian Humanism* (Princeton: Princeton University Press, 1991), 46–72.

48. Ugo Dotti, *Vita del Petrarca* (Bari: Laterza, 1987), 447: "Egli è infatti certo che la propria vocazione sia qualcosa che riguarda tutti e il suo isolamento, in realtà, rappresenta soltanto la condizione per poter partecipare con maggiore impegno e serietà alla vita e ai destini della communità umana."

49. Praising the humanist's intellectual virtues, Charles Trinkaus (for instance) concedes that the writer's "political naïveté is well known" (*In Our Image and Likeness*, 1: 16). By contrast, de Mattai delineates two distinct temperaments in the works, one idealistic and the other more pragmatic, keyed

respectively to the specificities of discrete circumstances (*Il sentimento politico del Petrarca* [Florence: Sansoni, 1944], 11–12). My ensuing remarks on *Seniles* 14.5 reconfirms just such a division.

50. For the most recent assessment of the Mount Ventoux ascent, see Lyell Asher, "Petrarch at the Peak of Fame," *PMLA* 108 (1993): 1050–63.

51. Sturm-Maddox, *Petrarch's Metamorphoses*, 104.

52. Regan, 187.

53. Frank Whigham, *Ambition and Privilege: The Social Tropes of Elizabethan Courtesy Theory* (Berkeley: University of California Press, 1984), 32 and 39.

Notes to Chapter Three

1. *Ricordi* B 156: "... whoever steers his life's course with nothing else in mind than to stand well among the people shows little sagacity, since to guess their preferences has more to do with chance than with judgment."

2. *Palladis Tamia* (1598), quoted in the Variorum edition of the *Sonnets*, ed. Hyder Edward Rollins, 2 vols. (Philadelphia: Lippincott, 1944), 2:53.

3. Philip Martin, *Shakespeare's Sonnets: Self, Love, and Art*, (Cambridge: Cambridge University Press, 1972), 2.

4. *Preface to Shakespeare*, in *Johnson on Shakespeare*, ed. Arthur Sherbo, 2 vols. (New Haven: Yale University Press, 1968), 1:91–92.

5. Citation from the third Arden edition of *The Poems*, ed. F. T. Prince (London: Methuen, 1960), 2. *Venus and Adonis* would see at least ten editions in Shakespeare's lifetime.

6. Speaking specifically of *Love's Labor's Lost*, William C. Carroll observes that one point the play emphatically teaches is "that dogmatic inflexibility, on the stage or in the audience, will sooner or later be shattered" (*The Great Feast of Language in* Love's Labour's Lost [Princeton: Princeton University Press, 1976], 87). See also the remarks of Louis A. Montrose in "'Sport by sport o'erthrown': *Love's Labour's Lost* and the Politics of Play," *Texas Studies in Literature and Language* 18 (1977): 528–52.

7. See Katherine Duncan-Jones, "Was the 1609 *Shake-speares Sonnets* Really Unauthorized?," *Review of English Studies* 34 (1983): 151–71. Other recent defenses of the Q version's integrity and order—which my own study assumes—include Joseph Pequigney, *Such Is My Love: A Study of*

Shakespeare's Sonnets (Chicago: University of Chicago Press, 1985), 209–24; and David K. Weiser, *Mind in Character: Shakespeare's Speaker in the Sonnets* (Columbia: University of Missouri Press, 1987). Even Robert Giroux, who views the *Sonnets* as an unauthorized publication, holds that "The order of the poems as printed in Q is *on the whole* right, though imperfect" (*The Book Known as Q: A Consideration of* Shakespeare's Sonnets [New York: Vintage, 1982], 17). See also Joel Fineman's judicious remarks in his extended note on 319–21 of *Shakespeare's Perjured Eye: Poetic Subjectivity in the* Sonnets (Berkeley: University of California Press, 1986).

8. Bruce R. Smith, *Homosexual Desire in Shakespeare's England: A Cultural Poetics* (Chicago: University of Chicago Press, 1991), 233–34.

9. Thomas P. Roche, Jr., *Petrarch and the English Sonnet Sequences* (New York: AMS, 1989), 402: "There is no fair young man—beyond Will's narcissistic projection.... Will is addressing the higher reaches of himself, that fair young man in all of us that needs will and urging." Compare Smith's opinion about the *Sonnets'* "surprisingly undramatic" character: "Shakespeare's speaker evokes friend and mistress not as real presences, but as mental images.... Shakespeare's persona speaks to himself" (231–32).

10. Cf. Fineman, note 7 above.

11. Anne Ferry, *The "Inward" Language: Sonnets of Wyatt, Sidney, Shakespeare, Donne* (Chicago: University of Chicago Press, 1983), 178.

12. Heather Dubrow, *Captive Victors: Shakespeare's Narrative Poems and Sonnets* (Ithaca: Cornell University Press, 1986), 190.

13. Sandra L. Bermann, *The Sonnet Over Time: A Study of the Sonnets of Petrarch, Shakespeare, and Baudelaire* (Chapel Hill: University of North Carolina Press, 1988), 56; Gerald Hammond, *The Reader and Shakespeare's Young Man Sonnets* (Totowa: Barnes, 1981), passim. For other passing comments on matters of audience, see Hallett Smith, *The Tension of the Lyre: Poetry in Shakespeare's Sonnets* (San Marino: Huntington, 1981), 1–12; and Murray Krieger, *A Window on Criticism: Shakespeare's* Sonnets *and Modern Poetics* (Princeton: Princeton University Press, 1964), 140–64.

14. Rosalie Colie, *Shakespeare's Living Art* (Princeton: Princeton University Press, 1974), 133.

15. Patricia Fumerton, *Cultural Aesthetics: Renaissance Literature and the Practice of Social Ornament* (Chicago: University of Chicago Press, 1991), 69. For the development of her

argument in reference to the sonnet, see esp. 85–104.

16. Lars Engle, "Afloat in Thick Deeps: Shakespeare's Sonnets on Certainty," *PMLA* 104 (1989): 833.

17. Engle, 838. For another version of this approach, see Adena Rosmarin, "Hermeneutics versus Erotics: Shakespeare's *Sonnets* and Interpretive History," *PMLA* 100 (1985): 20–37 ("the explanation that best explains the literary text...is identical with the explanation that best explains its interpretive history, itself treated as a text" [32]). See also Margreta de Grazia's comments on the *Sonnets'* progress in her *Shakespeare Verbatim: The Reproduction of Authenticity and the 1790 Apparatus* (Oxford: Clarendon Press, 1991), 132–76.

18. All quotations from the poems refer to *Shakespeare's Sonnets,* ed. Stephen Booth (New Haven: Yale University Press, 1977.

19. I take issue with Fineman's offhand reference to the line's "*almost* public 'we'" (200, my emphasis): his curious and unsubstantiated overqualification misleads, by muting the impact of the word's crucial plurality.

20. Pequigney, 11.

21. Martin, 27.

22. Stephen Booth observes that we are not absolutely certain until the next poem that "engraft" refers specifically to the subject's poetic preservation (158). For a challenge to Booth on this point, see 115–16 of Raymond B. Waddington, "Shakespeare's Sonnet 15 and the Art of Memory," in *The Rhetoric of Renaissance Poetry: From Wyatt to Milton,* ed. Thomas O. Sloan and Raymond B. Waddington (Berkeley: University of California Press, 1974).

23. Wordsworth inscribed the comment in his copy of Anderson's *British Poets;* published in Markham L. Peacock, Jr., *The Critical Opinions of William Wordsworth* (1950; New York: Octagon, 1969), 348. For an instance of the sentiment's endurance, cf. Robert Crosman: "As arguments for procreation, they are dazzling and impressive but also redundant and wearying" ("Making Love Out of Nothing at All: The Issue of Story in Shakespeare's Procreation Sonnets," *Shakespeare Quarterly* 41 [1990]: 477).

24. Colie, 53.

25. John Kerrigan (ed.), *The Sonnets and A Lover's Complaint* (Harmondsworth: Penguin, 1986), 27.

26. Marion Trousdale, *Shakespeare and the Rhetoricians* (Chapel Hill: University of North Carolina Press, 1982), 43.

27. Terence Cave, *The Cornucopian Text: Problems of Writing in the French Renaissance* (Oxford: Clarendon Press,

1979), 22. Cave's stands out as the best recent discussion of the topic: see his full argument, 3–34 passim. See also the remarks by Arthur F. Kinney, *Continental Humanist Poetics: Studies in Erasmus, Castiglione, Marguerite de Navarre, Rabelais, and Cervantes* (Amherst: University of Massachusetts Press, 1989), esp. 19–24; and Trousdale, esp. 39–55. For investigations more specifically of the Erasmean source, see esp. J. K. Sowards, "Erasmus and the Apologetic Textbook: A Study of the *De duplici Copia verborum ac rerum*," *Studies in Philology* 55 (1958): 122–35; and Alvin Vos, "*De copia* and Classical Rhetoric," *Classical and Modern Literature* 7 (1987): 285–94. For a consideration of *copia*'s relation to matters of gender in the Renaissance, see Patricia Parker, "On the Tongue: Cross Gendering, Effeminacy, and the Art of Words," *Style* 23 (1989): 445–65.

28. Erasmus, *De copia*, tr. Craig R. Thompson in vol. 24 of the *Collected Works* (Toronto: University of Toronto Press, 1978), 302.

29. Erasmus, 295 and 301.

30. *The Scholemaster*, in *English Works of Roger Ascham*, ed. William Aldis Wright (Cambridge: Cambridge University Press, 1904), 261. Posturing initially as a pedagogue who responsibly sets out to indoctrinate the young man in those social conventions he reveres, Shakespeare's poet himself comes to dramatize the indignities of what Seneca contemptuously termed the *elementarius senex*, the old man put back to school (*Epistulae morales* 36).

31. Judith Kegan Gardiner, "The Marriage of Male Minds in Shakespeare's Sonnets," *Journal of English and Germanic Philology* 84 (1985): 334. See also Katherine M. Wilson's notion of the *Sonnets'* marriage argument as a "parody" of the *encomium matrimonii* tradition, in her *Shakespeare's Sugared Sonnets* (New York: Barnes, 1974), 146–67.

32. Engle, 832.

33. Northrop Frye observes in passing how "Rationalizing readers tell us that the poet is urging the youth to marry, but only one of these sonnets—the eighth—has any serious treatment of marriage. True, the youth is urged to marry as the only legal means of producing offspring, but apparently any woman will do: it is not suggested that he should fall in love or that there is any possibility of his producing daughters or even a son who takes after his mother, which seems curious when the youth himself does" ("How True a Twain," in *Fables of Identity: Studies in Poetic Mythology* [New York: Harcourt, 1963], 88–89). More recently, cf. Eve Kosofsky

Sedgwick: "Neither desire for women nor even mastery seems to be an explicit issue; what is at stake is preserving the continuity of an existing dominant culture" (*Between Men: English Literature and Male Homosocial Desire* [New York: Columbia University Press, 1985], 34).

34. Erasmus, 584.

35. Cave, 5.

36. See, for instance, Northrop Frye's estimate of the poems as "mere literary exercise" (104); and Joseph Pequigney's dismissal, "The reduplication is puzzling and pointless.... One version would do, and one would do much better than the other (178). For more supportive readings, see Peggy Muñoz Simonds, "Eros and Anteros in Shakespeare's Sonnets 153 and 154: An Iconographical Study," in *Spenser Studies VII*, ed. Patrick Cullen and Thomas P. Roche, Jr. (New York: AMS Press, 1987), 261–86; and esp. John Kerrigan's remarks in his Introduction: "In some respects a buffer group... [153 and 154] about Cupid and his brand are also the logical outcome of the dark lady sonnets, since they make visible the erotic principle at work in them. Not 'obviously linked' with what precedes them, they are nevertheless inseparable from 127–52, and essential to those poems' effect" (61).

37. Gardiner, 335.

38. See, for example, John D. Bernard's argument that the prevailing inclination here is toward the quest for a "metaphysical essence accessible to the loving imagination alone" ("'To Conctancie Confin'de': The Poetics of Shakespeare's Sonnets," *PMLA* 94 [1979]: 77). On another register, Murray Krieger emphasizes the speaker's "utopian" nostalgia for a former time that contemporary society has undone ("The Conversion from History to Utopia in Shakespeare's *Sonnets*," in Words *about* Words *about* Words*: Theory, Criticism, and the Literary Text* [Baltimore: Johns Hopkins University Press, 1988], 242–55).

39. Jane Roessner, "The Coherence and the Context of Shakespeare's Sonnet 116," *Journal of English and Germanic Philology* 81 (1982): 341.

40. For a sustained consideration of the erosion of confidence in art's preservative power, see Anne Ferry, *All in War with Time: Love Poetry of Shakespeare, Jonson, Donne, Marvell* (Cambridge: Harvard University Press, 1975), 3–63; for a challenge to this outlook, see Bernard's article (note 38 above).

41. See Booth's long note delineating the difficulties, 364–72; the quoted passages are found on 366 and 369.

42. Jane Roessner, "Double Exposure: Shakespeare's Sonnets 100–114," *ELH* 46 (1979): 376.

43. Cf. Gary Schmidgall's observation that "many of the Young Man poems offer an impressive if grim view of the fierce competition among *all* classes of suitors at court" (*Shakespeare and the Poet's Life* [Lexington: University of Kentucky Press, 1990], 176). Schmidgall's is one of the best discussions of the poems from this "courtly" standpoint: see esp. 174–79.

44. Howard Felperin, "The Dark Lady Identified, or What Deconstruction Can Do for Shakespeare's *Sonnets*," in *Shakespeare and Deconstruction*, ed. G. Douglas Atkins and David M. Bergeron (New York: Peter Lang, 1988), 80.

45. On his way to the rival subsequence, the poet has occasion several times to follow the youth's wider circulation. Sonnet 38, for example, articulates a tension between the young man's capacity to inspire even meager talents to great verse ("For who's so dumb that cannot write to thee / When thou thyself doth give invention light?" [7–8]), and the subject's status as one "too excellent / For every vulgar paper to rehearse" (3–4). He seems torn between a pride in his own public performance, the ability he claims "to please these curious days," and an implicit, protective reflex to fear that others will usurp his poetic office. Especially after his emotional exclusivity is violated by poem 40, the poet feels compelled to vent his resentment against one who opens himself as "prey of every vulgar thief" in 48, and likewise ponders the youth's distant comforts, "with others all too near," in 61. The betrayal evokes the speaker's admonition in 69 "that thou dost common grow"; the awareness of exclusivity's breakdown over the course of events, intimated in the poet's frustrated reactions to his beloved's many encounters, lurches towards the rival poet subsequence's showdown.

46. Should we read the Q text's "fild" as "filed" rather than the "filled" for which Booth opts, the construction of "countenance" as "appearance of favor" is further enhanced: the youth's favor completes his poet's lines by "filing" or polishing them up—by applying the necessary "finishing touch," so to speak. See Booth's note, 289–90.

47. "Pitiful Thrivers: Failed Husbandry in the Sonnets," in *Shakespeare and the Question of Theory*, ed. Patricia Parker and Geoffrey Hartman (New York: Methuen, 1986), 239.

48. Booth observes that "The metaphor of a building far from accident gives the poem overtones of the many Latin poems in praise of the independent country life far from the

follies and dangers of Roman politics and society" (421).

49. See also Thomas Greene's interesting evaluation of 125's enemy as an "internal" antagonist: "The poet's real enemy is not the 'informer' as slanderer, but the voice within himself through whose forming action feeling comes into being" (242).

50. Engle, 835.

51. See Ovid's *Medicamina faciei*: "ingenio facies conciliante placet. /.../ sufficit et longum probitas perdurat in aeuum, / perque suos annos hinc bene pendet amor" [44, 49–50: The face is pleasing so long as the mind is true.... Probity stands up and endures throughout time, and love leans well upon this for many years].

52. Approaching the sonnet (and the subsequence) from another direction entirely, Nona Feinberg observes that "the Dark Lady commands a discourse which compels the speaker to question his own eloquence" ("Erasing the Dark Lady: Sonnet 138 in the Sequence," *Assays* 4 [1987]: 99).

53. Cf. James Winny: "It is a reasonable assumption that when Sonnets 138 and 144 were published in 1599 the sequence was complete; for the latter of them reads like a commentary on the whole matter of the Sonnets" (*The Master-Mistress: A study of Shakespeare's Sonnets* [London: Chatto, 1968], 73–74). The precise circumstances under which these variant readings actually appeared unfortunately elude us, disabling any definitive conjecture about their versions' status or authority. For a recent discussion of the texts, see 150–54 of Arthur F. Marotti, "Shakespeare's Sonnets as Literary Property," in *Soliciting Interpretation: Literary Theory and Seventeenth-Century English Poetry*, ed. Elizabeth D. Harvey and Katherine Eisaman Maus (Chicago: University of Chicago Press, 1990).

54. William Kerrigan, "The Personal Shakespeare: Three Clues," in *Shakespeare's Personality*, ed. Norman Holland *et al.* (Berkeley: University of California Press, 1989), 181; Sedgwick, 39.

55. See Booth's note, 521.

56. Leon Battista Alberti, *I libri della famiglia*, tr. Renée Neu Watkins as *The Family in Renaissance Florence* (Columbia: University of South Carolina Press, 1969), 71. Cf. John Klause's reflection that the sonneteer "is a manipulator of lies, not their victim, for his prevarications are primarily rhetorical" ("Shakespeare's *Sonnets*: Age in Love and the Goring of Thoughts," *Studies in Philology* 80 [1983]: 312).

57. Pierre de La Primaudaye, *The French Academy* (1586),

tr. T. Bowes, in James Winny (ed.), *The Frame of Order* (London: Allen, 1957), 108.

58. For instance, Margreta de Grazia's scrutiny of John Benson's 1640 publication of the sonnets, in modified form, seriously assails claims for the work's novel impact: "Most of the 1609 sonnets lost their distinctive form in Benson's edition: while it printed 146 of the 154 sonnets, it regrouped them into units of from one to five sonnets to form seventy-two poems and assigned each a title... that abstracted and universalized its content. The pronouns used in the titles... suggest a representative rather than an individuated subject and object" (163). Fundamentally sympathetic to Fineman's psychological focus, Sara van den Berg likewise finds his conclusions too extreme. See her "'Mutual Ordering': Subjectivity and Language in Shakespeare's Sonnets," in *Contending Kingdoms: Historical, Psychological, and Feminist Approaches to the Literature of Sixteenth-Century England and France*, ed. Marie-Rose Logan and Peter Rudnytsky (Detroit: Wayne State University Press, 1991), 178–79.

59. Fineman, 131.

Notes to Afterword

1. Jorge Luis Borges, "Averroes' Search," in *Labyrinths*, ed. Donald A. Yates and James E. Irby (Harmondsworth: Penguin, 1970), 188.

2. Paul de Man, "Lyrical Voice in Contemporary Theory: Riffaterre and Jauss," in *Lyric Poetry: Beyond New Criticism*, ed. Chaviva Hošek and Patricia Parker (Ithaca: Cornell University Press, 1985), 55.

3. The foremost example remains Stephen J. Greenblatt, *Renaissance Self-Fashioning: From More to Shakespeare* (Chicago: University of Chicago Press, 1980).

4. Speaking about Ovid, Petrarch and Sidney from a standpoint other than my own, Paul Allen Miller offers a formulation representative of the critical orthodoxy I wish to challenge, when he states that "the sonnet sequence, as developed by Petrarch and practiced by Sidney, offered occasion for the creation of a more complex and highly self-reflexive lyric subjectivity than any seen in the poetry of the Middle Ages. The rigidly hierarchical social system of feudalism left little room for the virtually autonomous ego, which the sonnets of a Sidney, a Shakespeare, or a Donne require" ("Sidney, Petrarch, and Ovid, Or Imitation as Subversion," *ELH* 58 [1991]: 499).

"Autonomy" of the brand he cites is exactly what I take issue with: these poets boasted such an ego, while remaining keenly aware of the contingencies which animate rather than inhibit their aesthetic self-presentations.

5. Roland Barthes, *A Lover's Discourse: Fragments*, tr. Richard Howard (New York: Noonday, 1978), 121.

Index

Achilles, 26, 62, 65, 203
"Ad grammaticos," 1–4
Adonis, 63, 151
Adorno, Theodor, 4, 197
Aeneas, 63
Aeneid, 19
Affective criticism. *See* Reader-Response criticism.
Africa, 128
Agamemnon, 26
Agon, 33
Ajax, 47
Alberti, Leon Battista, 188, 218
Albright, Daniel, 196
Alexander, 14
Almansi, Guido, 76–77, 88, 208
Amor, arguments of, 123–26
Amores, the, 6, 9, 15, 59, 131, 190–91: abortion in, 51–54; abuse in, 46–49; afternoon tryst in, 38–40; arch comedy in, 42–44; art and loss in, 24; audience and, 67–68; as Augustan elegy, 8–9; barriers in, 40–42; compromise and, 16–33; deals and capitulations in, 32; on death, 61–66; defense of poetics in, 23–24; denouement of, 40–41; doorkeeper in, 40–41; Elegy and Tragedy in, 27–29; elegy format of, 32–33; first version of, 202; futility of opposition, 19–21; Gallus in, 24–25, 57, 65; hands in, 54–55; impotency in, 42–44; melancholy in, 46–49; mistress-beating in, 46–49; mistress game in, 34–38; mistress's self-inflicted damage, 49–51; modesty in, 23; money's sexiness in, 44–45; negotiation in, 21–23; paired elegies in, 17; poet-*amator* in, 16–17; *quod licet,* 30–33; racecourse analogy in, 29–30; second book of, 19–20, 25; self-control in, 55–56; soldier in, 45–46; survival and, 57–58

André, Jean-Marie, 200
Apollo, 13, 67, 77, 98, 131
Ariadne, 47
Arno, 120
Ars amatoria, 15, 31, 58, 203
Ascham, Roger, 146–47
Asher, Lyell, 212
Astrophil, 163
Atalanta, 47
Audience, 198: ambiguity of, 10–11; authors' consciousness of, 6; between Petrarch and Shakespeare, 128–29; imperial, 56–69; interaction, 198–99; lyric poetry and, 4–12; Ovid's, 18, 27; Petrarch's, 71–74; poet as, 114; as Protean entity, 10; Shakespeare's, 131–32
Augustine, St., 76, 82, 110, 113, 116, 122, 124–25

221

222 Index

Augustus Caesar, 2, 8–9, 13–14, 33, 56–61, 66–67, 199–200
Autonomy (autonomous ego), 194, 219–20
Averroes, 192

Barolini, Teodolinda, 102, 207, 210
Barthes, Roland, 195, 220
Basia, 196
Bate, Jonathan, 197
Beatrice (Dante's), 99, 210
Bembo, Pietro, 92, 93
Benjamin, Walter, 198
Benson, John, 219
Bergin, Thomas G., 206
Bermann, Sandra, 133
Bernard, John D., 216
Bernardo, Aldo S., 74, 205, 206, 208
Blau, Herbert, 198
Blind hands, 17, 51, 54
Boccaccio, 78, 127, 128, 209
Booth, Stephen, 162, 184, 214, 216, 217–18
Borges, Jorge Luis, 192, 219
Bosco, Umberto, 72, 206
Boucher, Jean-Paul, 202
Boyle, Marjorie O'Rourke, 209
Braden, Gordon, 86, 198, 209
Briseis, 203
Brunt, P. A., 199

Caecas manus, 17
Caesar Augustus. *See* Augustus Caesar
Cahoon, Leslie, 15, 26, 47, 62, 63, 201, 203, 205
Calderwood, James, 99, 210
Callimachus, 9
Canzoniere, the, 7, 9, 68, 190–91: adaptation in, 121–22; appeal of mortal things, 117; audience in, 71–72, 111–13, 128, 138; commonplace vs. distinctive, 87–88; death's witness, 97–116; dual agent of, 78; duplicity in, 96; erotic and political concerns, 91–92; exasperation in, 94–96; *favola* and, 81–84; grief in, 114–16; humor in, 85–86, 91–92; irony in, 76–77; Laura's speech in, 107–9; laurel tree in, 113; Lau-re-ta canzone, 97–99; metamorphoses in, 88–91; mortal ties in, 109–10, 113, 114–16; palinodic prefix of, 79–81; pervasive influence of, 197; poetic survival in, 74–75; politics in, 118–21; prodigal ambition, 120–21; Reason, 126; religious conerns in, 82, 209; satire in, 93; selfhood and, 83–85; selfishness in, 106; spirituality in, 122–27
Carraram, Francesco da, 118
Carroll, William C., 212
Cassandra, 47
Castelvetro, Ludovico, 209
Catullus, 9, 61, 150
Cave, Terence, 146, 214–15
Ceres, 42
Cicero, 70, 103, 104, 119
Colie, Rosalie, 133–34, 145, 213, 214
Colonna, Giacomo, 76, 77
Confessions, 82
Conte, Gian Biagio, 18–19, 202
Controuersiae 2.2, 34–35
Copeley, Frank O., 203
Copia, 145–47, 151–53, 184, 215
Corinna (Ovid's), 32–33, 39–41, 51, 53, 61, 66–67
Corpus, 205
Cristo moro, 100
Crosman, Robert, 214
Cupid, 20–22, 24, 31, 55, 62–63, 126, 153, 216
Cypassis, 55

Dante, 8, 9, 73, 74, 79, 99, 103, 207, 210
Daphne, 86, 99, 113
Dark Lady, 133, 135, 176–91, 216, 218
De amicitia, 119, 205
Death: in *Canzoniere*, 97–116; Ovid on, 61–66; Petrarch on, 116–29, 210; Shakespeare on, 99, 157, 165, 171–72

Delia, 64
de Man, Paul, 192–93, 219
de Mattai, Rodolfo, 118, 211–12
De remediis utriusque fortunae, 116–17
De re publica, 103
De rerum natura, 56
Dio, Cassius, 202
Donne, John, 4, 8, 121, 219
Dotti, Ugo, 117–18, 211
Dubrow, Heather, 133, 213
Duncan-Jones, Katherine, 212
Du Quesnay, I. M. LeM., 201
Durling, Robert M., 103, 104, 206

Elegy, 202: epic and, 19–21; Ovid's compromise of, 17–33; Tragedy and, 27–29
Eliot, T. S., 4–5, 197
Elliott, Alison G., 35, 200
Engle, Lars, 135–36, 148, 176, 214, 215, 218
Epic, 202: cancellation of, 25–26; elegy and, 19–21
Epistola metrica, 71
Epistulae ex Ponto, 51, 66, 75–76, 203
Epitome, 146–47
Erasmus, 145–46, 147, 149, 215, 216
Eros, 21, 49, 56, 148, 150–51, 153
Euphorbus, 130
Everard, Jan, 1. *See also* Secundus, Janus.

Favola, 81–84, 100–1, 209
Feinberg, Nona, 218
Felerpin, Howard, 164, 217
Ferry, Ann, 133, 213, 216
Fineman, Joel, 132–33, 189–90, 194, 213, 214, 219
Folts, James D., 117, 211
Franciscus, 76
Fränkel, Hermann, 46, 47, 203
Freccero, John, 73, 207
French Academy, The, 9–10, 198
Frye, Northrop, 215–16
Fumerton, Patricia, 134, 213–14
Fyler, John M., 203

Gallus, Cornelius, 24–25, 57–59, 65, 194, 201–2, 204
Gamel, Mary-Kay, 15, 52, 201, 203, 204
Gardiner, Judith Kegan, 147, 154, 215, 216
Ginsberg, Warren, 201–2
Giroux, Robert, 213
Grazia, Margreta de, 214, 219
Green, Peter, 24, 45–46, 50, 59, 203, 205
Greenblatt, Stephen J., 219
Greene, Roland, 197
Greene, Thomas, 73, 174, 207, 218
Griffin, Jasper, 199
Guicciardini, Francesco, 130
Gyas, 25

Hades, 65
Hammond, Gerald, 133, 213
Harrison, Robert Pogue, 207, 208
Hector, 26
Heroides, 31
Hologernes, 147
Homer, 62, 64, 97
Horace, 6, 14, 56, 68, 82, 209

Ilithyra, 53
Iser, Wolfgang, 198

Jaeger, Werner, 196
Johnson, Samuel, 131
Johnson, W. R., 6, 197, 200, 201
Jones, Frederic J., 209–10
Jove, 25

Kennedy, William J., 7, 11, 197, 199
Kenney, E. J., 202
Kerrigan, John, 145, 214, 216
Kerrigan, William, 86, 184, 198, 209, 218
Kinney, Arthur F., 215
Klause, John, 218
Klemp, P. J., 92, 208, 209
Krieger, Murray, 216

Lais, 39
La Primaudaye, Pierre de, 9–10, 188–89, 198

224 Index

Latin verses, 2–3
Laura (Petrarch's), 7, 77, 83–116, 121–27, 210
La vita nuova, 73
Leishman, J. B., 197
Leuir, 33
Lex Iulia de adulteriis coercendis, 14
Lex Iulia de maritandis ordinibus, 14
Love's Labor's Lost, 131, 212
Lover's Discourse, A, 195
Luck, Georg, 15, 200
Lucretia, 56, 63, 108, 130
Lyne, R. O. A. M., 200
Lyric, 196: audience and, 4–12; voice, 4

Macer, 19–20, 31–33
McKeown, J. C., 46, 201, 202
Macrobius, 103
Mars, 54, 202
Marsyas, 13, 67
Martial, 13
Martin, Philip, 142, 212, 214
Martines, Lauro, 68, 205
Medea, 34–35
Medicamina faciei, 218
Memnon, 62
Meres, Francis, 130, 131
Messala, 61
Metamorphoses, 51, 55, 60, 67
Metamorphoses, in the *Canzoniere*, 88–91
Midsummer Night's Dream, A, 131
Milanion, 47
Miller, Paul Allen, 219–20
Miner, Earl, 199
Montrose, Louis A., 212
Mount Ventoux, 122, 211
Myerowitz, Molly, 15, 201

Naso, 18, 19
Nel commune dolor, 97–116
Nemesis, 64
Nequitae, 25–26
Nichols, Fred J., 196
Noferi, Adelia, 206, 208, 209
Nolhac, Pierre de, 211
Non iudicium, sed animus, 34–56

Noyer-Weidner, A., 208

Odysseus, 26
Odyssey, the, 65
Ong, Walter, 10, 198
Orestes, 47
Orpheus, 62, 64
Otis, Brooks, 201
Ovid, 14–68, 75–76, 130, 131, 165, 179, 186, 190, 218: abuse and suffering vignettes, 35; *Amores* character of, 16–17; *Amores* inaugural statement, 17–18; *apologia* of, 59; audience in, 192–93, 195, 201–2; autonomy of, 219; banishment and, 14, 57–59; classical prejudices and, 200; comedy in, 201; conditions of restraint, 34–56; *corpus*, 205; counter-classical sensibility of, 33; Daphne legend of, 113; on death, 61–66; eccentricity of, 34–35; elegiac compromise of, 17–33; epigram of, 18–19; exile of, 14–15; *favola*, 82; Golden Age theme, 200; on Gallus, 24–25, 57–59, 65; influence of, 9; limitation and failure in, 33; persona of, 17; Petrarch and, 70–71, 86, 89, 197; self-awareness and, 67; selfhood in, 193; Shakespeare and, 136, 197; soldier's appeal, 203; subjectivity and, 194; survival and imperial audience, 56–69; view of elegy, 17–18; vulnerability to audience, 6–7; words' shortcomings, 203
Ovidius Naso. *See* Ovid

Padua, 118–19
Palladis Tamia, 212
Parker, Douglas, 50, 203
Passionate Pilgrim, The, 182–83
Pequigney, Joseph, 139, 212–13, 214, 216
Perilla, 60
Perseus, 41–42
Petrarca, o dell'insignificanza, 76–77

Petrarch, Francesco, 68–69, 70–128, 190: attraction in, 150; audience and, 6–7, 74–75, 128, 192–93, 195, 208; autobiographical allegory and, 209–10; autonomy of, 72–73, 76–78, 219; and brother, Gherardo, 211; Dante relationship, 207; death and, 97–116, 210; elitism of, 117–18, 206; hegemony, 1; human nature and, 117–18, 211–12; influence of, 9; irony in, 78–79; laurel and, 75, 127–28; Lauretta and, 210; Ovid and, 70–71, 89, 197; pain of survival, 100; persona of, 121; personal sinfulness of, 210–11; political outlook of, 118–20; prodigal ambition, 120–21; selfhood and, 83–85, 193; Shakespeare and, 136, 177–82, 197; and son, Giovanni, 211; subjectivity and, 194; tradition of, 131
Petrie, Jennifer, 197
Phaeton, 94
Phoebus, 38
Piacenza, Luca da, 71
Po, 120
Policy, definition of term, 8–10, 173–74, 176–77, 190–91
Polonius, 147
Powell, Jonathan, 6, 197
Praxis, 15–16
Price, David, 196
Propertius, 8, 23, 50, 61, 201
Proteus, 146
Pythagorus, 130

Quinn, Kenneth, 30, 201, 203
Quintilian, 34
Quod licet, 17–33, 66

Raaflaub, Kurt A., 199
Radista, Leo Ferrero, 199
Rawski, Conrad H., 211
Reader-response criticism, 11
Reason, 123, 126
Recusatio, 3

Regan, Mariann S., 126, 210, 212
Renaissance, 68, 128, 135, 147, 188
Restraint, conditions of, 34–56
Rhetorical criticism, 11
Rhetorical Norms in Renaissance Literature, 11
Ricordi, 212
Roche, Jr., Thomas P., 132, 197, 209, 213, 216
Roessner, Jane, 154, 162–63, 216, 217
Romulus, 14
Rosmarin, Adena, 214

Santagata, Marco, 86, 209
Schmidgall, Gary, 217
Scipio, 103, 104
Secretum, 76, 113, 117, 124–25
Secundus, Janus 1–4, 196
Sedgwick, Eve Kosofsky, 184, 215–16
Semiramis, 39
Seneca, 34, 55, 116, 215
Seniles, 75, 118, 127, 208, 212
Shakespeare, William, 1, 9, 128: audience and, 7–8, 131–32, 192–93, 195; boundaries in, 154–76; copiousness and, 145–47; and death, 99, 157, 165, 171–72; disregard for fame, 131; duality in, 163; human growth in, 153–54; intimacy in, 164–65; Nature and, 149–50; oath and perjury, 11–12; familiarity with Ovid, 197; persona of, 129, 163; Petrarch and, 177–82, 197; poetic capability of, 130–31; public honor vs. private joy, 158–60; public manners in, 176–91; public means, 154–76; Q text of, 212–13, 217; rival claims in, 154–76; selfhood in, 193; social commitment in, 138–39; society and, 160–62; speaker and, 213; subjectivity and, 194
Shakes-peares Sonnets. Neuer before Imprinted, 130–31
Shawcross, John T., 199
Sidney, Sir Philip, 163, 219

Index

Sloan, Thomas O., 214
Smarr, Janet Levarie, 209
Smith, Bruce R., 7–8, 132, 197, 213
Socrates, 77
Sonnets, 7–8, 9: Benson's 1640 publication of, 219; betrayal in, 163–66; boundaries in, 154–76; conformity in, 180–81; conservative disposition in, 144–45; copiousness, 145–46; court life, 128–29, 217; duality in, 136, 163; duty in, 139–40; femininity in, 148–49; intimacy in, 164–65; isolation in, 175–76, 187–89; lust in, 184–85; marriage parody in, 215–16; Nature and, 139, 149–50, 179; perjury in, 188–90; private scrutiny in, 142–43; procreation, 137–54, 214; public acceptance and, 137–38, 140–44, 172–73; public honor vs. private joy, 158–60; public manners in, 176–91; public means in, 154–76; public witness, 133; rival, 166–76, 217–18; selfhood in, 132–33, 193; social temper of, 133–34; societal context and, 131–36, 138–39, 160–62; will, 184–85
Spence, Sarah, 68, 205
Steiner, George, 13
Stella, 163
Sturm-Maddox, Sara, 124, 209, 210, 212
Suetonius, 67
Suleiman, Susan R., 199
Survival, imperial audience and, 56–69
Syme, Ronald, 199

Theseus, 47, 131
Thibault, John C., 200, 205
Tiber, 120
Tibullus, 23, 57, 61–65, 201
Toher, Mark, 199
Tomis outpost, 14, 60–61, 56–58, 60–61, 66
Tragedy, 27–29, 209
Trinkaus, Charles, 116, 206, 211–12
Tripet, Arnaud, 72, 207
Tristia, 56–61, 66–67, 203
Trojan War, 31
Trousdale, Marion, 146, 198, 214, 215
Tudor court, 163

Uir, 35–37, 41

van den Berg, Sara, 219
Venus, 22, 31, 56, 62, 151
Venus and Adonis, 130, 131
Vickers, Nancy, 74, 208
Virgil, 14, 19, 33, 56, 202

Waddington, Raymond B., 199, 214
Wallace-Hadrill, Andrew, 200
Waller, Marguerite, 75, 208
Whigham, Frank, 128–29, 212
Wilkins, Ernest H., 208, 210
Williams, Gordon, 199, 200
Wilson, Katherine M., 215
Winny, James, 218
Woodman, Tony, 6, 197
Wordsworth, William, 145, 214

Zeitlin, Jacob, 205

About the Author

Christopher Martin is a member of the English Department at Boston University. His previous work on classical and Renaissance authors has appeared in *Illinois Classical Studies, English Literary Renaissance, Spenser Studies, Essays in Criticism* and *Shakespeare Quarterly*. He is currently editing the Ovid volume of Penguin Book's *The Poets in Translation* series, and is also at work on a study of nostalgia in Jacobean literature.

Duquesne Studies
LANGUAGE AND LITERATURE SERIES

VOLUME SEVENTEEN

General Editor:
Albert C. Labriola
(Department of English, Duquesne University)

Advisory Editor:
Foster Provost
(Department of English, Duquesne University)

Editorial Board:
Judith H. Anderson
Donald Cheney
Ann Baynes Coiro
Mary T. Crane
Patrick Cullen
A. C. Hamilton
Margaret P. Hannay
A. Kent Hieatt
William B. Hunter
Michael Lieb
Thomas P. Roche, Jr.
Mary Beth Rose
John M. Steadman
Humphrey Tonkin
Susanne Woods